THE LIVING CHAUCER

THE Living Chaucer

By

Percy Van Dyke Shelly

NEW YORK / RUSSELL & RUSSELL

REISSUED, 1968, BY RUSSELL & RUSSELL
A DIVISION OF ATHENEUM HOUSE, INC.
BY ARRANGEMENT WITH THE
UNIVERSITY OF PENNSYLVANIA PRESS
L. C. CATALOG CARD NO: 68-25060
PRINTED IN THE UNITED STATES OF AMERICA

Preface

IN the making of this book on Chaucer I have confined myself to a consideration of his poetry and have said little or nothing about the man or his life or his times. So much has been written in the past twenty-five or fifty years on the facts of his life and on the chronology, texts, and sources of his works that there is perhaps some danger of our losing sight of his significance as a poet, and I have therefore felt that a book which should stress his poetry and dwell upon Chaucer as an artist rather than as a subject for scholarly research or as an historian and illustrator of his age might not be unwelcome. I have written of certain aspects of his poetry that have interested me and I have had in mind the general reader and lover of poetry more than the specialist.

No one can write on Chaucer without being indebted to the many scholars, American, British, and other, who have added so much to our knowledge of the poet and his work. My obligations to them are great, and I take pleasure in acknowledging the fact and in paying tribute to their painstaking and often brilliant labors. This book, I trust, will be found to be in harmony with the soundest of their conclusions. But fundamentally it is based upon the reading of Chaucer rather than the reading of his commentators. One cannot hope, at this late day, to say anything new of a poet who has been a subject of comment and criticism for more than five hundred years. But one may reasonably hope to present a slightly different point of view, to say again some things which though said before may have been forgotten, and to bring within the compass of a single volume a great many things that should be known to the lover of poetry today about the work of one of the greatest of English poets and artists, albeit one of the oldest.

In particular I have sought to stress the fact that Chaucer's poetry is of value and interest not alone as an historical phenomenon, of significance chiefly to the student of literary history, but as a joy and inspiration to the general reader of this twentieth century, however "modern," "advanced," or "sophisticated" he may pride himself on being.

My thanks are due to my colleagues in the field of English in the University of Pennsylvania for their friendly and sustained interest in this attempt to evaluate Chaucer as artist. Especially am I indebted to Professor Clarence Griffin Child, under whose inspiring teaching I first pursued the advanced study of Chaucer, and to whom I owe the happy suggestion of the book's title. Professor Child has also most generously read the entire manuscript of the book and given me the benefit of his wide knowledge and profound scholarship in valuable criticisms and suggestions. I am indebted, too, to Professors Albert C. Baugh, Matthew W. Black, and Alfred B. Harbage for their having read and criticized various chapters.

In addition, I wish to thank the following organizations for their kind permission to make use of certain quotations from various books published by them:

The Connecticut Academy of Arts and Sciences, E. P. Dutton and Company, Messrs. Faber and Faber and the executrix of the late G. K. Chesterton, Messrs. Harper and Brothers, the Harvard University Press, Houghton Mifflin Company, Alfred A. Knopf, Inc., Longmans, Green and Company, The Macmillan Company, and Charles Scribner's Sons.

In quoting from the works of Chaucer I have made use of Skeat's text as published by the Oxford University Press.

P. V. D. S.

University of Pennsylvania
October 19, 1939

Contents

THE LIVING CHAUCER

The teachings of most of the great prophets and poets are simply protests against the "law of kind." Chaucer does not protest, he accepts. It is precisely this acceptance that makes him unique among English poets.

—Aldous Huxley, ON THE MARGIN, pp. 196–97.

. . . —this meditacioun
I putte it ay under correccioun
Of clerkes, for I am nat textuel.

CANTERBURY TALES, *I, 55–57*

CHAPTER I

On Not Reading Chaucer

IN 1880, in a criticism of Chaucer that was at once admirable and inadequate, Matthew Arnold expressed the opinion that Chaucer "will be read, as time goes on, far more generally than he is read now." That prophecy has been fulfilled. As modern scholarship has made Chaucer more accessible and more easily and fully understood—and no poet save Shakespeare has been better served by modern scholarship—he has come to be read by hundreds where tens read him before. Outstripping Spenser and Milton, he stands next to Shakespeare, I suppose, among the great classics of English poetry, in the number of readers he can claim.

And yet, much of this widespread reading of Chaucer today is not all it should be. Often it is the reading not of Chaucer at all, but of some modernization or translation of Chaucer—sometimes in prose. Often it is no more than the reading of a few selections from the *Canterbury Tales* listed as required reading in school or college, with the addition perhaps of certain selections not on the reading lists but read voluntarily and eagerly (and with little complaint as to the difficulties of the language) in the youthful and quite human pursuit of the naughty. Few have read the *Canterbury Tales* in their entirety, and fewer still are familiar with Chaucer's other works. One of the greatest of English poets, Chaucer is known only in fragments. He is not the Unknown Poet, as he has recently been called, but the Little Known, the Half Known, and the Wrongly Known. Even mature lovers of literature and certain critics who have written about him with assurance think of him as the author only of the *Canterbury Tales,* as a poet of manners, a humorist and satirist, and nothing more. Such was the view of Hallam in 1818, who held that Chaucer excels "chiefly as a comic poet and a minute observer of manners and circumstances." Chaucer the poet of beauty, the poet of love, who until he did the *Canterbury Tales* wrote virtually nothing but poems dealing in one way or another with the subject of love, is practically unknown, though as long ago as 1895 Professor Ker averred that Chaucer's finest work is to be found outside the *Canterbury Tales* and especially in *Anelida and Arcite, Troilus and Criseyde,* and the Prologue of the *Legend of Good Women.*[1] The Complaint of Anelida Professor Ker described as the "most exquisite deliverance of Chaucer's finest poetical sense." That was more than forty years ago, but we are still getting hold of our Chaucer, when we get hold of him at all, by the wrong end. And many a criticism of him leaves us in doubt whether the critic has read any of his works but the *Canterbury Tales.* This is true of Hallam's view above; it is true of Arnold's criticism. And when A. E. Housman only yesterday remarked that "perhaps no English poem of greater than lyric length, not even the Nonne's Priest's Tale or the Ancient Mariner, is quite so perfect as the Rape of the Lock," [2] we wonder whether he had only forgotten Chaucer's *Troilus and Criseyde* or had not read it. The second alternative is almost incredible, but it is difficult on other grounds to account for the mention of the *Nun's Priest's Tale* and the omission of *Troilus and Criseyde.*

This one-sided and imperfect knowledge of Chaucer's work, this lack of a full and adequate recognition of his genius, is nothing new. In 1817 Leigh Hunt complained bitterly that "Chaucer is considered as a rude sort of poet, who wrote a vast while ago, and is no longer intelligible. . . . Chaucer is nothing but *Old* Chaucer or honest Geoffrey." De Quincey in 1835 spoke of "those divine qualities" in Chaucer "which,

[1] W. P. Ker, *Essays on Medieval Literature,* Macmillan, 1905, p. 82.
[2] A. E. Housman, *The Name and Nature of Poetry,* Macmillan, 1933, p. 15.

even at this day, are so languidly acknowledged by his unjust countrymen." In 1841 Richard Hengist Horne, in the introduction to *Poems of Geoffrey Chaucer Modernized,* said that although Chaucer "is one of the great poets for all time, his works are comparatively unknown to the world. Even in his own country, only a very small class of his countrymen ever read his poems. Had Chaucer's poems been written in Greek or Hebrew, they would have been a thousand times better known. They would have been translated." Alexander Smith, in an essay in *Dreamthorp* (1863) says that Chaucer is not frequently read, and although his essay leaves one in doubt as to how much of Chaucer Smith himself had read, his statement is probably true. In 1873 Dr. Furnivall referred to Chaucer as "that tenderest, brightest, most humourful sweet soul, of all the great poets of the world, whom a thousand Englishmen out of every thousand and one are content to pass by with a shrug and a sneer." In 1923 Mr. Aldous Huxley remarked that "Between those who are daunted by his superficial difficulties and those who take too much delight in them Chaucer finds but few sympathetic readers." [3] And in 1932 Chesterton was able to say with perfect truth that the English "have never realized the nature, let alone the scale, of the genius of Geoffrey Chaucer," and that "what seems to me altogether missed is the *greatness* of Chaucer." [4]

The reason for this comparative neglect of Chaucer and for the less than full perception of his genius lies, in the opinion of many, in the difficulty and antiquity of his language. It is believed that were he modernized, translated, or simplified, he would come into his own, would be read by the general reader and lover of poetry as much perhaps as Shakespeare, and be revealed as the truly great poet he is. This conviction is at the bottom of all those attempts by

[3] Aldous Huxley, *On the Margin,* N.Y., 1923, p. 195.
[4] G. K. Chesterton, *Chaucer,* N.Y., 1932, p. 3.

Dryden, Pope, Wordsworth, Leigh Hunt, and others, down to Professor Tatlock, Mr. Mackaye, Mr. Hill, and Professor Krapp, to modernize Chaucer and to make the "well of English undefiled" palatable to the modern reader. But in such works the well is no longer undefiled. And it should be sufficiently obvious that Chaucer translated is no longer Chaucer. Chaucerian scholars thoroughly understand this, and most of them accept it as a principle, and instead of countenancing or producing modernizations, direct their efforts to the establishing of the best text; that is, the text that seems nearest to Chaucer's original, which can be approximated only by the most careful collation of all the manuscripts and by the application of the most expert knowledge of linguistic forms. They subscribe to Leigh Hunt's remark, made over a hundred years ago, that "every alteration of Chaucer is an injury." They rest secure in the faith that Chaucer's poetry will win more and more readers in spite of the antiquity of his English. And they might even agree with Landor's judgment that "as many people read Chaucer as are fit to read him." "I would rather see Chaucer quite alone," said Landor, "in the dew of his sunny morning, than with twenty clever gentlefolks about him, arranging his shoe-strings and buttoning his doublet. I like even his *language*. I will have no hand in breaking his dun but rich-painted glass to put in (if clearer) much thinner panes."

The plea of the difficulty or antiquity of Chaucer's language is not quite convincing, or altogether honest. The difficulty of learning to read Chaucer in the original is not really great. We learn Lowland Scotch in order to read Burns. We learn Latin to read Horace and Virgil, Greek to read Homer, and Italian to read Dante. The "difficulty" of Chaucer has never prevented the poets from reading him, and reading him for the most part with high appreciation. Earlier poets, such as his contemporaries and his immediate successors in the fifteenth century, would of course find no difficulty, and probably his sixteenth- and seventeenth-century admirers, such as Sidney, Spenser, Shakespeare, and Milton, read him with ease, as being so much nearer to him in point of time than were their followers. But to many latter-day poets, from Dryden to Mr. Masefield, Chaucer seems to have been an open book in spite of all difficulties. We see the Wordsworths—Dorothy, Mary, and William—reading him aloud while seated snugly about the fire of winter nights. Wordsworth describes him as "one of the greatest of poets" and speaks of "my love and reverence for Chaucer." He quoted him in his letters, referred to him in his poems, and modernized some of his tales. For fifty years Leigh Hunt read him enthusiastically and wrote about him, quoted him, and alluded to him in essay, letter, and conversation. Hunt seems to have been one of the few great men of letters in the nineteenth century who knew pretty much *all* of Chaucer, who had read the *Book of the Duchess,* the *House of Fame, Troilus and Criseyde,* and the *Legend of Good Women* as well as the *Canterbury Tales,* and to have had a better idea of the beauty and melody of Chaucer's verse than most men of his day. Southey in 1803 wrote, "I am now daily drinking at that pure well of English undefiled, to get historical manners, and to learn English and poetry," and later said, "Whoever aspires to a lasting name among the English poets must get the writings of Chaucer, and drink at the well-head." He placed Chaucer above Petrarch and Dante in "versatility of talents" and held that "only Shakespeare has surpassed him in his intuitive knowledge of human character, and the universality of his genius." Scott admired and quoted and referred to Chaucer extensively, and showed that his interest was a poetic and not merely an antiquarian interest. Lamb's library included a Speght Chaucer, a black-letter folio of 1598. Coleridge in 1804 contemplated doing an essay on the "Genius and Writings of Chaucer" and in later years said, "I take unceasing delight in Chaucer. His manly cheerfulness is especially delicious to me in my old age." Hazlitt lectured upon him and referred to him frequently in his essays. Campbell wrote an essay and an article on Chaucer. De Quincey referred to Chaucer as "a poet worth five hundred of Homer," and in this respect agreed with Lowell, who likewise preferred Chaucer to Homer, "except in the single quality of invention." Landor paid the highest tributes to Chaucer, in poem, letter, and imaginary conversation, placing him next to Milton and Shakespeare among English poets, and holding him to be "fairly worth a score or two of Spensers." William Morris and Burne-Jones read Chaucer together at Oxford, and Tennyson, we are told, "enjoyed reading Chaucer aloud more than any poet except Shakespeare and Milton." Swinburne, Ruskin, Mrs. Browning, Edward Fitz Gerald, George Meredith, and Aubrey De Vere read and praised him. Clough lectured upon him, as Thoreau did in this country. And Lowell wrote one of the best critical essays on Chaucer that we have. On the other hand, Byron found Chaucer "obscene and contemptible," Tom Moore found him "unreadable," and Shelley, Rossetti, and Pater seem to have read him little if at all. But most of the great writers of the Romantic and Victorian periods read him with enthusiasm and with few or no complaints of the difficulty or antiquity of his language. Indeed Alexander Smith, in his essay of 1863, minimized these when he said, "A very little trouble on the reader's part, in the reign of Anne, would have made him as intelligible as Addison; a very little more, in the reign of Queen Victoria, will make him more intelligible than Mr. Browning." And one may add that today, with the aids to be found in any elementary book on Chaucer, the reader can, with a little effort, learn to read him not only with understanding and pleasure but with a fair approximation to what we believe to have been Chaucer's pronunciation. The truth of this statement is demonstrated in many a class in college and university each year.[5]

Most of these lovers of Chaucer were able to read him no doubt with a fairly full grasp of his meaning and a more or less accurate sense of the regularity of his verse. But they could have had little or no knowledge of the pronunciation of his vowels, for such knowledge did not exist much before 1870, and then for a long time was in the possession only of special students of Chaucer and of Middle English. Hence they could not appreciate to the full the melody of his verse. When Landor in one of his *Imaginary Conversations* says to Southey that he prefers Chaucer to Spenser in all points "excepting harmony," he shows that he lacked the secret of Chaucer's pronunciation. To the fully equipped modern reader Chaucer's verse is as harmonious, as beautiful in its melody, as is Spenser's. "Poetry," as Housman truly observes,[6] "is not the thing said but a way of saying it." And we may add that the way of saying it is not alone a matter of diction, figure of speech, accent, and rhythm, but of all the subtle play and interplay of vowels and consonants. And no one can appreciate to the full the melody of Chaucer's verse who has not mastered his pronunciation. If we would know Chaucer *the poet* and not merely Chaucer *the story-teller,* we must learn to read his lines as he read them. There is no other way but that.

In simplifying Chaucer for the modern reader, it has been urged, the thing to do is to keep the lines virtually as they stand, even though this may necessitate the retention of endings that no longer exist. Such is Chesterton's advice, and he offers as an example three lines from the dying speech of Arcite in the *Knight's Tale:*

[5] For many of the above references to Chaucer I am indebted to Miss Caroline F. E. Spurgeon's admirable book, *Five Hundred Years of Chaucer Criticisms and Allusions,* 3 vols., Cambridge University Press, 1925.

[6] Housman, *op. cit.,* p. 35.

What is this world? What asken man to have?
Now with his love, now in his colde grave,
Alone withouten any company.[7]

Chesterton prefers this slight modification of Chaucer's original to Mr. Hill's rendering—

What is this world? What asketh man to have?
Now with his love, now cold within his grave,
Alone, alone, with none for company.[8]

Mr. Hill would of course reply that his aim was to render the *Knight's Tale* in modern English and that Chesterton's lines are neither modern English nor Chaucerian English. Chaucer's actual words, we believe, were:

What is this world? What asketh men to have?
Now with his love, now in his colde grave,
Allone, withouten any companye.

Both of the modern versions, it will be observed, discard or ignore the feminine endings of all three lines and the feminine cæsura in the second line; and they substitute an eye-rime or spelling-rime for the true rime of the first two lines. They also ignore the assonance in the u-sounds of *now, love, withouten,* and possibly *companye.* To miss so many things and to miss the strong cæsura after *Allone* is to miss much of the beauty of Chaucer's music, especially of the last line. Chesterton is right in describing that line as "a desolate yet living cry, echoing in a vault of stone," and he is right in saying that Mr. Hill "has broken the backbone of the tragic line with a load of repetition." But its tragic desolation is more striking in the original than in either of the modified forms given here. In part, its effect is undoubtedly due to the two preceding lines and to its climactic rela-

[7] Chesterton, *op. cit.,* p. 226.
[8] Frank E. Hill, *The Canterbury Tales,* Longmans, Green and Company, 1930, p. 104.

tionship to them. Chaucer uses the very same line in the opening of the *Miller's Tale,* but in an entirely different setting. He is telling of "hende Nicholas," who lodged with the carpenter and his wife in Oxford:

> A chambre hadde he in that hostelrye
> Allone, withouten any companye.

The effect is totally different, not merely because the figure is far less imaginative when used in connection with a room in a lodging-house than it is when associated with the "colde grave," but because here the preceding line is brisk and business-like and lacks those vowels which in the second of the three lines from the *Knight's Tale* make assonance with vowels of the third line. The effect in the *Knight's Tale* is largely due to the fact that the third line comes so fittingly and strikingly immediately after "now in the colde grave." In short, the retention of Chaucer's endings, though it may help to maintain for the modern reader the regularity of his verse, cannot by itself reproduce Chaucer's music. For that, we must use, in reading his lines, the sounds that he used. Obviously these cannot be given in any translation or modernization. They are not revealed by Chaucer's text, for many a line looks exactly or almost exactly like modern English. To the eye the line

> Now with his love, now in the colde grave

is modern in every respect save for the *e* in *colde.* But to the ear, at least five of its nine words are not modern but Chaucerian. And the appeal of poetry is to the ear, not the eye.

To read Chaucer in translation is better than not to read Chaucer at all. But let no one suppose that, in doing so, he is reading Chaucer or is in position to judge aright of Chaucer's merits as a poet. To translate Chaucer is not only difficult, it is impossible. Chaucer without Chaucer's melody—

with somebody else's melody—is not Chaucer. To know Chaucer one must learn to read him in the original with his pronunciation. To do this is, as I have said, not difficult. But however difficult it may be, the effort must be made, for the lover of poetry can ill afford to neglect one of the greatest poets of all time, or to read him with anything less than full appreciation of his genius.

To neglect Chaucer is to neglect the poet who, historically, is the most important of all English poets, and the poet who, from the purely absolute point of view, must be placed, when all things are considered, second only to Shakespeare in the hierarchy of English poets.

This is a large claim, but it is neither new nor extravagant. The grounds upon which it is made, however, need to be emphasized and consolidated.

To gain a proper sense of the profound change wrought in English poetry by Chaucer, one must read first what has been preserved of the verse, Old English and Middle English, that precedes him. Turning from that to Chaucer, one enters a new world. Or rather, upon the old world the sun has risen and the poetic landscape is literally transformed. Tennyson's phrase about "the morning star of song" is inadequate. Chaucer was more than the forerunner and herald of day; he was day itself, come at last to the north, bringing warmth and beauty and joy where, before him, what was for the most part a drear and solemn literature alone reached permanent record. As Leigh Hunt said, English poetry "burst into luxuriance in his hands, like a sudden month of May."

It was not merely that Chaucer's verse had a grace, melody, and perfection of form unknown to English poetry before, but that he looked upon poetry as an art and himself as an artist. So far as we can judge by what is extant, earlier English poetry, although some of it possessed artistic merit of one kind or another, had, with few exceptions, been preserved only when it served the cause of religion or was weighted with moral purpose. That which was not serious was allowed to perish. There was little that ventured to stand alone, to put its trust simply in the power of beauty and truth. To find justification it must glorify God and fight the seven deadly sins. This is true even of many romances. Their authors had as much eye to knightly, Christian, or courtly virtues as they had to absorbing story. In historical or pseudo-historical verse, such as Layamon's *Brut,* the celebration of the national glory is the central motif, and this of course is a didactic motif. Even in the most powerful poems of the earlier Middle English period, such as the *Debate of the Body and the Soul* and the *Owl and the Nightingale,* the religious and didactic note predominates, and (except perhaps in the latter) outweighs poetic and artistic interest. And in Chaucer's own age, Langland and Gower are moralists and reformers throughout. Even the *Confessio Amantis,* in which Gower set out to write "something between earnest and game," is at bottom, and in spite of its many stories, a moral discourse. In this, the last of his major works, "the moral Gower" is moral still. The anonymous poems *Pearl* and *Sir Gawain and the Green Knight,* which are perhaps the most artistic poems made in England in the fourteenth century with the exception of Chaucer's, are nevertheless also still in the bonds of morality.

This is obvious in *Pearl;* it is not so obvious, but yet plain enough, in *Sir Gawain.* For example, the poet goes out of his way, though, as he says, "my tale tarry thereby," to tell why the knight bore the pentangle on his shield and to explain its symbolism, which is purely moral and religious. The passage runs to the length of forty lines, and is clearly a digression in the interest of didacticism. But not only single passages such as this betray the influence of the cloister; the story as a whole, in spite of its varied merits and interests, has in it the tedium of the moral. In plot and character-portrayal it is governed by the moral purpose of the writer. He is not a free artist. He must prove that Gawain is a paragon of knighthood, "the most faultless knight that ever trod earth." The story is a sort of Temptation of St. Anthony, in terms of medieval chivalry and romance—a test of Gawain's courtesy, honor, bravery, and chastity. "Cursed be ye, cowardice and covetousness, for in ye is the destruction of virtue." This is the text, of which the poem is virtually an exemplum. This, and another—that " 'tis no marvel if one be made a fool and brought to sorrow by women's wiles." [9]

This poem, written about 1370, has been extravagantly praised as "incomparably the best of the English romances," but one has only to recall Chaucer's *Knight's Tale* to see at once the immense superiority of the latter. Both poems are romances, but otherwise they belong to different categories entirely. One is the work of a free artist, the other of a moralist—of a moralist with considerable artistic taste, to be sure, and with a lively interest in nature, costume, armor, jewels, furniture, and the ways of the courtly circle, but one who nevertheless conceives of art and poetry as handmaids to virtue and religion.

Chaucer freed English poetry from her leading strings, brought her out of the monastery and the church into the world, and tacitly affirmed that her proper concern is beauty and truth, and life in all its fascinating fullness and variety. He knew little or nothing of Aristotle, but he worked upon the Aristotelian principle that the business of poetry is to give pleasure—intellectual and emotional pleasure. So far from being a moral, religious, philosophical, or edifying poet, he deliberately made himself a love poet and thought of and described himself as a love poet in all his works down to the *Canterbury Tales*. Even in these he was still largely

[9] The quotations are from the translation of Miss Jessie L. Weston, N.Y., Scribner's, 1909.

earnestness and loftiness of spirit. Chaucer's sense of humor, the immense range of his sympathies, his sanity, his sweet and joyous savoring of so many and such varied phases of life, his pathos, his sense of pity, his love of beauty—these things, together with the fact that he is always the artist and seldom or never the reformer or preacher or moralizer, raise him above Spenser, Milton, Dryden, Pope, Wordsworth, and Browning, and explain why this medieval poet of England is still a living force, and why, as his work has become more fully understood, he has more and more come to be recognized as standing second only to Shakespeare, among English poets, in his knowledge of life and in the truth and beauty with which he has portrayed and revealed so many of its aspects.

CHAPTER II

Chaucer and the Critics

OF the four or five great critics of whom the history of English literary criticism can boast, three have written of Chaucer. This perhaps is as high a percentage as we have any right to expect. But the fact is that no one of the three has given us a criticism of Chaucer's poetry that is either comprehensive or satisfying, and Chaucer still awaits the adequate critic. Dryden's criticism, generous though it is, and in some ways the best of all, suffers in certain respects from the limitations of Dryden's literary taste and of the taste of his age. And it was written of course without benefit of the results of modern Chaucerian scholarship. Hazlitt's criticism of Chaucer is fragmentary and scattered. Matthew Arnold's consists of but a single passage in his essay on the *Study of Poetry* and is the work of one who allowed himself, in this case more so than usually, to be ridden by a phrase and a critical dogma. In America the only outstanding critic who has written of Chaucer is Lowell. His essay of 1870 is worthy to stand with the best in Chaucerian criticism, but it is but a single essay and is far from exhaustive. Moreover, in a number of important points it needs correction in the light of modern scholarship. Lesser critics in great number have written of Chaucer, especially in the first half of the nineteenth century, and some have written well, notably, as we have seen, Leigh Hunt. But many of them necessarily worked with imperfect texts and with imperfect knowledge of Chaucer's language, and in most instances their criticism of Chaucer took the form of brief essays or scattered passages.

Chaucerian scholarship of the modern kind—factual, accurate, scientific, and based upon the historical method—is not more than sixty or seventy years old. It dates from the appearance of Professor Child's paper, "Observations on the Language of Chaucer," in 1863, from the founding of the Chaucer Society in 1868, and from Ten Brink's *Chaucer Studien* of 1870. Since then the work of English, American, and German scholars has enormously enriched our knowledge of Chaucer's life and time, of his text and language, of the sources and analogues of his works. And to the labors of these men and women every reader of Chaucer today is profoundly indebted. By them have been made available to the critic the materials needed to serve as the basis for a sound, thorough, and illuminating criticism.

But the curious fact is that with this advance in Chaucerian scholarship and with the outpouring of scholarly books and articles that has accompanied it, there has been no increase, but on the contrary a decrease, in Chaucerian criticism. I am thinking of literary criticism written by a poet or a critic rather than by a specialist, and addressed to the general reader and the lover of poetry rather than to the scholar. Lowell's essay in the *North American Review* in 1870, Arnold's pronouncement in 1880, a few pages in Swinburne's article "Some Notes on English Poets" in the *Fortnightly Review* in 1880, and more recently Sir Henry Newbolt's "The Poetry of Chaucer" in the *English Review* in 1913, Mr. Noyes's review in the *Bookman* in 1929, Mr. Aldous Huxley's essay in *On the Margin* in 1923, Mrs. Virginia Woolf's essay in *Common Reader* in 1925, and Mr. Masefield's brief paper on Chaucer given as the Leslie Stephen Lecture in 1931 are about all we have from pens of distinction in the literary, as distinct from the scholarly, world. The bulk is surprisingly small. And of the papers by living writers in this list, the one we should expect to be the best, as coming from the poet who has felt so greatly the power and inspiration of Chaucer, and who has elsewhere so generously acknowledged his debt, is far from being either a penetrating or a satisfying piece of work.

Chaucer, in a word, has been taken over by the scholars and the specialists and has become a Field of Research. The men of letters have surrendered to the professors and doctors of philosophy, overborne and awed by learning. If, now and again, a man of letters ventures to write on Chaucer, he confines himself to a brief essay, personal and familiar, as have Mr. Huxley and Mrs. Woolf; or to a page or two on a single phase of Chaucer's poetry, as did Hudson in a memorable passage in *A Hind in Richmond Park*. Only Chesterton had the courage to write a *book* upon Chaucer. It is a book that contains some excellent things, but its subject is not Chaucer's poetry or the greatness of Chaucer as an artist, but Chaucer's philosophy, and the philosophy and religion of his age, and the superiority in general of the social order of the fourteenth century to that of the twentieth.

It must not be inferred that specialists are incapable of excellent criticism or that scholars are necessarily deficient in poetic judgment and taste. On the contrary, the best Chaucerian criticism of the past twenty or twenty-five years is to be found in the books of some of the most eminent of Chaucerian scholars. But most of these are books of lectures that were delivered before academic audiences, and too frequently they are weighted with matter that is of interest only or chiefly to the specialist. Moreover, the output of modern Chaucerian scholars is for the most part buried in learned periodicals or in uninviting books intended only for specialists, and is concerned with anything but Chaucer's poetry. It is concerned with the facts of his life and times, with the influences upon his work, with the source of this story or that line. Scholarship, as distinct from criticism, is interested not in literature as such but in facts, the facts of literary history. Dominated by the spirit of science, by the scientist's reverence for facts, its ambition is to do what may be acclaimed by the academic world as a "contribution to knowledge." Chaucer's Criseyde and Pandarus, the Wife of Bath, the Host, the Pardoner are among the most masterfully drawn characters in all literature. But the scholar's interest in them is centered in their prototypes and sources, not in the art and truth with which they are portrayed. He seeks to identify the individuals who may have sat for these portraits, or to discover the hints, details, and similar characters that Chaucer may have found in his reading of Jean de Meun, Boccaccio, and other writers. The Prologue of the *Canterbury Tales* is treated much as an historical document, of value as illustrating the customs and costumes of the time. And Chaucer is made to seem to possess only an historical and philological interest, with little or no truly poetic interest. All of this, of course, has a specific value. It is part of the process known as "extending the bounds of knowledge." And bit by bit it gathers the materials out of which some day an imposing edifice of Chaucerian criticism will no doubt be built. But it is not criticism and it does little to attract readers to Chaucer or to reveal his true position as a poet.

"What," it has been asked, "is the difference between a literary critic and a literary historian?" And the jesting answer was, "The literary historian knows what he is talking about." But it would be as true an answer and as good a jest to say that the literary critic knows the difference between literature and history; he also knows the quick from the dead. Too often the literary historian is concerned with matters that, strictly speaking, are not literary but social, political, religious, or philosophical. To him a book is a book and a fact a fact. All is grist that comes to his mill, for all illustrates the history of literature. To command his attention a thing need not be excellent; it need only be in the past tense. Frequently he ignores the distinction between "antiquarian interest" and æsthetic value, the "distinct æsthetic value for the reader of today," which Pater considered to be the critic's proper concern. Dryden is sometimes criticized for having called Chaucer the "Father of English Poetry." Was there no English poetry before Chaucer? But Dryden was speaking as a poet, and as the great critic that he was, not as a literary historian. He was thinking of poetry, not of versified history, philosophy, morality, or social criticism. He was thinking of great poetry, possessed of imagination, grace, and the vitality that assures long life. He was thinking of English poetry, not of Anglo-Saxon poetry in the alliterative long-line.

But if the scholar and literary historian are sometimes lacking in judgment and taste, so too is the critic, and the critic is often deficient in that accurate and detailed knowledge which is the possession of the scholar and the literary historian. The right combination is one of the rarest things in the world. And in Chaucerian criticism it is hard to say whether the critic or the poet or the scholar is to be charged with the most deplorable errors, the most bizarre judgments, or the most grotesque suggestions. It was a reputed critic who, in 1920, said that "Chaucer is not what we understand by a great poet; he has none of the imaginative comprehension and little of the music that belong to one."[12] It was no less a poet and critic than Swinburne who called Chaucer "the poet of the sensible and prosperous middle class in England" and who considered that Wordsworth's sublimity is worth all the excellences of Chaucer put together. And it was Mr. Noyes who wrote,

> On the whole, the "Prologue" must be set down as his greatest achievement . . . the greatness of Chaucer elsewhere is to be found in the incidentals rather than the finished structure and full body of his work. . . . Chaucer was, above all things, a maker of preludes—preludes to narrative, preludes to character painting,

[12] J. Middleton Murry, *Aspects of Literature,* N.Y., Knopf, 1920, p. 153.

the first vital touches of portraiture, and preludes to the confident and full-fledged lyricism of the Elizabethans.

When Mr. Masefield writes, "We gather from the poems that Chaucer's own marriage was one of the utmost and liveliest unfortunate horror. The Wife of Bath describes her fifth marriage as being to much such a Clerk as Chaucer's description of himself. Can it possibly be that the Wife of Bath is a portrait of Mrs. Chaucer?" [13] he is indulging in neither scholarship nor criticism, but in a jest, if he is jesting, such as, if allowable at all, is allowable only to genius.

Judgments such as these compel us to ask, "What, precisely what, of Chaucer has the critic read?" Did Swinburne ever read the *Book of the Duchess,* the *House of Fame,* the *Parliament of Fowls, Troilus and Criseyde,* the *Legend of Good Women?* If so, how could he speak of Chaucer as "the poet of the sensible and prosperous middle class" when in point of fact he was much more the poet of the court and the poet of Courtly Love? Has Mr. Noyes read *Troilus and Criseyde?* That poem is one of the few triumphant examples of "finished structure and full body" in our literature. And in it and in many parts of the *Canterbury Tales* are to be found not "preludes to narrative, preludes to character painting," but masterpieces of narrative, masterpieces of character painting.

It was a scholar and a specialist, on the other hand, who expressed the opinion that Chaucer's work "in the last analysis . . . impresses us inevitably as superficial and remote"; that it "has no vision; it is scarcely at all interested in the human heart or the ways of the soul"; that "of anything approaching profound passion or really tragic conception, he has nothing . . . we go to him to be amused, to be en-

[13] John Masefield, *Chaucer,* Macmillan, 1931, p. 27.

tertained, to watch the shows of things. He is the poet of the eye, not of the heart or the soul" and he belongs to "the third or the fourth class of great poets." This writer holds it against Chaucer that he "exhibits scarcely a sign of any reforming spirit," that "in all his work there is not an allusion to English politics . . . not a single patriotic utterance," and that in his treatment of the representatives of the Church "there is no word against the system, no condemnation of the personages. He expresses no indignation. . . . He did not take the matter to heart." [14]

Well, neither did Shakespeare take the matter to heart. Yeats in one of his essays reminds us that the business of a poet is "revelation and not reformation," and he praises Shakespeare as one who understood this and was content to "watch the procession of the world with sympathy for men as they are." Great literature, he says, "has always been written in a like spirit, and is, indeed, the Forgiveness of Sin, and when we find it becoming the Accusation of Sin, as in George Eliot . . . it has begun to change into something else." [15] In another essay Yeats sets it down as a fault

[14] J. E. Wells, *Manual of the Writings in Middle English,* New Haven, 1923, pp. 602–606.

[15] W. B. Yeats, *Ideas of Good and Evil,* Macmillan, 1924, pp. 125–26. Ruskin expresses much the same thought. He remarks that Shakespeare seems to have been sent into the world to portray human nature without warp or bias, and adds, "It was necessary that he should lean *no* way; that he should contemplate, with absolute equality of judgment, the life of the court, cloister, and tavern, and be able to sympathize so completely with all creatures as to deprive himself, together with his personal identity, even of his conscience, as he casts himself into their hearts. He must be able to enter into the soul of Falstaff or Shylock with no more sense of contempt or horror than Falstaff or Shylock themselves feel for or in themselves; otherwise his own conscience and indignation would make him unjust to them; he would turn aside from something, miss some good, or overlook some essential palliation. He must be utterly without anger, utterly without purpose; for if a man has any serious purpose in life, that which runs counter to it, or is foreign to it, will be looked at frowningly or carelessly by him. Shakespeare was forbidden by Heaven to have any *plans.* . . . Not, for him, the founding of institutions, the preaching of doctrines, or the repression of abuses. Neither he, nor the sun, did on any morning that they arose together, receive charge from their Maker concerning such things. They were both of them to shine on the evil and good; both to behold unoffendedly all that was upon the earth, to burn unappalled upon

of most of the Victorian poets that they failed to keep to the proper subjects of poetry. He saw, he says, "that Swinburne in one way, Browning in another, and Tennyson in a third, had filled their work with what I called 'impurities, curiosities about politics, about science, about history, about religion, and that we must create once more the pure work." [16] These are fundamental points and are understood by most critics and by most scholars. Chaucer, so far from being condemned, deserves the highest praise for refusing to make his poetry a vehicle of moral indignation and reform and for keeping out of it the politics, religion, and social ills of his time. This is one of the things in which he is superior to Langland and Gower. Like Shakespeare, Chaucer wrote as one whose business was "revelation and not reformation" and he watched "the procession of the world with sympathy for men as they are."

The view that Chaucer has but little interest "in the human heart or the ways of the soul" and nothing of "profound passion or really tragic conception" may be put down to sheer blindness and insensibility. Chaucer's characters come trooping in crowds to refute it. Well considered, the drama of the *Canterbury Tales* proves that from first to last Chaucer's supreme interest was precisely his interest in the human heart and the ways of the soul. What else explains the greatness of the Wife of Bath's Prologue, of the Pardoner's confession, of the *Nun's Priest's Tale,* or of such of the fabliaux as the *Miller's Tale* and the *Merchant's Tale?* Is there no profound passion, no real tragedy, in *Troilus and Criseyde?* It is its passion and tragedy that make it one of the world's great love stories, and Chaucer's telling of it

---

the spears of kings, and undisdaining, upon the reeds of the river." *Modern Painters,* vol. IV, chap. XX.

There is another remark by Yeats which it is well to remember in this connection: "Only that which does not teach, which does not cry out, which does not persuade, which does not condescend, which does not explain, is irresistible." *Op. cit.,* p. 423.

[16] W. B. Yeats, *The Trembling of the Veil,* Macmillan, 1927, p. 207.

superior to Boccaccio's, Shakespeare's, and Dryden's. What else but Chaucer's interest in the heart and soul of Criseyde has made her one of the most fascinating and baffling of the heroines of fiction? The world has wondered at his pity for her, his sympathy. Well, his sympathy is due to his depth of understanding, to that vision, that insight into the ways of the human heart and soul, which he is said to lack.

In much of this adverse criticism of Chaucer there is, as I have said, the suggestion that the critic has failed to read Chaucer, to read all of him, and to read with sufficient care and sympathy. But there is in it, too, something of the limitation of the characteristic Victorian, or indeed English, view of poetry and of the function of the poet—the view that the poet partakes, or should partake, of the character of the priest, the prophet or *vates,* and be an instrument in the hands of God for the ennobling of human life—a view inherited from Spenser and Milton, represented strongly in Carlyle's conception of the poet and writer, seen in practically all of Ruskin's criticism of painting and architecture, and present as perhaps the chief though veiled motif in the literary criticism of Matthew Arnold. It is seen in Arnold's definition of poetry and of all literature as at bottom "a criticism of life," in his declaration that "the noble and profound application of ideas to life is the most essential part of poetic greatness" and that poetry should answer "the question *How to live."* It is seen in his conviction that Goethe's "most important line of activity" was as "a soldier in the war of liberation of humanity." We must "turn to poetry to interpret life for us, to console us, to sustain us," and he prophesies that "most of what now passes with us for religion and philosophy will be replaced by poetry."

It is a commonplace that the English have seldom been interested in art as art. They have looked upon art as they have looked upon beauty, and in dealing with either have been entirely comfortable only when enlisting them in the cause of morality or the "liberation of humanity." Ruskin's view "that a thing be beautiful is not enough" is thoroughly English. With few exceptions English critics, from Sir Philip Sidney down, have stressed the moral, didactic, and edifying aspects of poetry. Even in Coleridge there was much of the prophet, as much perhaps as there was of the poet, the critic, or the philosopher. And one suspects that it was this aspect of the English mind which led to the exaltation of Milton as the greatest of English poets next to Shakespeare. When, in the *Biographia Literaria,* Coleridge speaks of the "two glory-smitten summits of the poetic mountain" on which Shakespeare and Milton are seated—Milton "his compeer not rival"—he is in part voicing critical tradition and making the necessary modification of Addison's view of *Paradise Lost* as "the greatest production, or at least the noblest work of genius, in our language," but he is also writing as one to whom beauty and art are not enough, or to whom grandeur and sublimity, if joined with the didactic and edifying, are sufficient, however remote they may be from life in all its fullness and variety. When Arnold says, "we all of us recognize . . . Shakespeare and Milton as our poetical classics," he is doing the same thing. Arnold is fully alive to the shortcomings of *Paradise Lost* and mentions some of them: it is not really a theological poem but a commentary on a biblical text; in form it is "the copy of a copy, a tertiary formation";[17] its incidents awaken only "the most languid interest"; the theological speeches are not "attractive poetry," but poetically tiresome; "the afflictions and sentiments of Adam and Eve" fail to move the reader "passionately at all." But in Arnold's opinion these weaknesses are all outweighed and compensated for by the grandeur of Milton's style, his "unfailing level of style." And it is on this score that Arnold gives Milton his distinguished place next to Shakespeare. No one has said so much about

[17] Arnold is here quoting Scherer.

the grand style as Arnold has. But if one looks closely, one sees that his interest in it, his sense of its value, springs from moral considerations more than artistic. The soul of the power of poetry and art, he says, "resides chiefly in the refining and elevation wrought in us by the high and rare excellence of the great style," and "our grand source" for these "influences of refining and elevation" is Milton.

From this stress upon the edifying aspects of literature and art there was a definite reaction even in Victorian times, especially by the Pre-Raphaelites, by Pater, Wilde, Whistler, and subsequently by Arthur Symons, Yeats, and George Moore. Pater, like Arnold, had much to say about the elevation and adornment of the human spirit, but while Arnold stressed its elevation, Pater emphasized its adornment. His interest in art was an æsthetic interest, and he defined and practised "æsthetic criticism." More than any other English critic he subscribed to the doctrine of art for art's sake, though both Wordsworth and Coleridge had given lip-service to the Aristotelian principle of pleasure as the end of art. It is a matter for regret that Pater never wrote on Chaucer. A critic who exclaimed, "To live ever in the concrete! to be sure, at least, of one's hold upon that!"—who laid so much stress upon "the here and now," who praised Wordsworth's poetry for its "precise and vivid incidents," and who exalted Lamb because "in the making of prose he realizes the principle of art for its own sake, as completely as Keats in the making of verse . . . working ever close to the concrete, to the details, great or small, of actual things . . . with no part of them blurred to his vision by the intervention of mere abstract theories"—such a critic should have found much to praise in Chaucer's art. But Pater seems to have known little of Chaucer. In the whole of Pater's work there is but one reference to him, a brief passage on the *Knight's Tale*.

All of this bears definitely upon the criticism of Chaucer,

for Chaucer did not write as a vicar of God or as a reformer. Not even in his satire is he a reformer. Nor did he write as one who believed that the business of the poet is to answer the question How to live, or that "the noble and profound application of ideas to life is the most essential part of poetic greatness." Chaucer conceived of and practised poetry in its broadest sense—in the sense of Hazlitt's definition [18] and in the sense of Keats's famous lines about beauty and truth. He would have subscribed not only to the view that Beauty is Truth but to the view that Truth is Beauty.

It will not do, of course, in this day, to take Matthew Arnold too seriously. But his pronouncement on Chaucer was made with so much authority and appearance of finality that it carried great weight and its influence may be seen even yet. It is present in the recent critic's statement that Chaucer is "not what we understand by a great poet." Arnold did not go so far as this, but he said something very much like it. It is seen in Mr. Noyes's statement that

> Chaucer definitely falls short of the highest poetry. He never touches the sublime; he never gives us that deep understanding of the eternal harmonies that we hear in that other Catholic poet of the Middle Ages:
>
> In la sua volontade è nostra pace.

Here Mr. Noyes uses the identical line from Dante that Arnold uses for the same purpose, and in another place he follows Arnold in claiming that "Chaucer does not write great single lines."

In many ways Arnold's criticism of Chaucer is generous and even handsome.[19] Chaucer's "power of fascination" is enduring and his poetical importance is real. "He is a genuine source of joy and strength, which is flowing still for us

[18] See the opening pages of Hazlitt's lecture "On Poetry in General" in *Lectures on the English Poets.*

[19] It is found in the essay, "The Study of Poetry" in *Essays in Criticism,* 2nd Series.

and will flow always." His "large, free, simple, clear yet kindly view of human life" gives his poetry "truth of substance." He is "the father of our splendid English poetry; he is our 'well of English undefiled,' because by the lovely charm of his diction, the lovely charm of his movement, he makes an epoch and founds a tradition. In Spenser, Shakespeare, Milton, Keats, we can follow the tradition of the liquid diction, the fluid movement, of Chaucer; at one time it is his liquid diction of which in these poets we feel the virtue, and at another time it is his fluid movement. And the virtue is irresistible. . . . The virtue is such as we shall not find, perhaps, in all English poetry,,outside the poets whom I have named as the special inheritors of Chaucer's tradition." And in illustration of the excellence of Chaucer's style he quotes a stanza from the *Prioress's Tale.* He concedes that Chaucer's poetry "transcends and effaces, easily and without effort, all the romance-poetry of Catholic Christendom . . . all the English poetry contemporary with it . . . all the English poetry subsequent to it down to the age of Elizabeth."

All this is excellent and, as I have said, even handsome. But Arnold goes on to insist that "Chaucer is not one of the great classics. He has not their accent. . . . The accent of such verse as

In la sua volontade è nostra pace

is altogether beyond Chaucer's reach. . . . Something is wanting, then, to the poetry of Chaucer, which poetry must have before it can be placed in the glorious class of the best," and that something is "the high and excellent seriousness, which Aristotle assigns as one of the grand virtues of poetry. The substance of Chaucer's poetry, his view of things and his criticism of life, has largeness, freedom, shrewdness, benignity; but it has not this high seriousness. Homer's criticism of life has it, Dante's has it, Shakespeare's has it. It is this chiefly which gives to our spirits what they can rest upon." And he adds, "the voice of poor Villon . . . has at its happy moments . . . more of this important poetic virtue of high seriousness than all the production of Chaucer." And he quotes in illustration the last stanza of Villon's *La Belle Heaulmière.*

The first thing to be said of all this is that though in general Arnold quoted much in his literary criticism—indeed, it was part of his critical method, and he quoted frequently from Homer, Virgil, Dante, Shakespeare, Milton, and Wordsworth—the quotation here, in the essay on the *Study of Poetry,* of a line and a stanza from the *Prioress's Tale,* is the only quotation from Chaucer to be found in the whole of Arnold's work. We thus have evidence that he had read the *Canterbury Tales,* at least in part, but no evidence that he had read any other work by Chaucer, not even *Troilus and Criseyde* or the *Legend of Good Women.*[20] The impression Arnold gives is that his knowledge of Chaucer is slight and thin. The quotation from the *Prioress's Tale* is far from being the happiest choice he could have made to illustrate Chaucer's verse at its best. Many lines in Chaucer's poetry, even in the *Canterbury Tales,* have more of the grace and melody, the unmistakable accent, of great poetry, than have these. And when Arnold quotes the line from Dante and says that the accent of such verse "is altogether beyond Chaucer's reach," we wonder just how much he knew about Chaucer's pronunciation, even as late as 1880; and this in spite of what he says in appreciation of Chau-

[20] The only reference to his reading of Chaucer occurs in a letter dated November 1880, and written while he was at work upon this essay, "The Study of Poetry." But it gives no indication as to how much or as to what individual works of Chaucer Arnold had read: "I have been reading Chaucer a great deal, the early French poets a great deal, and Burns a great deal. Burns is a beast, with splendid gleams, and the medium in which he lived, Scotch peasants, Scotch Presbyterianism, and Scotch drink, is repulsive. Chaucer, on the other hand, pleases me more and more, and his medium is infinitely superior." George W. E. Russell, ed., *Letters of Matthew Arnold,* N.Y., 1895, vol. II, p. 214.

cer's "divine liquidness of diction, his divine fluidity of movement." There is more than one indication that Arnold was not altogether at ease in reading Chaucer. In his earlier essays *On Translating Homer* (1861–62) he speaks several times of the difficulty of Chaucer's English: "The diction of Chaucer is antiquated"; "numbers of Chaucer's words are antiquated for poetry"; "When Chaucer . . . is to pass current amongst us, to be familiar to us . . . he has to be modernized"; "Chaucer's words . . . are yet not thus an established possession of an Englishman's mind." And in the 1880 essay he writes that Chaucer's "language is a cause of difficulty for us." Neither Leigh Hunt nor Landor had such complaints to utter or was embarrassed by the difficulty of Chaucer.

When, for example, Hunt comes to the description in the *Knight's Tale* of the great "Emetreus, the kyng of Inde," with its line

> Cam ryding lyk the god of armes, Mars,

he exclaims, "There's a noble line, with the monosyllable for a climax!" It *is* a noble line, and, if I am not mistaken, in the grand style. Chaucer's poetry contains many a line in the grand style; some of them, like this, notable for their force and a certain majesty; others more touched with sweetness and tenderness, but in equal degree the perfect expression of the thought and examples of the melody that is so peculiarly Chaucer's own. But in order to appreciate them, to perceive that they *are* in the grand style, one must understand both Chaucer's pronunciation and his prosody. Here are a half dozen of them, set down as separate lines:

> And in a tombe of marbul-stones clere
>
> Of olde Britons, dwellinge in this yle
>
> That Gawain, with his olde curteisye

Doun at the rote of Vesulus the colde

Hir olde povre fader fostred she

O tendre, o dere, o yonge children myne

Such lines come to Chaucer easily and naturally, it seems, for they often occur in passages of rather matter-of-fact narrative. In such a setting their beauty startles and delights us all the more:

So longe he seyled in the salte se

Of olde stories, longe tyme agoon

They occur even in the fabliaux, the last place where Matthew Arnold would find them:

The dede sleep, for wery bisinesse

Wery and weet, as beste is in the reyn

Again, when the Pilgrims reach the little town of Bob-up-and-Down and the drunken Cook falls off his horse, Chaucer describes the difficulty they had in getting him up again:

Ther was greet showving bothe to and fro,
To lifte him up, and muchel care and wo,
So unweldy was this sory palled gost.

Here the last line is worthy of Dante at his best, whether in vivid imagery, in strength of imagination, or in accent and movement. But this example would run foul of Arnold's dogma that "the subject must be a serious one (for it is only by a kind of license that we can speak of the grand style in comedy)." [21]

The high seriousness which Arnold insists upon as necessary to the greatest poetry is no doubt a noble thing, and

[21] Chesterton very happily speaks of Chaucer as "a humorist in the grand style." *Op. cit.*, p. 10.

perhaps it springs, as he says it does, from "a noble nature." But to a broader criticism and to a critic possessed of a larger humanity it might well seem to spring from weakness, from too great an intensity and narrowness, from the weakness of taking things too seriously, and of taking one's self too seriously along with everything else. Homer, Dante, Milton, and Wordsworth might have been greater poets even than they are had they possessed a sense of humor. It is uncritical, not to say a little absurd, to degrade or disparage a writer for having a sense of humor. The high seriousness of a Dante, a Milton, a Wordsworth—a persistent, unrelieved, and chronic high seriousness—is impossible to men like Chaucer, Shakespeare, Fielding, Lamb, or Thackeray, not alone because they have a sense of humor, but because of their rich and abundant knowledge of life and the breadth of their sympathies. Where it exists, it is the product, it may be, of a noble nature, but also certainly of an intense egotism and a comparatively pale and bloodless humanity. Milton's soul was like a star and dwelt apart, and it was Wordsworth who so described it.

Arnold concedes that Chaucer's criticism of life has "largeness, freedom, shrewdness, benignity." But it has more than this; it has also high seriousness—where high seriousness is called for. The outstanding examples are the *Knight's Tale* and *Troilus and Criseyde.* Dryden preferred the *Knight's Tale* "far above all" Chaucer's other stories. And in dedicating his translation of it to the Duchess of Ormond, he goes even further.

> The bard who first adorned our native tongue
> Tuned to his British lyre this ancient song;
> Which Homer might without a blush reherse,
> And leaves a doubtful palm in Virgil's verse:
> He matched their beauties, where they most excel;
> Of love sung better, and of armes as well.

High seriousness or no high seriousness, Dryden here places Chaucer with two of "the great classics" and sets him above them in the treatment of love, though on that count the *Knight's Tale* cannot compare with the *Troilus*. In modern times Pater has praised the *Knight's Tale* as a noble and powerful handling of the theme of friendship, and he rightly describes this as "especially a classical motive." The poem is conceived and executed in the spirit of the highest art. And of specific passages that illustrate the quality of high seriousness, one may mention the famous death of Arcite, or, at the end of the poem, Theseus's speech on the death of all things. The latter strikes the moral and philosophical note and is obviously and directly a criticism of life. The former is something better than this, a bit of life itself, a very moving and tragic bit of life portrayed with perfect truth and art. Both have "the high seriousness which comes from absolute sincerity"—the quality Arnold denied to Chaucer and acknowledged only in "the great classics" he named.

But the supreme example of high seriousness in the poetry of Chaucer is to be found in *Troilus and Criseyde,* in the poem as a whole and in many of its parts. The love of Troilus and Criseyde, set against the background of the siege of Troy, entangled with the enmities and treacheries of war, destined to a tragic end by the gods and a hostile fate, and overshadowed even in its moments of bliss by the impending doom of the city, is one of the triumphant examples of high seriousness in English poetry. And this is true whether we think of high seriousness in its moral or in its artistic aspects. The interest deepens as the story unfolds, the action rises to a higher and higher plane, until in the last book Troilus is revealed as a figure of high tragedy, helpless in the toils of "fatal destyne," with no hope but to find early death in battle. Moreover, in style and in the handling of details of character and scene Chaucer's art is commensurate with the greatness of his theme.

It is strange that one who laid so much stress as Arnold did upon the importance of the action or the story in great poetry, who wrote that "the eternal objects of poetry, among all nations, and at all times" are "actions, human actions" and that "A great human action of a thousand years ago is more interesting . . . than a smaller human action of to-day," who praised the Greeks because with them "the poetical character of the action in itself, and the conduct of it, was the first consideration," who found fault with Keats's *Isabella, or the Pot of Basil* and with the moderns in general because they neglect structure, suffer the action to "go as it will, with occasional bursts of fine writing and with a shower of isolated thoughts and images"—it is strange that such a critic did not value Chaucer more highly, did not see that Chaucer is the supreme master of the story in English poetry, with as fine an instinct for what will make a great story as art in managing it. When Arnold bids us read the story of Keats's poem in Boccaccio to see "how pregnant and interesting the same action has become in the hands of a great artist, who above all things delineates his object; who subordinates expression to that which it is designed to express," he is sending us abroad for a model when there was a better one at home, and to a model upon whose art the first great English poet so greatly improved in the very points at issue. Chaucer more than any other English poet "succeeds in effacing himself and in enabling a whole action to subsist as it did in nature." And the outstanding instances of his success are the *Knight's Tale* and *Troilus and Criseyde.*

It is strange, too, that Arnold, with his love of the classical, of order and sanity, did not see that order and sanity are of the essence of Chaucer's poetry. "Sanity," he exclaims, "that is the great virtue of the ancient literature: the want of that is the great defect of the modern, in spite of all its variety and power." But it is not wanting in Chaucer. Chaucer is the sanest of English poets. And as Professor Lounsbury said forty years ago, "Of all the English poets no one is so fully the representative of the Hellenic element as Chaucer. . . . In him . . . can be recognized the Hellenic clearness of vision which saw human nature exactly as it was, and did not lack the courage to depict it."

Lastly, it is strange that one who defined literature as a criticism of life, who found fault with Shelley's poetry for its "unsubstantiality," its "incurable want, in general, of a sound subject-matter" and called him "that beautiful spirit building his many-coloured haze of words and images

'Pinnacled dim in the intense inane' "

should not have been more responsive to the fullness and truth of life in Chaucer. Again and again in reading Chaucer we realize that it is this quality that constitutes his greatest appeal. In this particular, only Shakespeare has excelled him. His poetry is steeped in life, and his subject-matter is as sound today as Shakespeare's, though two hundred years older—sounder far than Spenser's or Milton's. But Arnold ignored all this, or sacrificed it to a formula about high seriousness and the grand style. As a result his criticism of Chaucer is open to the charge of blindness and inconsistency. Probably he never read Chaucer thoroughly. Perhaps he objected to Chaucer's humor, realism, and occasional coarseness. And yet, one remembers that he gave high praise to Burns's *Jolly Beggars* and despite its "hideousness and squalor" and "bestiality," pronounced it "a superb poetic success." In any case, Arnold's criticism of Chaucer lacks the weight and authority its manner seems to give it, and he must be charged with doing less than justice by one of the greatest of English poets. This is the more to be regretted because Arnold is on the whole the greatest of modern English literary critics and because he is one of the most readable. A fuller and sounder criticism of Chaucer from his pen—as full and sympathetic, let us say, as his criticism of Wordsworth—might have drawn many readers to Chaucer from other than the academic circles to which readers of Chaucer today seem so largely to be confined.

CHAPTER III

The Development of Chaucer's Art

I

CLASSIFICATION OF HIS MAJOR WORKS

THE transformation wrought in the poetic scene in England by the work of Chaucer was sudden and striking. But the transformation or development within Chaucer's poetry itself is no less remarkable than that which the work of Chaucer brought about in the nation's poetry as a whole. There is nothing quite equal to it in any other poet's career—unless it be Shakespeare's. The early *Book of the Duchess,* for example, and the later *Troilus and Criseyde* are obviously the work of the same poet; they are both unmistakably Chaucer. And yet they are worlds apart. It is not that relatively the earlier poem is markedly immature; on the contrary, it has great merit and shows high promise. Nor is it that the earlier poem is largely imitative and conventional. The essential point is that it belongs to the medieval world of allegory and dream and looks backward to the *Roman de la Rose,* while the *Troilus* is of the modern world and points forward to the later glories of play and novel, to Shakespeare and Fielding. The earlier poem, it is true, gives evidence that even then the poet was finding his way toward a more lifelike art, a truer realism, than was to be found in his French models. But there is in it no hint of the splendors of *Troilus and Criseyde* or of the varied drama and masterly grasp of life we find in the *Canterbury Tales.* And yet the gulf between the *Book of the Duchess* and the *Troilus and Criseyde* or the *Canterbury Tales,* great though it is, is bridged by the intervening works. It is one of the most fascinating of studies to read Chaucer's major poems in what we believe to be their chronological order and to perceive the gradual broadening and deepening of his art, the eager assimilation of new knowledge, the steady gain in confidence and sureness of touch, until the poet who at the start was to a great extent conventional and imitative has produced not only two masterpieces, but two masterpieces unlike anything in the world before. The change was revolutionary and amounted to nothing less than the making of a new art in England, the creation of new literary types, of new verse and stanza patterns, and the introduction of a new grace and melody into English poetry. And it was freighted with enormous significance to subsequent English literature—in the drama, the novel, the short story, and in both narrative and lyric poetry.

It was once an accepted commonplace that Chaucer's career might be divided into three periods—the French, in which he imitated the French love-poets; the Italian, in which he was inspired and supposedly "emancipated" by Dante, Petrarch, and Boccaccio; and the English, in which he freed himself from foreign influence and came to the full maturity of his powers in dealing with English life of his own day. The scheme is neat and has some warrant in fact. It is roughly suggestive of certain phases of Chaucer's literary development. But its shortcomings are many, and in some ways it is downright misleading. Professor Kittredge pointed out certain of its weaknesses some years ago.[22] But there are still others. It leaves altogether out of consideration the Latin influence, which was great, especially that of Ovid. It implies that during the French and Italian periods there was little or no originality in Chaucer's work. It seems to indicate that his escape from the dominance of the French school was due to Italian influence alone, and that Chaucer did not reach his full stature or achieve mastery in his art

[22] G. L. Kittredge, *Chaucer and His Poetry,* Cambridge, 1915, pp. 26–28.

until the period of the *Canterbury Tales,* although the *Troilus and Criseyde,* done in the so-called Italian period, is as great and perfect a work of art as the *Canterbury Tales,* and in the opinion of some a greater and more perfect work. But its chief defect is that it lays too much stress upon influences and tends to underrate Chaucer's contribution to his own development. It seems to imply that his growth was chiefly from without, that there was little virtue or genius, other than a power of assimilation, in the man himself. It is part and parcel of the naïve belief that the explanation of all things is to be sought in the indication of influences and the determination of sources.

For critical purposes and for a clearer view of the progress of Chaucer's art, it is better to ignore for the moment this conventional threefold division of his career and to examine briefly the two strikingly different groups into which his major poems fall. Influences and borrowings are found in all his works—his latest and most mature as well as his earlier. But so also is originality. And I suspect that far the more important was his originality, and that the triumphs he achieved in the end were the result of his native powers and temperament, of more or less consciously formed artistic perceptions and ideals, and of a constant searching and experimenting calculated to satisfy these, quite as much as the result of subjection to influences from abroad. It is possible, for instance, that Chaucer was a capital story-teller long before he ever read Ovid or Virgil or Boccaccio. There are such things as born story-tellers, and Chaucer seems to have been one of them. And he appears to have had from the first an instinct or a taste for the concrete, the real, and the natural—to say nothing of his sense of humor—which would account for many of his most characteristic excellences.

Chaucer's major poems in their probable chronological order are the *Book of the Duchess,* the *House of Fame,* the

Parliament of Fowls, Troilus and Criseyde, the *Legend of Good Women,* and the *Canterbury Tales.* Of these, the first three and the *Legend of Good Women* may be placed in one group and recognized as Experimental Works. *Troilus and Criseyde* and the *Canterbury Tales* form the second group and may be called The Masterpieces. These titles fail to suggest all the differences between the two groups, but they at least stress the important fact that Chaucer's mastery came only after long and varied experiment, without implying that it was the result only or chiefly of foreign influence, especially from Italy.

Of the poems of the first group, two are unfinished—the *House of Fame* and the *Legend of Good Women.* The *Canterbury Tales* is also unfinished, but only, presumably, on account of the poet's death; not, as seems to have been the case in the earlier instances, because the artist in him was dissatisfied with the experiment and was pushing on to new and more ambitious things. One of these two poems, the *House of Fame,* is peculiarly of a transitional and experimental nature, as we shall see. Two certainly, and probably all four, of the poems in the first group are occasional poems —a fact especially significant. Lastly, three of the four, and part of the fourth—the Prologue of the *Legend of Good Women*—are dream-poems belonging to the familiar French genre of love-vision made so popular by the *Roman de la Rose* and still much in vogue in Chaucer's day in England as well as in France.

The love-vision is a highly conventional thing. It opens characteristically with an account of the poet's falling asleep and having a marvelous dream. In the dream he finds himself in a meadow full of daisies, a walled garden, a great forest, or in a richly decorated chamber, or a temple of glass. There are conventional decorations—a May morning, singing birds, painted walls. The story does not begin until the dream introduces it, and what happens happens in a dream. The setting is not of this world but of a dream-world. And the characters are dream characters. Usually they are not actual persons from real life, but abstract or symbolic personages. They have no names, other than "the man in black" and his "lady bright," or the Eagle, the Goddess of Fame, Nature, the God of Love, and the well-known personifications of allegory—Beauty, Youth, Delight, Foolhardiness, Flattery, Desire, and the like. Nor has the place of action a name, for it is really not a place at all. It never was, on land or sea; it has neither latitude nor longitude. Thus, everything in the vision-poem is shadowy and remote. The story is a story within a story, and the telling of it the imitation of an imitation. The love-vision as a literary type, at least from the modern viewpoint, is weak in substance and wanting in definition and dramatic realism. In its remoteness and its element of "strangeness in beauty" it is thoroughly romantic, and in its allegory and symbolism typically medieval.

The poems of the second group belong to a very different category. *Troilus and Criseyde* and the *Canterbury Tales* represent an art that is modern rather than medieval. And with them may be placed the individual legends of the *Legend of Good Women,* as distinct from its Prologue. These are not in any sense masterpieces comparable to *Troilus and Criseyde* and the *Canterbury Tales,* but in their substance and their art they belong with these rather than with the dream-pieces.

In the poems of the second group Chaucer has escaped from the dream and the garden of the Rose. He has given up allegory and gone to life directly, whether the life of classical and medieval myth and story or the life that he knew in his own England. His characters are individuals, with definite habitation and a name—Troilus, Pandarus, and Criseyde in the besieged city of Troy; Cleopatra, Queen of Egypt; Pyramus and Thisbe in Babylon; Dido and Aeneas in Carthage; Duke Theseus of Athens, Hippolyta his queen, and her fair sister Emily; John the carpenter of Oxford, and his young wife Alison, and Nicholas, and Absolon; Symkyn the parlous miller of Trumpington near Cambridge; Harry Bailly of the Tabard in Southwark, and so on. Everything has become more vivid, concrete, lifelike, and dramatic. In fact, in the *Canterbury Tales* the characterization is so highly specific that scholars have spent much labor in attempting to identify some of the pilgrims and some of the characters in the stories with actual persons of Chaucer's day. Certain features of the code of Courtly Love have been retained in such things as *Troilus and Criseyde* and the *Knight's Tale,* but only because they are true to human nature and are psychologically sound. In the matter of structure and form there has likewise been a great advance. The long proem or approach to the story is eliminated; the action is more direct and generally more swift; the design is carefully blocked out; and the individual scenes and the work as a whole have acquired nicer proportion and symmetry.

Chaucer the poet never conceived of art as a vehicle of religious or moral instruction, for such things as the *Tale of Melibeus* and the *Parson's Tale* are not only in prose but are dramatic in intention and must be considered as rightly a part of the dramatic scheme of the *Canterbury Tales* as a whole. The *Parson's Tale* is introduced as appropriate to the character of the Parson, and the *Tale of Melibeus*

> —a litel thing in prose,
> That oghte lyken yow, as I suppose—

is told by Chaucer in his character as pilgrim not in revenge upon the Host for so rudely interrupting his tale of *Sir Thopas,* nor really in the spirit of irony, but simply as certain to appeal to his hearers as affording sound practical advice. Chaucer was, however, of his time in his acceptance of the medieval love-vision and its conventions. And the cardinal feature of his development as an artist consists in his escaping from the dream world of the poems of Group I to the real world of those of Group II. In one sense, of course, this progress was in part really a return to the past, to the methods and ideals of classic art, as Chaucer discovered them in Ovid and Virgil and saw them adapted in Boccaccio. There is more in common between ancient and modern literary art than there is between either and medieval. And Chaucer is more modern in his great masterpieces than Ovid or Virgil or Boccaccio.

Chaucer began his poetic career, then, by accepting the form and conventions of the medieval dream-poem or love-vision as the prevailing popular mode of the day. And yet he did not accept it altogether. From the first he seems to have been aware of its limitations. And through the whole period of his dream-poems, which extended over the greater part of his literary career, he was apparently experimenting with ways of improving it, of making it more vital and human, and at the same time seeking new modes and new subjects upon which he could spend the full measure of his genius. This will become clear, I think, if we examine the poems of Group I in their probable chronological order, especially the *Book of the Duchess* and the *House of Fame.*

II

THE BOOK OF THE DUCHESS

The change from the art of the poems of Group I to that of the poems of Group II is usually ascribed to Italian influence, to Dante and Boccaccio in particular. Professor Lowes, for example, has recently said that Chaucer's "private Renaissance" began when he returned to England from his first visit to Italy in 1372–73, bringing with him manuscripts of Dante, Boccaccio, and Petrarch; and he adds that the demand "of Genoese merchants for a port in England changed the current of English poetry." [23] The late Professor Ker was of opinion that Chaucer did not really know how to tell a story until he learned the art from Boccaccio. The "intuition of the right lines of a story," he said, "was what Chaucer learned from Boccaccio. There is nothing more exhilarating in literary history than the way in which Chaucer caught the secret of Boccaccio's work, and used it for his own purposes." Again, "Chaucer had all the medieval tastes, the taste for exorbitant digressions and irrelevances, the love of useful information, the want of proportion and design," and then he read Boccaccio and from him learned "the lesson of restraint and coherence." And lastly, "Chaucer learned from Boccaccio the art of construction . . . the lesson of sure and definite exposition." [24]

The Italian influence upon Chaucer, especially that of Boccaccio, was undoubtedly great. But its importance has been exaggerated and its nature widely misunderstood. No doubt "the current of English poetry" was changed by Chaucer's first visit to Italy, but it had already been changed before this when Chaucer first wrote, in the tradition of French poetry, as artist and love-poet and lover of beauty rather than as moralist. And Chaucer's "own particular and private Renaissance" began, I should say, not with his reading of the Italians, but before this, with his reading of Ovid, or of Ovid and Virgil. That Chaucer knew much about the art of telling a story and about construction, design, proportion, restraint, and coherence before he had read the Italians is clear, I think, in the *Book of the Duchess*. That he learned something of these things from Dante and Boccaccio there can be no doubt, but he knew much about them before, either from his reading of Ovid and Virgil or from the instinct of his own genius or both.

[23] J. L. Lowes, *Geoffrey Chaucer*, Boston and New York, 1934, pp. 55–56.
[24] W. P. Ker, *Medieval Literature*, Macmillan, 1905, pp. 69, 71, 84, 87.

Moreover, the critics who stress Boccaccio's influence recognize and applaud the improvements Chaucer made upon Boccaccio, in these very respects, when in the *Knight's Tale* and *Troilus and Criseyde* he told again the stories of Boccaccio's *Teseide* and *Il Filostrato.* It is a bit odd to maintain that Chaucer learned design, proportion, and "the right lines of a story" from the very man he so improved upon in these regards. The preferable view is that he was learning these things all the time—partly from his reading in the French poets and in Ovid and Virgil, and partly through his own experience and experimentation. What he found in Boccaccio was the right kind of subjects. And the influence of Dante and Boccaccio consisted rather in stimulating and strengthening powers and qualities already present in Chaucer's work than in bringing to it something entirely new. In this matter of Chaucer's development the terms "bondage" and "emancipation" are much too strong. He was never emancipated because he was never in bondage—not even to the French school. The *Book of the Duchess* has as much freshness and originality as the early work of many another poet, and in point of design, management of the story, and "restraint and coherence"—though restraint is by no means one of its outstanding virtues—it excels, for example, the narrative poems of Shakespeare, *Venus and Adonis* and the *Rape of Lucrece.* And there is no trace of Italian influence in it. It was written, indeed, before Chaucer went to Italy, and therefore when he had presumably not read a word of Dante or Boccaccio.

Chaucer's debts to others in the *Book of the Duchess* are many. It has been shown that he borrowed freely from Ovid, from several poems by Machaut, from Froissart, from the *Roman de la Rose,* and from other sources. And yet, as Professor Lowes admirably says, "the incredible result is a poem which is pure Chaucer." [25] The element of originality

[25] *Op. cit.*, p. 127.

in this the first of Chaucer's major poems and the one in which he is supposed to have been most in bondage to the French poets, is by no means small. It has been noted by various scholars, more recently by M. Legouis and Professor Kittredge. M. Legouis finds that Chaucer "has introduced into the most factitious of all poetic styles a sense of reality and a dramatic force, which brought life and colour to the conventions he dealt with." Under the influence of Machaut "he substituted human beings for the personified abstractions of the *Roman de la Rose*" but "went much further than Machaut in the way of realism"—in the brisk and natural conversation between the Dreamer and the Knight in Black and in "the dramatic tone of the narrative." And M. Legouis concludes that "nearly all the characteristics of Chaucerian poetry can be found indicated here in this still somewhat clumsy poem." [26]

Professor Kittredge, in what is by far the best appreciation of the poem we have, praises its originality and art even higher. He points out that here for the first time the love-vision and the lover's lament are "turned to the uses of a personal elegy" and that with great art Chaucer makes the elegy "spoken, not written merely," and spoken "by the lady's husband, who can best describe her beauty." The poet does not lament the Duchess in his own person but "detaches himself completely, to concentrate our attention on the theme, which is, as it ought to be, the bitter grief of the despairing husband." He thus achieves artistic detachment and this "becomes from this time forward a marked feature of Chaucer's method." Professor Kittredge praises the original character of the Dreamer, his childlike wonder, "the artless artfulness" with which he draws out the Knight and enables him to assuage his grief while telling of the beauty and graciousness of his lost Lady; the way in which "the

[26] E. Legouis, *Geoffrey Chaucer*. English translation by L. Lailavoix, London, 1913, pp. 81–82.

whole poem is developed out of the Dreamer's mood"; and the harmony of mood between the character of the Dreamer, the tale of Alcyone which he was reading before he went to sleep, and the bereavement of the Knight. The poem "is really like a dream," is true to dream psychology. And in the description of the Lady we have a veritable portrait, not a catalogue of items. It is heavily indebted to Machaut, and yet "nowhere in the poem does his [Chaucer's] originality appear more strongly." It is an example of the "admirable selective art that distinguishes the later work of the poet." And Professor Kittredge concludes that already in this early poem Chaucer "shows himself in immediate contact with the facts and experiences of human life—even with the life of dreams. . . . Never was there a more conventional situation. . . . Yet somehow the conventions are vitalized." [27]

From all this it is clear that in his first original poem of any length, and without benefit of Dante or Boccaccio, Chaucer achieved no little unity of effect, dramatic force, and truth to life. He also revealed touches of his characteristic humor, as in the description of Morpheus and the other gods of sleep in the dark cave in a deep valley—gods

> That slepe and did non other werk.
>
> . . . .
>
> They had good leyser for to route
> To envye, who might slepe beste;
> Some henge hir chin upon hir breste
> And slepe upright, hir heed yhed,
> And some laye naked in hir bed,
> And slepe whyles the dayes laste.

Again, when the messenger of Juno breaks in upon this group of masterful sleepers—not Iris, as in Ovid, but simply a messenger, a male messenger—he hails them with a gruff and hearty familiarity that anticipates the homely directness

[27] Kittredge, *op. cit.*, Chapter II.

of certain passages in the *Parliament of Fowls* and the *Canterbury Tales,* or the bluff manner of some of Pandarus's speeches to Troilus:

> This messager com flying faste,
> And cryed, "O ho! awak anon!"
> Hit was for noght; ther herde him non.
> "Awak!" quod he, "who is, lyth there?"
> And blew his horn right in hir ere,
> And cryed "awaketh!" wonder hyë.
> This god of slepe, with his oon yë
> Cast up, axed, "who clepeth there?"
> "Hit am I," quod this messagere.

A third instance is in the description of the feather-bed the poet vows to Morpheus if he will grant him the boon of sleep:

> Of downe of pure dowves whyte
> I wil yive him a fether-bed,
> Rayed with golde, and right wel cled
> In fyn blak satin doutremere,
> And many a pilow, and every bere
> Of clothe of Reynes, to slepe softe;
> Him thar not nede to turnen ofte.

Here we have not only the beautiful verse "In fyn blak satin doutremere," unexpected in this humorous passage, but the capital last line, slipped in as an aside and all the more effective by being so unobtrusive.

These instances of Chaucer's humor are also examples of his realism, which pervades pretty much the whole poem. It is seen, as we have noted, in his making the characters individuals instead of personified abstractions, in the success of the dream atmosphere and psychology, and in his use of the language of real life in the dialogue. The dialogue is not yet the vivid and fascinating thing it was later to become in *Troilus and Criseyde* and the *Canterbury Tales,* but it has the genuine accent of living speech. There is realism, too, in the description of the hunt, which accords in detail with the practice of the time; and in such little touches as the picture of the hunter blowing a blast

> Tassaye his horn, and for to knowe
> Whether hit were clere or hors of soune—

or the description of the whelp:

> Hit com and creep to me as lowe,
> Right as hit hadde me yknowe,
> Hild doun his heed and ioyned his eres,
> And leyde al smothe doun his heres.

And there is realism in the larger matters of character and human passion—in the portrayal of the anguish of Alcyone waiting in vain for the return of her shipwrecked husband, and in the rendering of the grief of the Knight in Black and of the beauty and charm of his Lady. The Knight is wholly taken up with his grief when the Dreamer comes upon him in the forest sitting with his back to an oak. He is bemoaning his lost Lady, and when addressed by the Dreamer, he does not hear him, is in fact unaware of his presence. He talks to himself and argues why and how his life should last. He has well-nigh lost his mind in his sorrow, and his words have the accent of genuine grief:

> "Allas, deeth! what ayleth thee,
> That thou noldest have taken me,
> Whan that thou toke my lady swete?
> That was so fair, so fresh, so free,
> So good, that men may wel [y]-see
> Of al goodnesse she had no mete!"

The description of the Lady is the most famous part of the poem and constitutes its chief note of beauty. Professor Lowes has justly described it as "a Portrait of a Lady unmatched (I think) save by Dante in medieval poetry." [28] And one may be excused for repeating that it was done, as we believe, before Chaucer had read a word of Dante or Boccaccio. It is the first thing of its kind in English—a full-length portrait of a woman, rendering successfully not merely her beauty but the sentiment of womanly charm, which Lowell felt so strongly and described so well. And it is but the first of a series of charming women that Chaucer was to give us. It is not a formal portrait, but one developed gradually and naturally in the course of the Knight's story. There is in it something of the schematizing or anatomizing that the Elizabethan poets were so fond of, but nothing at all mechanical. Chaucer describes her hair, her eyes and face, her neck, shoulders, arms, hands, and nails, her round breasts, her hips "of good brede," her long body and "straight flat bak." And though much of all this is found in his French models and is in accord with the conventions of the time, it seems entirely fresh and unconventional. Her hair

. . . "was not rede,
Ne nouther yelw, ne broun hit nas;
Me thoghte, most lyk gold hit was."

Nothing could be more commonplace than this comparison of a fair one's hair with gold, and yet the last line here, in the personal note it strikes, and in its accent and movement, rises to great poetry. Her face

"Was rody, fresh, and lyvely hewed;
And every day hir beaute newed."

How exquisitely this last line suggests the youthful freshness of her beauty! But her character is stressed quite as much as her beauty, and the poet—or the bereaved husband—dwells alternately upon her physical attractions and her

[28] *Op. cit.*, p. 125.

grace of mind, her "goodly softe speche," her thought set upon gladness and inclined to all good, her joy in life, her gayety tempered with dignity—

"Therwith hir liste so wel to live,
That dulnesse was of hir adrad.
She nas to sobre ne to glad."

Neither capricious nor petty, she had no desire to queen it over a lover, and for a whim send him to Prussia or Tartary, Alexandria or Turkey—

"She ne used no suche knakkes smale."

A thorough aristocrat, a lady of "noble port and meyntenaunce," her open and friendly manner is free from all hauteur or pride, and her truth and goodness are in no point insipid, but spring from her natural goodness of heart:

"She used gladly to do wel."

In a word, she is, as Lowell said, the fresh and charming young woman one would expect to find in the dewy woods rather than in a ballroom. And she has something too of the "violet nature of the girl," which Hawthorne found in many English girls. But she is also a woman of the world with knowledge of good and evil:

"I sey nat that she ne had knowing
What was harm; or elles she
Had coud no good, so thinketh me."

The picture is done with such truth and so strong a personal touch that we feel it must be not only a portrait of Blanche, Duchess of Lancaster, and an affectionate tribute to her from one who knew her well, but a revelation also of Chaucer's ideal of womanhood. He is writing from the heart. And his heart, it is clear, is set not on beauty alone but on goodness and truth, and especially on all that is suggested by the word "charm." Here at the beginning of his career the poet already possesses the art of portraying a woman vividly and of conveying to us a living sense of her beauty and character. The Lady in the *Book of the Duchess* is cousin to Criseyde, Constance, Griselda, Emily, and to some of the ladies in the *Legend of Good Women,* in that, though all are different, they are all women of gentle and tender heart, winsome and charming.

In this early poem Chaucer shows too his power of conveying the delicate beauty of nature. Whether he is describing the green ways of the forest-side with their thick, soft, sweet grass and their flowers—more than there are stars in the sky—

> As thogh the erthe envye wolde
> To be gayer than the heven—

or the forest itself with its noble trees and many living creatures, we feel the personal touch, the touch of one who no doubt had found suggestions for these passages in the French poets but who had also seen and loved these things himself, these

> . . . grete trees, so huge of strengthe,
> Of forty or fifty fadme lengthe,
> Clene withoute bough or stikke,
> With croppes brode, and eek as thikke . . .

and who had seen with loving eye the

> . . . many squirelles, that sete
> Ful hye upon the trees, and ete,
> And in hir maner made festes.

In faithful observation of animal life, and in tender sympathy with it, these last lines anticipate Burns, and yet they are unmistakably Chaucer and no one else—neither Burns, nor de Meun, nor Machaut, nor Froissart. The poet is working from within and giving us his characteristically delicate, simple, and homely feeling for nature, for winter and "hys colde morwes" that had made the earth suffer, or for the "swetnesse of dew" that made the woods again grow green.

We are introduced also in this poem to Chaucer's world of gentle breeding and high courtesy, and this may be counted as another of its beauties. The best example occurs in the conversation between the Knight and the Dreamer when the Knight is surprised and interrupted in his revery by the appearance of this stranger, who might well have been looked upon as an intruder and meddler. But so far from showing resentment or superiority because of higher rank, the Knight, truly gentle, apologizes for not hearing or perceiving the Dreamer sooner:

> He sayde, "I prey thee, be not wrooth,
> I herde thee not, to sayn the sooth,
> Ne I saw thee not, sir, trewely."
> "A! goode sir, no fors," quod I,
> "I am right sory if I have ought
> Destroubled yow out of your thought;
> Foryive me if I have mistake."
> "Yis, thamendes is light to make,"
> Quod he, "for ther lyth noon therto;
> There is nothing missayd nor do."
> Lo! how goodly spak this knight . . .

In spite of his grief and his apparent desire to be alone, the Knight is friendly and gracious, and the conversation is carried on as between equals. The adroitness with which the Dreamer draws out the Knight's story is an example of the most delicate tact, the result of perfect breeding. And perhaps we may see here one of the secrets of Chaucer's success as a diplomatist and trusted emissary of two English kings. Certainly the world to which Chaucer introduces us is a world of gracious and finished manners, and of a breeding that springs from true goodness of heart, from a living and sensitive humanity within. And this is Chaucer's habitual world—much more indeed than the world of the Tabard Inn, or the Wife of Bath, or the Pardoner, the Miller, or the Cook. We meet it in poem after poem—in the *Parliament of Fowls,* the *Anelida and Arcite, Troilus and Criseyde,* the *Legend of Good Women,* and a number of the *Canterbury Tales,* even in some of the fabliaux. This instance of it in the *Book of the Duchess* is but the first, and I mention it as another of the truly Chaucerian characteristics present in this early work.

Finally, there is the beauty of Chaucer's verse. In this early poem his verse is not as regular or as musical as it later became. The short octosyllabic lines lack the graver beauty of the later decasyllabic verse and indeed at times have something of the wooden, sing-song quality that characterizes so much of Middle English verse. But for the most part the lines are graceful and beautiful, and already Chaucer is making effective use of the feminine ending:

> And in this boke were writen fables
> That clerkes hadde, in olde tyme,
> And other poets, put in ryme
> To rede, and for to be in minde
> Whyl men loved the lawe of kinde.
> This book ne spak but of such thinges,
> Of quenes lyves, and of kinges,
> And many othere thinges smale.

There are, too, not a few striking and beautiful individual lines, such as those I have already cited:

> Me thoghte most lyk gold hyt was

> And every day hir beaute newed

or such as these:

> To rede, and drive the night away

> Me mette so ynly swete a sweven

That was so fair, so fresh, so fre

And pitee of my sorwes smerte.

The poem must have been a great success in the courtly circle for which it was written. It was not only an elegy on the death of a Duchess, paying high tribute to her beauty and character, and while describing the grief of the Duke, a prince of the realm, portraying him as a perfect knight and ideal lover, but a story which in all points would meet the courtly taste of the time—a love-story of a young knight, a perfect servant of love, and of the beautiful and charming lady he saw and loved and wooed and won. And in addition to this central interest there would be the interest in the story of Ceyx and Alcyone, in the dream, in the hunt, the forest, and other decorative features of the poem. And many a hearer or reader at the court must have been aware that here was a work of poetic art that transcended anything done in English before, and that England at last had a poet worthy to stand beside the greatest of French poets.

But the point of most interest at the moment is not the realism, humor, or beauty of this early work of Chaucer's, but the question of its proportion and design and whether or not Chaucer learned "the right lines of a story" and "the lesson of restraint and coherence" only when he read Boccaccio.

That the *Book of the Duchess* is a carefully designed and admirably coherent poem must be clear, I think, to anyone who reads it with attention and sympathy—not as an "early poem." Everything is done in order. The story advances step by step as in Chaucer's later and best work. It is to be the story of a dream. He explains how he came to have the dream. He had long suffered from sleeplessness, the result of a love-sickness which has afflicted him "this eight yeer." So one night not long before, being unable to sleep, he had picked up a book and in it found a tale, the tale of Ceyx and Alcyone, from which he learned for the first time of gods that could make men sleep. In jest he vowed rich gifts to Morpheus and Juno if they would grant him the boon of sleep. But no sooner were the words out of his mouth than he was seized with such a lust to sleep that he fell asleep on his book and had the sweet and wonderful dream of which he will tell. Thus it is precisely Chaucer's rigorous sense of order and coherence, and his feeling that a story must, as I have said, proceed step by step, with each step given its just proportion, that is the cause of the prologue's perhaps undue length. And it is this same sense of order, together with the laws and conventions of the literary type in which Chaucer was working, that governs the rest of the poem, or the story proper. But though the management of the story is due in part to Chaucer and in part to the laws of the love-vision mode, it is strictly logical and coherent, and the poem achieves the highly important quality of artistic unity.

Its proportions, it is true, are not what we would make them today. Nor are they those that Chaucer observed in his most mature work. But they are entirely sound from the point of view of the art-form he was using, and they are defensible even from the point of view of modern taste. Much of the criticism of the *Book of the Duchess* and of Chaucer's other dream-poems is due to misunderstanding of the type or to our modern impatience with it. But it was as natural and proper for Chaucer to cast his story in the form of a love-vision as it was for Marlowe or Shakespeare to write drama. It was the mode of the day, and Chaucer simply observed the demands of a special form. One of these was that the poet must explain how, where, and when he had the dream, and this of course necessitates a prologue and explains the delay in getting to the story proper. Another was that the love-story must accord with the system of Courtly Love and include an account of the Knight as a professed servant of Love, of the Lady's beauty and maidenly reserve, of the lover's pains, of his complaint against Fortune, of his long and faithful wooing and final winning of his love. These things, in the case of the *Book of the Duchess,* account for the somewhat protracted length of the story of the Knight in Black, which, however, Chaucer skilfully relieves by introducing bits of conversation between the Knight and the Dreamer.

But apart from all question of conventions, and considered from the modern point of view, is the Prologue or the Knight's story really too long? In a poem of 1,334 lines, the Knight's story covers 747 lines, of which 216 are given to a description of his Lady. But since the Knight's story of his love and his loss and the tribute to the beauty and charm of his Lady are the very heart of the poem, this is as it should be. The Prologue runs to 290 lines, or slightly more than one-fifth of the entire poem, which is not greatly out of proportion, if at all. Of the 290 lines, 158 are devoted to the story of Ceyx and Alcyone. And it is this that certain critics have fallen foul of—as being too long, or as being a digression pure and simple. The last point has been fully covered by Professor Kittredge, as we have seen. And that it is not too long is clear, I think, from its success. It is a little gem of story-telling in itself. Chaucer rightly judged that if it was worth telling at all, it was worth telling well. We must remember, too, that Chaucer seems at this time in his career to have been reading the classics—especially Ovid. And this tale from Ovid seems to have fascinated him. His own words—

> Whan I had red this tale wel,
> And overloked hit everydel—

point to the close and delighted attention he gave it.

That his attention and delight were born of the artist in him, I believe there can be no doubt. The story of Ceyx and

Alcyone is one of the best told of all the *Metamorphoses,* and in it Chaucer would find "the right lines of a story" if he had not found them before; of a story, moreover, full of the pathos he loved, dealing not with personified abstractions but human beings, and rendering human passion truly and dramatically; a story of a devoted husband and wife—especially of the devoted wife, tender and faithful, in terror of the sea, and torn by grief at the death of her husband. Here he would find a stirring account, full of action, of a storm and wreck at sea; and again, vivid scenes—as definite and clear-cut as pieces of sculpture—such as that of Alcyone weeping on the shore and watching her husband waving good-bye from the high-curved poop of his ship; or the picture of Sleep on his high ebony couch, with the countless empty dream-shapes lying about him; or that of Morpheus, in the likeness of the drowned Ceyx, standing wan and naked and wet, his beard and matted hair dripping with water, before the couch of the sleeping Alcyone. From such passages Chaucer could learn much as to the artistic use of detail, the importance of definition, and the ways of achieving realism. How vividly and with what skilful use of detail, at once homely and poetic, for example, does Ovid describe the darkness and silence of the cave of the gods of sleep! The rays of the sun never enter there. No morning cock or watchdog or goose disturbs the silence—no wild beasts or cattle, or rustling trees, or sound of human voice. And how true to life is he when he makes Alcyone groan aloud as she sees in her dream the image of her drowned husband! She seeks to clasp him in her arms, she cries out to him to stay and wait for her, and in so doing wakes herself to the tragic realization of what has happened. It is only a brief scene, but it is dramatic and memorable, and it is based upon true knowledge of the human heart, especially of woman's heart.

Chaucer's development as an artist consisted largely in

his getting ever closer to the lifelike and the actual, the specific and the concrete; in his learning to put more and more life into his work. The conviction seems to have grown upon him that the proper subjects of poetry are human beings and human passions. As he went on, he acquired a deeper and livelier interest in character and came to perceive that a character and an action must be *placed,* must have a setting or background as definite and as highly individualized as the character itself. More and more he saw that saliency and vividness, whether of character or scene, depend upon details, the telling use of specific details. And in his best work nothing is more striking than his remarkable sense for the concrete, his genius in finding and using significant and felicitous detail.

Now in Ovid—whether in this tale of Ceyx and Alcyone, which he retold, or in such a story as that of Baucis and Philemon, which he did not retell but which he certainly knew—Chaucer would again and again find things that would urge him in the direction I have mentioned. Few things in literature are more vivid, for example, than the picture we get of the thatched cottage of Baucis and Philemon and of the old couple bustling about preparing food for their stranger guests. I quote from Professor Miller's translation:

> . . . over this bench busy Baucis threw a rough covering. Then she raked aside the warm ashes on the hearth and fanned yesterday's coals to life, which she fed with leaves and dry bark, blowing them into flame with the breath of her old body. Then she took down from the roof some fine-split wood and dry twigs, broke them up and placed them under the little copper kettle. And she took the cabbage which her husband had brought in from the well-watered garden and lopped off the outside leaves. Meanwhile the old man with a forked stick reached down a chine of smoked bacon, which was hanging from a blackened beam and, cutting off a little piece of the long-cherished pork, he put it to cook in

the boiling water. . . . The old woman, with her skirts tucked up, with trembling hands set out the table. But one of its three legs was too short; so she propped it up with a potsherd. When this had levelled the slope, she wiped it, thus levelled, with green mint.[29]

The scene is Homeric in its lifelike and homely detail, and we at once think of Chaucer's description of the poor widow's "narwe cotage" and her way of life in the *Nun's Priest's Tale,* and of his marvelous success in setting before us a whole household and its economy in the *Miller's Tale,* the *Reeve's Tale,* or the *Summoner's Tale.* Dryden noted this parallel between Ovid and Chaucer, in a sentence famous for its second part but usually forgotten as to its first: "I see Baucis and Philemon as perfectly before me, as if some ancient painter had drawn them; and all the pilgrims in the 'Canterbury Tales,' their humours, their features, and the very dress, as distinctly as if I had supped with them at the Tabard in Southwark." And he adds, "the figures in Chaucer are much more lively, and set in a better light."

I am not laying too much emphasis upon the influence of Ovid. I am simply pointing out that in Ovid—as also in Virgil, in the story of Dido, for example, which he used in what we believe was his next major poem, the *House of Fame*—Chaucer found admirably told stories and artistic methods and ideals such as might well have led to his becoming increasingly dissatisfied with the French modes of the day and eventually to his abandoning them, and might well have set his native genius and taste moving in the direction it took, though he had never met with Dante and Boccaccio.

It must be remembered too that very early in his career Chaucer had found remarkable examples of realism in the *Roman de la Rose.* Jean de Meun was not only a great sati-

[29] Frank Justus Miller, *Ovid's Metamorphoses,* Loeb Classical Library, G. P. Putnam's Sons, vol. I, pp. 451–53.

rist, but a satirist who at times made masterful use of the realistic method. His portrait of the Duenna is one of the most brilliant in all literature, worthy to be hung beside the Wife of Bath or the Nurse in *Romeo and Juliet.* And it is definitely a triumph of realism. The Duenna's long, thoroughly pagan, realistic, cynical, and worldly wise discourse on love and marriage and on how women may make the most of love—pointed and enlivened as it is by generous allusions to her own rich experience, especially in the days of her prime when her door swung on its hinges day and night—is an early illustration of what can be done by the use of dramatic monologue and abundant specific detail to breathe life into what would otherwise be a mere description. Likewise in the amusing anecdote which Genius tells as a warning to men never to trust their secrets to their wives. The picture there of the wheedling woman worming a secret from her husband at night in bed is as lively and vivid as you please, and it is done for the most part by direct discourse of a highly colloquial kind and with telling use of detail. Both passages illustrate the way realism emerged in the thirteenth century, even in works of traditional medieval romance and allegory. That Chaucer appreciated to the full Jean de Meun's satirical and realistic method at the time he wrote the *Canterbury Tales* is well known; it has been emphasized again and again because of its influence upon the characters of the Prioress, the Wife of Bath, the Pardoner, and the Friar. The essential point is that Chaucer was thoroughly familiar with it early in his career and perhaps from the beginning. It was part of his equipment, in all probability, even before he wrote the *Book of the Duchess.* And in any study of Chaucer's development it must be borne in mind as an ever present potential impulse toward the realistic in his own work.

That Chaucer's native powers of story-telling were considerable even when he did the *Book of the Duchess* is seen not only in the way he improved upon the Old French vision-poem and adapted it to his uses, but in the improvements he made upon Ovid in retelling the story of Ceyx and Alcyone.

For one thing, Chaucer's version is much shorter than Ovid's—158 octosyllabic lines against 338 hexameters. And this is but the first of many instances of compression and improvement of the works of others to be found in Chaucer's poems. That Ovid's narrative is a bit too long I think there can be no doubt. He devotes ninety-eight lines to the description of the storm and shipwreck, which thus becomes really a digression and a piece of virtuosity, existing for itself and not as a properly proportioned and subordinated detail of the story. Chaucer gives it just seven and a half lines. Alcyone's plea that Ceyx should not take the journey Chaucer altogether omits. He omits the scene of Ceyx's departure, the account of Alcyone's preparations against his return and of her going to the shore after her vision and finding the dead body. He brings the story more strictly within the scope of human life by omitting all reference to the transformation into birds. He happily avoids Ovid's tendency toward didacticism by omitting the explanation of the various offices of the sons of Sleep. He changes Ovid's plot, and in so doing betters Ovid's psychology. In Ovid Alcyone is ignorant of Ceyx's death. She counts the nights until he shall return, she weaves the robes he is to put on and those she herself will wear, she burns incense to the gods and prays to Juno that her husband may be safe. And it is Juno who, finding these entreaties for the dead intolerable, informs Alcyone of the truth by sending her a vision of the drowned Ceyx. In Chaucer, Alcyone has forebodings because her husband does not return. She fears that he is dead, she vows to eat no bread until she hears of her lord; and when she can get no word of him and no man can find him, she prays Juno to help her, to give her grace to see her lord or to know where he is, to send her a dream that she may know the truth. Ovid is at fault here, because he represents Alcyone as being full of foreboding before Ceyx's departure, but as suffering none apparently during his absence. And it is much more fitting that the vision should be sent in answer to Alcyone's anxious prayers to Juno than because of Juno's merely feminine and petty annoyance at a mortal's continued solicitation for the life of a man already dead.

By these changes and by a very clear division of his narrative into four nicely proportioned parts, Chaucer throws even greater stress upon Alcyone than does Ovid. Ceyx is subordinated, the story becomes really Alcyone's story, and she stands forth a figure of passionate, wifely devotion and of tragic suspense and grief. Especially admirable is Chaucer's brief, dramatic ending—an ending which anticipates the swift resolution of the *Pardoner's Tale,* for instance; and this is another improvement upon Ovid.

Here then in this tale of Ceyx and Alcyone, the first story that so far as we know Chaucer ever told, he shows that he possessed a strong sense of design, proportion, and emphasis, of human values, of the pathetic and the dramatic; a sense furthermore that is decidedly his own and that enables him to improve upon his sources. Machaut and Froissart had also told this story from Ovid, and Chaucer knew their versions as he knew Ovid's. But as Professor Lowes has remarked, Chaucer's is "at once all of them, yet none of them but Chaucer," and is eloquent of the "unmistakable, individual stamp which Chaucer, even at this early day, set upon everything he touched." [30] But it is important to add that this element of originality included artistic qualities and powers which Chaucer is supposed to have acquired only after reading Boccaccio—among others the art of telling a story well. For this tale of Ceyx and Alcyone *is* told well; it holds the reader's interest and leaves with him the memory of a piti-

[30] *Op. cit.*, p. 119.

able and tragic fate. And yet, it is highly probable that it does not represent Chaucer at his best even at the time it was written, for it is a story told merely by the way, as part of the introduction to another story, and the poet is in haste to resume his narrative and arrive at the point where he can begin to satisfy the taste of his fashionable and courtly readers for the May morning, the hunt, the forest, and the other trappings of romance.

III

THE HOUSE OF FAME AND AFTER

To the student of Chaucer's poetic development the *House of Fame* is in some ways the most significant and fascinating of all his works, for it is so clearly experimental and in so peculiarly full a sense transitional. There are many things about it which remain uncertain. A longish poem of 2,158 lines in three books, it is unfinished, breaks off abruptly, almost we may say in the middle of a sentence, and no one can tell what it was to have been or what the meaning and significance may be of the poem as it stands. Its date is a matter of dispute. We cannot be absolutely sure that it is the first of Chaucer's major poems after the *Book of the Duchess*. So far as objective evidence is concerned the *Parliament of Fowls* and even the *Troilus and Criseyde* may have preceded it. But this is wholly improbable, and scholarly opinion today favors 1379 or 1380 as the probable date of its composition, and leans strongly to the view that the *House of Fame* is the second of Chaucer's major poems, with an interval of approximately ten years between it and the *Book of the Duchess*. In those ten years Chaucer had been to Italy twice, in 1372–73 and 1378. He had come to know Dante's *Divine Comedy* and some of the works of Boccaccio, though not, it would seem, those that were later to attract him so strongly. What he had written in the course of those ten years we cannot with certainty say, but probably the *Life of St. Cecilia,* afterwards incorporated in the *Canterbury Tales* as the *Second Nun's Tale;* the greater part of the work which later became the *Monk's Tale;* and several Complaints, such as the *Complaint to his Lady,* the *Complaint of Mars,* and possibly the *Complaint unto Pity*—although this last may have been written very early and before the *Book of the Duchess.* In all of these poems, with the probable exception of the *Complaint unto Pity,* there is more or less influence from Dante; and in the *Monk's Tale* there is influence also from Boccaccio's *De Casibus Virorum et Feminarum Illustrium* and *De Mulieribus Claris.* In the *House of Fame* the influence of Dante is such that certain scholars—though without sufficient cause—have considered the poem to be in some sort a humorous imitation or take-off of the *Divine Comedy.* All these works belong in type to the older tradition. The *Life of St. Cecilia* is little more than a translation of a Latin life. The *Monk's Tale* is a series of short "tragedies" in the medieval sense; the various Complaints conform to the pattern of the formal Complaints of Old French love poetry; and the *House of Fame* is a dream-poem, of the same Old French genre as the *Book of the Duchess.*

After an introductory discussion of dreams and an invocation to the god of sleep, the poet tells of a wonderful dream he had on the night of December tenth. He is within a temple of glass, in which are many golden images, rich tabernacles, and curious and beautiful paintings. It is the temple of Venus and on its walls are pictured the story of Troy and all the wanderings of Aeneas. He marvels in particular at the beauty of these paintings, but knows not who wrought them, or where he is, or in what country. So he goes forth by a wicket to make inquiry. But outside he sees only a great field

As fer as that I mighte see,
Withouten toun, or hous, or tree,
Or bush, or gras, or ered lond.

At last he is aware of an eagle soaring in the heavens, apparently an eagle of gold, it shines so bright, and it seems to be bending its flight downward.

So ends Book I. It is slightly over five hundred lines long, and of these, more than three hundred are given to the story of Aeneas, which is really an epitome of the *Aeneid,* the first in English, with special emphasis upon the love of Dido and Aeneas, his desertion of her, and her complaint of his falseness.

In Book II the Eagle, seeing Chaucer alone in the field, swoops down suddenly, seizes him fleeing, and carries him aloft in his strong claws—"as lyghtly as I were a larke." Dazed and faint from fright, Chaucer lies still. Soon the Eagle speaks to him, calls him by name, and jokes about his weight—

And tho gan he me to disporte,
And with wordes to comforte,
And sayde twyës, "Seynte Marie!
Thou art noyous for to carie."

He tells Chaucer he is Jove's bird who has been sent to carry him to the House of Fame, where he can learn many wondrous things, especially tidings of love and of love's servants. This Jove has done in compassion for Chaucer's long devotion to the God of Love, and to give him some disport and some easement of his labors. The Eagle tells Chaucer where Fame dwells and explains how all tidings and sounds from earth are carried to Fame's abode. He prides himself on his learning and his powers of description, Chaucer meanwhile hanging helpless in his talons and forced to listen. His guide then points out the galaxy and other wonders of the heavens, and tells the story of Phaeton driving the chariot of the sun. Meanwhile they are still soaring upward. The loquacious bird offers to point out and name all the stars. But Chaucer is wearied and will hear no more—

> "Wilt thou lere of sterres aught?"
> "Nay, certeinly," quod I, "right naught;
> And why? for I am now to old."

Soon they hear a great rumbling, like the beating of the sea, and the Eagle tells him that it proceeds from Fame's house. Suddenly they arrive near the palace, and the Eagle sets Chaucer down on his feet and leaves him, promising to wait to take him back.

In Book III the poet approaches the palace or castle of Fame, set on a high rock of ice, on the sides of which names are engraved, some partly melted, others, on the north side, still entirely legible. He climbs to the castle and finds it wondrously beautiful, with many famous harpers, minstrels, and the like standing in niches and playing all manner of instruments. He enters the gate and in the hall finds Fame, a female creature, sitting on a dais holding court. Nine separate companies of petitioners approach her one after the other and ask various boons. She grants these, rejects them, or grants the reverse of what they ask, according to mere whim, and each time bids Aeolus to blow their fame on his trump of good or evil report to all corners of the world.

Finally a stranger approaches the poet and asks him if he has come in search of fame—

> "Nay, forsothe, frend!" quod I;
> "I cam noght hider, graunt mercy!
> For no swich cause, by my heed!"

He has come, he says, for tidings of love and such things glad. He is then directed out of the castle to a house called Labyrinthus standing in a valley. It is a wicker house that whirls incessantly at great speed, and from its apertures issue rumors and voices of all kinds. He beholds the Eagle perched on a stone and is carried into the whirling house by his former guide. The place is crowded with folk of many kinds, all telling each other news and stories—some true, some false, some compounded of true and false. Finally in one corner of the hall he hears a great noise where men tell tidings of love. He goes thither and in the crowd sees "a man of gret auctorite"—and the poem breaks off just as Chaucer apparently is to hear the tidings of love for which he sought.

It is a gay and lively poem, in which imagination and humor vie for the honor of making it the success it is. It deals with matters that we associate usually with poetry of high seriousness. There is many a name and story and allusion from classical sources; there is Jove's Eagle and a flight through the heavens; and the action takes place on a stage that suggests Dante and Milton. And yet the whole is pitched in a colloquial and consistently humorous key. It is the earliest and one of the best of mock-serious poems in English. And it shows that Chaucer is already a master of humorous situation, humorous character, and humorous dialogue. The conversation between the Eagle and the poet, though mostly monologue by the Eagle, is true dialogue, in natural and living speech. The Eagle is Chaucer's first humorous character and one of the first in English literature. He is also the first of several loquacious characters that Chaucer was to paint. But to view the Eagle's loquacity and inveterate love of lecturing as evidence of an "educational bent" in Chaucer's verse, as Sir Arthur Quiller-Couch does, is to miss wholly the humor of the thing and to fail altogether to perceive the dramatic quality that Chaucer's art had achieved at this relatively early date. The poet's portrait of himself—of his fear and helplessness in the Eagle's claws and before the Eagle's endless discourse, his pretending to think that Jove was about to "stellify" him, his mock-heroic comparison of himself with Enoch, Elias, Romulus, and Ganymede, his representing himself as unfortunate in love, and the Eagle's remark that there is but little wit in Chaucer's head—is another humorous success. Book II, in which these features occur, is no doubt the best of the poem. But Book III, with its shrewd satire upon fame and its picture of the crowd of gossip-mongers, each whispering in the other's ear, is full of matter, as well as of delightful fancy and humor. The poet has seen through the fickleness and shallowness of fame. And the throng of shipmen and pilgrims that he sees in the whirling house of rumors, "With scrippes bretful of lesinges," and of pardoners, couriers, and messengers

> With boistes crammed ful of lyes
> As ever vessel was with lyes [i. e., lice]

points forward to the motley world of the *Canterbury Tales,* especially to some of its more precious rascals.

But what is the poem's meaning? Many conjectures and theories have been advanced, some that necessitate our reading into the poem symbolical and allegorical meaning that it seems altogether to lack.[31] Ignoring these, it is essential to note that the occasion and purpose of this journey to the House of Fame are made perfectly clear by the poet himself. The Eagle explains in detail just why he has been sent to carry Chaucer off on this fearsome and marvelous flight. Jupiter has had great pity for the poet who has served Cupid and Venus so long without reward, who has made books, songs, and ditties in honor of Love and Love's servants and with great humbleness and virtue has sat many a night in his study until his head ached, ever writing of love, praising

[31] For a review of some of these, see W. O. Sypherd's *Studies in Chaucer's "Hous of Fame,"* Chaucer Society's Publications, 1907. Sypherd emphasizes the fact that the poem is a love-vision of the same genre as the *Book of the Duchess,* the *Parliament of Fowls,* and the Prologue of the *Legend of Good Women,* and that it can be properly understood only if studied in connection with these.

and furthering Love's cause. Jupiter has considered also that Chaucer has no tidings of Love's folk, either from far countries or from the very neighbors at his door, for after working all day at his reckonings in the Customs he goes home and sits over a book as dumb as any stone, and thus lives as a very hermit—though to be sure he is little given to abstinence. Therefore Jupiter in his grace has sent the Eagle to give Chaucer "some disport and game" in recompense for his labor and devotion to the God of Love, and to carry him to the House of Fame where he shall hear many wonderful and diverse tidings of love:

Of Loves folke mo tydinges,
Bothe sothsawes and lesinges;
And mo loves newe begonne,
And longe yserved loves wonne,
And mo loves casuelly
That been betid, no man wot why,
But as a blind man stert an hare;
And more iolytee and fare,
Whyl that they finde love of stele,
As thinketh hem, and overal wele;
Mo discords, and mo ielousyes,
Mo murmurs, and mo novelryes,
And mo dissimulaciouns,
And feyned reparaciouns;
And mo berdes in two houres
Withoute rasour or sisoures
Ymaad, then greynes be of sondes;
And eke mo holdinge in hondes,
And also mo renovelaunces
Of olde forleten aqueyntaunces;
Mo lovedayes and acordes
Then on instruments ben cordes;
And eke of loves mo eschaunges
Than ever cornes were in graunges . . .

Near the end of the poem, as the Eagle is about to carry Chaucer into the whirling House of Rumors, he again explains that Jove in his grace wishes to "solace" the poet with new "sights and tidings," to relieve his "heaviness" and "distress," and to that end has commanded the Eagle to show Chaucer where he may hear "most tidings." Finally the poet wanders to that corner of the hall where men tell "love-tidings" and there he sees the "man of great authority."

From all this it is clear that Chaucer is describing himself and thinking of himself as a poet of love and of nothing else. As such he is known to his world of courtly readers, and even to the gods on high. And it is in recognition of his services as a love-poet that Jupiter grants him this boon of a holiday. He is suffering from some heaviness and distress, is in need of solace, of "disport and game." But his suffering is not, it seems, that of an unsuccessful lover, though in one passage he humorously refers to himself as one whom Love sees fit not to advance. Nor, I think, is the poet complaining of his job in the Customs, of its confining and exacting duties, or of his having too little time for poetry. The stress throughout is upon Chaucer as poet, not as lover or overworked Customs official. Here as elsewhere he keeps his diplomatic and political and business life out of his work, and as always saves his poetry for poetry. Chaucer the man of affairs is one thing, Chaucer the poet another. Here he is poet, a poet of love, as he is in all his poems down to the *Canterbury Tales,* and surely, in large measure in these also. And the poet of love has, it seems, gone stale, is at a dead end, is at loss for a subject. The adventure Jove sends him is designed to afford him a holiday to be sure—to give him some respite from his poetical labors—but it is also to be an inspiration, to supply the means for the making of still greater love-poetry, to give him just such tidings as would be of most interest and worth to a poet of love. He is in need of new material, of fitting subjects, subjects suitable for an avowed love-poet—subjects which, while meeting the taste of the time for poetry of Courtly Love, would satisfy also the taste of this particular love-poet, who, as the *Book of the Duchess* and this latest poem the *House of Fame* show, was by no means satisfied with the conventional love-poems of his day, who had been reading his Ovid and Virgil and Dante, whose interest in the realities of life must at all times have been intense, and whose experience of life must by now have been rich and varied—subjects such as he had found treated incidentally in poems other than love-poems by Ovid and Virgil, and such as he was to find only a year or two later in Boccaccio's *Teseide* and *Filostrato* made the themes of independent and self-sufficient works; the right subjects for a love-poet—stories of great passions, of the passion of Dido for Aeneas, of Palamon and Arcite for Emily, of Troilus for Criseyde.

This interpretation is the more likely by reason of the stress laid not merely upon Chaucer as a love-poet but upon the fact that he has no tidings of Love's folk and that he is to be taken to the one place in the world—

Betwixen hevene, erthe, and see—

where he will hear the *most* tidings of love, the *most diverse* tidings—tidings, indeed, of all sorts of love-affairs and not of one particular affair, whether of the court or not. Moreover, the adventure is granted him that he may "be of good chere." And this, it seems, means of good cheer as a poet of love, for, the Eagle goes on to say, when they come to Fame's palace Chaucer will hear more wonderful things of love than there are grains of sand by the sea or grains of corn in granaries.

But what, it may be asked, of the "man of great authority"? His presence seems to imply that it was from him the poet was to get the tidings of love he sought, that these were to be special tidings, of interest to the court, and that the poem was in all probability intended to be an occasional poem celebrating some affair or event in the royal family or the court, some wedding or betrothal.

Such is the view most widely held. But the fact is, we know nothing whatever of the man of great authority save that he was a man of great authority and that the poet saw him in that corner of the whirling House of Rumors where men told tidings of love—

> Ther men of love tydings tolde.

To hold that he was to communicate tidings of love to the poet, or indeed that he possessed any to communicate, is pure supposition. And the view that the tidings to be communicated were special tidings, tidings of some particular affair or event at the court or elsewhere, is not only supposition, but supposition that goes in the teeth of all we have been told about them down to this point; that is, down to the end. It contradicts the stress laid by the Eagle, in the passage quoted above, on the poet's learning the most tidings, and the most diverse tidings, of love. It contradicts the answer the poet gives to the stranger who accosts him in the House of Fame and asks him why he has come there. He has come, he says,

> Som newe tydings for to lere:—
> Som newe thinges, I not what,
> Tydinges, other this or that,
> Of love, or swiche thinges glade.
> For certeynly, he that me made
> To comen hider, seyde me,
> I shulde bothe here and see,
> In this place, wonder thinges.

And it contradicts the Eagle's remarks just before he conducts the poet into the House of Rumors. "I was instructed by Jove," he once more tells Chaucer, "to take you where you will hear the most tidings. Here you will learn many a one."

> Wher thou maist most tydinges here;
> Shaltow anoon heer many oon lere.

Thus in three distinct places the number and variety of the tidings are stressed, and nowhere is there mention, or even a hint, of any special tidings. If we are to suppose the man of great authority was to tell the poet anything, we must suppose he was to tell him many things, many stories, rather than one, or to supply him with the inspiration for many stories. This is not to imply that the *House of Fame* was intended to be a Prologue to a series of stories of love, comparable in some ways with the legends in the *Legend of Good Women,* as has been argued.[32] It may mean nothing more than that, as the Eagle says, the poet is to be rewarded and refreshed after his labors in the interests of love by learning numerous stories of the kind that as a love-poet he delights in most and that will best serve his art. Because the *Book of the Duchess,* before the *House of Fame,* and the *Parliament of Fowls* after it, are occasional poems, dealing supposedly with events within the royal family, is no sufficient grounds for believing that this too is an occasional poem. Chaucer was more than a poet of the court. He was a poet of love.

Significant in this connection is the ending of the *Parliament of Fowls.* Wakened out of his dream by the noise of the many birds as they flew away after singing their song in welcome of summer, the poet says that he took up other books to read, that he reads always, in the hope that some day he will have a dream by which he will fare the better:

> I wook, and other bokes took me to
> To rede upon, and yet I rede alway;

[32] J. M. Manly, *Kittredge Anniversary Papers,* Boston, 1913, pp. 73ff.

I hope, ywis, to rede so som day
That I shal mete som thing for to fare
The bet; and thus to rede I nil not spare.

This, of course, may be an appeal for some sort of court preferment, but considered in the light of Chaucer's whole literary career, of the poems he had already done and those he was yet to do, it seems more likely to be an expression of the hope that some day he will come upon, or dream, some thing (i. e., some subject) by which he will "fare the bet" *as a poet*—perhaps as a poet of love, but in any case as a poet.

A striking feature of the *House of Fame* is its wealth of new matter out of the classics; and if, as we suppose, it is the next of Chaucer's major works after the *Book of the Duchess,* this is all the more significant. Chaucer had long been familiar with Ovid, but in the interval between the *Book of the Duchess* and the *House of Fame* he seems to have read him more widely—the *Heroides,* the *Ars Amatoria,* and the *Fasti* as well as the *Metamorphoses.* He had also, it appears, recently read Virgil's *Aeneid,* Dante's *Divine Comedy,* and possibly, though by no means certainly, Boccaccio's *Amorosa Visione* and the *Teseide.* And he had done his reading, one must believe, with the same closeness of attention and delight as he had read the tale of Ceyx and Alcyone before writing the *Book of the Duchess.* Especially had he seized upon the *stories* he found in this reading—in particular the love stories. Thus he came to the writing of the *House of Fame* with a mind full of new matter—of stories out of Ovid and Virgil and of new ideas from these poets and from Dante—and perhaps fired with the hope of making a poem of greater originality and of freer and richer art than anything he had done before.

The list of classical figures he alludes to or whose stories he tells in the *House of Fame* is impressive. It includes Aeneas and Dido and other persons in the story of the

Aeneid, Phyllis and Demophoön, Achilles and Briseis, Paris and Oenone, Jason and Hypsipyle, Hercules and Deianira, Theseus and Ariadne, Romulus, Ganymede, Alexander of Macedon, Scipio, Daedalus, Icarus, Phaeton, Plato, Medea, Circe, Calypso, Calliope, the goddess of Fame, Aeolus, Triton, Julius Caesar, Pompey, Pluto and Proserpina; the constellations of Orion, Castor and Pollux, Delphinus, and the seven daughters of Atlas or the Pleiades; famous "harpers" such as Orpheus, Arion, Chiron, the Centaur, Marsyas, Apollo, and Misenus; and famous authors—Statius, Homer, Virgil, Ovid, Lucan, and Claudian. The story of Dido he tells at length. To that of Theseus and Ariadne he gives twenty-two lines, and to Phyllis and Demophoön only nine lines; and he merely alludes to the stories of Achilles and Briseis, Paris and Oenone, Jason and Hypsipyle, Jason and Medea, and Hercules and Deianira. To five of these he turned again in later years in the *Legend of Good Women,* telling them with greater fullness and a more mature art. But in the *House of Fame* he is interested in the story of Troy and its sequel more than in any other. He mentions with admiration the writers who have upheld the fame of Troy, and Virgil who is responsible for the renown of "the Troian Eneas." He mentions also

> . . . Venus clerk, Ovyde,
> That hath ysowen wonder wyde
> The grete god of Loves name.

And Fame's hall was full "Of hem that writen olde gestes."

Thus, in the *House of Fame* Chaucer shows that he is alive to the greatness of classical story and classical tradition, and he seems to be turning definitely to it and away from the tradition of the *Roman de la Rose.* He has come to know it at first hand, and not, as in his references to the story of Troy in the *Book of the Duchess,* from secondary sources such as Benoit de Sainte Maure or Guido delle

Colonne. And this is really the secret, I think, of the length of the introductory matter in Book I, of which some critics have complained as violating proportion and unnecessarily delaying the opening of the story proper. Chaucer has read in Virgil the story of Troy with its sequel of the wandering of Aeneas and the founding of Rome, and he has felt its fascination. In Virgil, moreover, he has found a love story, of Dido and Aeneas, which he knew also from Ovid's *Heroides*—a much greater and more passionate love story than that of Ceyx and Alcyone, which he had used in the *Book of the Duchess.* So, with swift masterful strokes, he outlines the whole plot of the *Aeneid,* dwelling at length upon the love of Dido for Aeneas, giving it indeed some two hundred of the three hundred lines he devotes to the *Aeneid* as a whole. He recognized it at once for the great story it is and saw in it a subject ready made to the hand of an avowed love-poet. So he tells it, but in his own way, following Virgil in the main, but changing the characterization and the emphasis, in conformity partly with Ovid and partly with the conventions of Courtly Love and his own interest in the woman of gentle and compassionate heart.

Virgil's Dido is beautiful, queenly, magnificent in hospitality, and not without her moments of tenderness and pity. But she is also a woman violent in temper and fierce in passion, whether of love or hate. Her love for Aeneas consumes her like a fire—*caeco carpitur igni.* Restless and unhappy she visits the temples, sacrifices to the gods, and studies the omens. Burning and in a frenzy she roams through the city—

> Uritur infelix Dido totaque vagatur
> Urbe furens.

A second night she goes to the banquet and madly (*demens*) craves to hear more of the Trojans' toils. She hangs on the lips of Aeneas as he tells of them, and when the company has at last dispersed, she mourns alone and throws herself on the empty couch. After winning Aeneas and while living with him through most of the winter as his mistress, she is happy. But as spring approaches and she learns that he is secretly arming his ships and preparing for flight, she becomes a perfect Fury. Aflame with anger, she rages through the city in search of him—

> Saevit inops animi totamque incensa per urbem ,
> Bacchatur . . .

And finding him by the ships, she vents her fury upon him, accusing him of falseness and treachery, of planning to leave her and her kingdom by stealth, of hardness, ingratitude, and cruelty. After a torrent of reproaches and pleadings, she bids him go and seek his Italy, and suffer shipwreck, as she hopes, and be haunted evermore by her relentless shade. Later, when from her tower she sees in the early light the fleet under sail, her rage rises to even higher pitch. She regrets she did not burn his ships, seize him and his men, and put them to the sword. She calls upon the Sun, Juno, Hecate, the avenging Furies, and the gods of Elissa, and prays that if by decree of Fate Aeneas is to reach Italy, he may there be met by hostile arms, be driven from his lands, witness the slaughter of his folk, and himself die before his time and lie unburied in the sand. She pleads for some avenger to rise from her ashes and pledges her people to undying hatred of the whole stock and race of Aeneas:

> Litora litoribus contraria, fluctibus undas
> Imprecor, arma armis; pugnent ipsique impotisque.

It is a magnificent picture, but a picture of a woman distraught, desperate, bitter, fierce, vindictive,—and a little theatrical. Virgil's Dido is much of a Juno. Beneath her golden hospitality she hides a tigress and a Fury. And there is no doubt that something of the stress laid upon this side of her character is due to the poet's theme of empire and his desire to account not only for the founding of Rome but also for the long feud between Rome and Carthage.

Chaucer's Dido on the other hand, whether here in the *House of Fame* or later in the *Legend of Good Women,* is a very different person. No less queenly and generous, the keynote of her character is womanly tenderness; and when she discovers that Aeneas will leave her, she complains of his falseness, it is true, but in words that reveal her continued great love for him:

> "Allas!" quod she, "my swete herte,
> Have pitee on my sorwes smerte,
> And slee me not! go noght away!"

There is no hatred here, no vindictiveness or passion for revenge, and nothing to suggest that Aeneas may have had his own good reasons for going. Her tragedy lies simply in the fact that one who deserves so well of love has been dishonored, shamed, and deserted, and by a lover who, hero though he is, has proved no better than other men—

> "O, have ye men swich goodliheed
> In speche, and never a deel of trouthe?"

She retains her dignity and wins and holds our sympathy and pity.

In this departure from Virgil Chaucer is undoubtedly to some degree under the influence of Ovid. The strength of Ovid's Dido, as of Chaucer's, is in her constancy. She does not hate her betrayer, she only complains of his falseness. And in her passionate fondness she goes much further than Chaucer's heroine; she begs him to give up his wanderings, to return to her, to share or rule her kingdom, and make her his wife or mistress or what he will—

Si pudet uxoris, non nupta, sed hospita dicar;
Dum tua sit, Dido quidlibet esse feret.

But Chaucer is really following the ideals of Courtly Love even more than he is following Ovid—especially the dogma that the lady can do no wrong but is all goodness and truth, and the further doctrine that fidelity in love is the greatest of virtues and falseness the greatest of sins. He stresses Aeneas as a typical faithless lover, who has broken one of the chief commands of love. And though he mentions the compulsion of the gods as Aeneas's excuse, he does so half-heartedly and as something "the book seyth." We must remember, however, that the system of Courtly Love is itself in part a far-off inheritance from Ovid.

In the portrayal of Dido Chaucer is following also, I believe, the dictates of his personal taste. His works afford numerous examples of women of great sweetness and gentleness, whose strength is in their tenderness and the constancy of their affection. Blanche the Duchess is such a one. Anelida in *Anelida and Arcite,* a work done, it would seem, at about the same time as the *House of Fame* or very soon after, is another. She too has been betrayed. But in the elaborate and formal complaint she utters against the false Arcite, the sweet constancy of her love prevails over her momentary bitterness. If in one breath she exclaims:

"Almighty god, of trouthe sovereyn,
Wher is the trouthe of man? who hath hit sleyn?
Who that hem loveth shal hem fynde as fast
As in a tempest is a roten mast . . ."

in the next she is all tenderness again:

"Now mercy, swete, if I misseye,
Have I seyd oght amis, I preye?
I not; my wit is al aweye."

Constance in the *Man of Law's Tale* and Griselda in the *Clerk's Tale* are additional examples. And in the *Legend of Good Women* there are several more. This type of woman is indeed more characteristically Chaucerian than Alison or May or the Wife of Bath.

The story of Dido is the only one Chaucer ever told out of Virgil. It is the only story in the *Aeneid*—apparently the one work of Virgil's that Chaucer knew—that would serve his need, for he was a poet of love, not of adventure or of conquest and battle. And he told it twice—the second time better than the first. Here in the *House of Fame,* for instance, he omits all account of the wooing, which he describes so skilfully in the *Legend of Good Women.* He has not the time for it; his scheme permits only a brief outline. Perhaps, too, his art is not yet equal to it. But even in this his first telling he makes the story of Dido a thing of simple and fascinating beauty. In his poetic development up to this time he seems to have been seeking, as a poet of love, stories more substantial than the pale abstractions of medieval allegory, and characters more human than the shadowy unrealities of much of the French love-poetry. In Virgil's Dido and Aeneas he found flesh-and-blood lovers, to all intents and purposes historic figures. And yet, though they were real enough, they were but puppets on strings in the hands of the gods. He found them entangled with the destiny of Rome, in a story big with empire. In Virgil the whole action is determined by the gods. Dido is fired with love by Cupid, whom Venus sends to her in place of Ascanius. Aeneas and she enter the cave by the will and contrivance of Juno. And Aeneas is adamant in his purpose to go, and deaf to her pleas, because the fates oppose and the gods have closed his ears—*Fata obstant, placidasque viri deus obstruit auris.* Chaucer brings the story to earth, rationalizes it, and makes it move by the laws of human character. Though in the more detailed telling in the *Legend of Good Women* he mentions Cupid's impersonation of Ascanius, he does so with obvious skepticism, as something that "oure autour telleth us," and not until he has fully accounted for the infatuation by purely natural means. Thus he makes the story modern. As a poet feeling his way to a new art he has on the one hand escaped for the moment from medieval allegory and on the other avoided or minimized the element of the mythical and supernatural, which he found so marked in the classics. He relegates the gods to minor rôles or uses them in a merely decorative or allusive way, with the result that his Dido and Aeneas have wills and passions of their own. Moreover, though newly steeped in Virgil and Dante, Chaucer has no ambition to write an epic or to essay the epic style. He feels no urge to undertake such proud themes as the founding of a nation or the theological economy of Hell, Purgatory, and Paradise. As a modest poet of love he will continue to write of love, seeking new and more interesting subjects, and by making use of new matter from his reading with the help of his own best judgment and taste, work forward to a truer and firmer, fuller, gayer, and more lifelike art.

In his use of classical matter in the *House of Fame*—whether in the story of Aeneas and Dido and of other false lovers and betrayed women in Book I, or in the description of the Eagle and the flight through the heavens in Book II, or in that of the goddess of Fame and the many companies of suitors in Book III—Chaucer very definitely gives the impression that he is enjoying himself hugely, that he is reveling in this brave new world of the imagination. At times, as in Book III, we feel there are too many marvels and allusions, an excess of detail, and that the story is in consequence slowed up and unduly prolonged. Chaucer the craftsman is enjoying himself too much, full of the zest of "making." He has more matter than he can well digest and has not as yet mastered to the full the art of compression, pregnant reference, omission. That the sense of proportion and design is strong within him is shown by the admirable division of the poem into three books, the mechanical units agreeing perfectly with the logical. That he is alive to the need of artistic restraint is seen in his referring the reader to Virgil and Ovid for a full account of Dido's death and of all she said and then adding, with an emphasis compounded of gusto and regret,

> And nere hit to long to endyte,
> By god, I wold hit here wryte.

But at times his enthusiasm, his absorption and delight in his material, seems to get the better of him and to beguile him, for instance, into a lengthy and disproportionate account of the nature and fickleness of fame while he is still in search of the tidings of love for which he set out. Why the poem ends so abruptly and is left unfinished we do not know, but possibly because it had got out of hand, had taken a wrong turn and become unmanageable. But though it seems thus to have lost direction and to be an experiment that was a success not so much in itself as in its clearing the way for, and making possible, greater things to come, it is full of the joy of the artist—of the artist reaching out into new fields, discovering new beauty, and finding fresh realms of the imagination in which to disport. In Book I he tells the story of the *Aeneid* in little more than outline, but he makes it interesting and gives it charm. And if he seems to be in haste, it is because this is introductory matter and he knows that an introduction must not be too long. Here and there he delights us with little pictures charged with classical or Renaissance feeling for beauty—such as that of Venus

> Naked fletinge in a see,

or the picture of the disguised Venus as she appeared before Aeneas and Achates—

> Goinge in a queynt array,
> As she had ben an hunteresse,
> With wind blowinge upon hir tresse—

or the description of the God of Sleep

> That dwelleth in a cave of stoon
> Upon a streem that comth fro Lete,
> That is a flood of helle unswete;
> Besyde a folk men clepe Cimerie,
> Ther slepeth ay this god unmerie
> With his slepy thousand sones—

or the picture of Aeolus in his cave, controlling the winds with difficulty—

> This messanger gan faste goon,
> And found wher, in a cave of stoon,
> In a contree that highte Trace,
> This Eolus, with harde grace,
> Held the windes in distresse,
> And gan hem under him to presse,
> That they gonne as beres rore,
> He bond and pressed hem so sore.

Such descriptions are called quaint by some, but they are really of high art, done in the classical tradition, with imaginative power and entire simplicity. The line

> And there he stod, as still as stoon

may be set beside Keats's

> Sat gray-hair'd Saturn, quiet as a stone.

Chaucer's verse in the *House of Fame* is unequal, but in general it is more beautiful and more finished than that of the *Book of the Duchess.* And how great an advance it represents over earlier English verse is curiously illustrated by a passage in Book II. The first few lines of that book are very like the sing-song doggerel of the older English romances which Chaucer was later to burlesque in *Sir Thopas* —the "drasty rymyng" that made the Host's ears ache:

> Now herkneth, every maner man
> That English understonde can,
> And listeth of my dreem to lere.

But only seven lines further we have

> Now faire blisful, O Cipris,
> So be my favour at this tyme!
> And ye, me to endyte and ryme
> Helpeth, that on Parnaso dwelle
> By Elicon the clere welle—

and we have come to the Renaissance and the beauty that was Greece and Rome, and to English poetry with a new accent.

The theory has been advanced by Professor Shannon that Chaucer left the *House of Fame* unfinished because he found his classical material incompatible with the love-vision type upon which he attempted to graft it. The love-vision was in this case "merely a form to carry the ideas," and the poet "was carried so far away from his love-vision idea by his classical material that when he attempted to return to it, he found the spirit of the poem so changed that he gave it up." In the *Parliament of Fowls,* on the other hand, "he kept to medieval ideas and hence preserved the true love-vision spirit. In the *Legend of Good Women* he used classical material again, but not as an organic part of the love-vision. He wrote the Prologue with its May-day full of birds and flowers in true medieval fashion and told his stories from the Classics separately in the legends." And Professor Shannon sees in the *House of Fame* "the first attempt in English literature to engraft upon the formality of the Middle Ages the imaginative freedom of the Classics. Hence the poem may be said to mark a literary epoch." [33]

Whether or no this is the correct explanation of the unfinished state of the poem, which is improbable, there is much truth in this view of a conflict in Chaucer's poetic development between the old and the new, and in the notion of his experimenting, in the *House of Fame* and the *Legend of Good Women,* with methods of harmonizing them. But the beginning of the conflict is to be found in the *Book of the Duchess* with his first use of matter out of Ovid, as I have said, and not in the *House of Fame* as the fruit of his visit to Italy and his contact there with the spirit of the Renaissance. And in the contest there was on the side of the new not only the matter out of Ovid, Virgil, Dante, and other writers, but Chaucer's personal dissatisfaction with the old, and also a certain artistic ideal, I believe, which though ill-defined at first, was present with him all along and enabled him, even in the *Book of the Duchess,* to put new life into the love-vision form. His interest in the love-poetry of France and his sympathy with it were profound, and his loyalty to it as the poetry to which he went to school and to which he owed so much throughout his career, remained to the end. There was, moreover, the hold of fashion, upon him and upon his audience of the court. A court poet of that day, whether in France or England, was expected to be a love-poet and to write love-poems in the accepted modes. But these considerations did not blind Chaucer to the shortcomings of this older poetry, or deter him from seeking to improve it. So he experimented with the conventions and the established forms—with the love-vision in the *Book of the Duchess,* the *House of Fame,* the *Parliament of Fowls,* and the *Legend of Good Women,* and with

[33] Edgar Finley Shannon, *Chaucer and the Roman Poets,* Harvard University Press, 1929, pp. 117–19.

The reading of Boccaccio's *Teseide* and *Filostrato* was an event in Chaucer's life—one of the most important single experiences in his artistic career—but not because Chaucer learned from Boccaccio "the right lines of a story" or "the art of construction" or "the lesson of sure and definite exposition." Rather it was because he found in Boccaccio, as I have said, the right kind of subjects for a poet of love—love stories that stood alone and were not mere episodes in an epic or a romance; stories, moreover, whose setting was the actual world, not the garden of the Rose, and whose action took place in the full light of day, as it were, and not in the twilight of dreams; stories furthermore that declared the sufficiency of human character and human actions as subjects of art. From Boccaccio's example Chaucer got the courage to break with fashion, to throw over the dream and the garden, to let himself go, and to do the kind of thing he had long been wanting to do and indeed had been flirting with ever since he wrote the Ceyx and Alcyone in the *Book of the Duchess* or the Dido and Aeneas in the *House of Fame;* namely, to make that kind of realistic story not a mere incident in a vision-poem, but a book by itself. This he did in the *Palamon and Arcite* and the *Troilus and Criseyde,* for both poems are highly realistic as well as romantic, the passionate rivalry of Palamon and Arcite and their love for Emily being as realistic as the scene of the duel or the tournament, and the love of Troilus and Criseyde as true to life as the conversation of Pandarus. Once he had settled the question and by writing *Troilus and Criseyde* had convinced himself of the rightness of the realistic subject and method, he extended the principle to other than love stories and thus came upon the happy idea of the *Canterbury Tales,* in which the characters should be of many different sorts, including the very neighbors at his door, and in which he would be a poet not alone of love but of the whole contemporary scene.

Chaucer's search, I think it may be said, had all along

been for the interesting—for that which we moderns call interesting, rather than for what was interesting to Gower or to the author of *Sir Gawain* or to the courtly circles of England and France who delighted in the poems of Machaut and Deschamps. He found it, though mixed with other elements, in Ovid, Virgil, Boccaccio, and other writers; and he found it in the life about him. And in *Troilus and Criseyde* and the *Canterbury Tales* he produced works that are possessed of greater *modern* interest than any he used.

What it was that enabled Chaucer thus to anticipate modern taste it is perhaps idle, but none the less fascinating, to speculate. Certainly it was something besides the influence of Boccaccio and the contact with the Renaissance. No doubt his wide culture had something to do with it. His enormous intellectual curiosity and appetite explains much of his growth and center-of-the-road quality. It led him on from one interest to another and allowed him to rest in no one thing too long. Thus he did not get too much either of the popular romance literature, or of the religious, didactic, or scientific writings of his age, or of the poetry of the *Roman de la Rose* tradition, or of the classics, or of the Italians. His interest in all these was great, and they all went to the feeding of his genius and the broadening of his art. But other poets were possessed of perhaps equal culture. Gower's was possibly as great as Chaucer's, and Dante's was no doubt broader as well as deeper.

Chaucer's modernity is to be explained, I believe, by other things than his breadth of culture—by his realistic temperament, his admirable sanity and balance of mind, his sense of humor, his instinct for the concrete, and above all his humanity, his native interest in men and women. The qualities of mind that made him a successful public servant, diplomatist, and man of affairs determined the realistic bent of his literary taste and led to his turning more and more to life, to the actual world of men and women, in the successive poems he wrote. It was his zest for life—the zest of one whose abstinence was little—and his wide experience in the world of affairs—the experience of one whose work in the course of his life brought him into contact with all manner of men—that enabled him to perceive more and more clearly as he went on that the achievement of a new and sounder art lay in his turning less to books and more to life. His seeing eye and the delight he took in the infinite variety and color of human character convinced him that the thing to do was to transfer as much as he could of that variety and color and concrete detail to the page before him if he would make his poetry more vivid and of lasting interest.

CHAPTER IV

On Chaucer's Borrowings

SOME forty years ago Professor Lounsbury reminded us that in the study of literature, and especially in the study of a great poet like Chaucer, questions of borrowings and of sources are not matters of the first importance. "Chaucer," he said, "is first and foremost a man of letters, and as a man of letters he must be judged. Where he got his materials may be of interest to the special student of comparative literature. It is of the slightest possible interest to the student of literature pure and simple. What he did with his materials after he got them is the supreme thing that concerns the latter." The greatness of genius, he remarked, "like that of nature, consists in the infinite ability it possesses to originate new effects by new combinations of old material." He spoke of the search for sources as a "perverse industry . . . having little else to exercise itself upon." And he added, "In nothing is the originality of Chaucer more strikingly seen than in the fact that his tales depend very slightly for their interest upon invention." [34]

It was a timely, and one would have thought, a sufficient warning. But the "perverse industry" has flourished uninterruptedly ever since, and a very large part of the scholarly work done upon Chaucer in the intervening years has been devoted to the tracing of sources and analogues, and even to the identification of hints, suggestions, and echoes from the writings of others. The modern editions of Chaucer are full of notes calling attention to his debts.

Let it be said at once that this kind of scholarship is not

[34] T. R. Lounsbury, *Studies in Chaucer,* Harper, N.Y., 1892, Vol. III, pp. 396–400.

without its value, and that its value is not alone to the special student of comparative literature but to the student of literature pure and simple as well. It makes possible a better understanding of Chaucer's work and a truer conception of the nature of his greatness—provided, always, the student possesses the requisite energy and insight to discover for himself the truth that though Chaucer is one of the greatest of borrowers, he is also one of the most original of poets. That the tracing and listing of debts and influences does not necessarily detract from Chaucer's genius or dwarf his stature as a poet, and even as a poet of invention, is seen in the fact that the very scholars who have shown the greatest industry and brilliance in the tracing of influences are the first to insist upon his originality.

At the same time, the excessive devotion to questions of indebtedness which has marked modern Chaucerian scholarship has without doubt put the stress in the wrong place and had the effect of giving the reader, and especially the general reader, an altogether inadequate conception of the poet's greatness. When the reader is told that possibly not one of the *Canterbury Tales* was original with Chaucer, that the very scheme of that immortal work may have been suggested by other works, that two of Chaucer's greatest stories —*Troilus and Criseyde* and the *Knight's Tale*—are retold from Boccaccio, and a third—the *Clerk's Tale*—from Petrarch, and that such masterpieces of character portrayal as the Pardoner and the Wife of Bath have their counterparts in Jean de Meun—when he is told these things, and a hundred more like them, he may be pardoned for getting the impression that the net result of modern Chaucerian scholarship has been to nullify every claim to originality that Chaucer may have had, and for looking upon the "Father of English poetry" as at most a master of mosaic—of mosaic and melody. Constantly reminded of Chaucer's indebtedness, the reader becomes skeptical of scholarly claims as to Chaucer's greatness and is inclined to attribute them to the natural but unjustified enthusiasm of specialists.

The danger, however, is not alone to the general reader. Even the special student may be misled into an exaggerated idea of Chaucer's indebtedness. He reads perhaps dozens of notes and articles that call attention to Chaucer's sources, but he seldom reads the sources themselves. In this way he gets an altogether false notion of the nature of a given influence and therefore of the extent of Chaucer's debt in a given case and of the degree of his originality. Without reading the *Roman de la Rose* and gaining a first-hand knowledge of the characters of False Seeming and the Duenna, he cannot possibly perceive how very different the Pardoner and the Wife of Bath are from their supposed prototypes, or how truly original Chaucer's two character portrayals are. Likewise, unless he reads Boccaccio's *Teseide* and *Filostrato,* he cannot realize how genuinely Chaucer's *Knight's Tale* and *Troilus and Criseyde* are works of creative genius and originality, although in one sense they are but retellings of Boccaccio's narratives and contain, indeed, here and there lines and passages translated almost verbatim.

The description of the Wife of Bath and the account of her life, as given in the general Prologue and in the Prologue to her tale, are indebted not only to the portrayal of the Duenna in the *Roman de la Rose* but to the discourse of the Jealous Husband in the same poem, and to various other works, both French and Latin, which treat satirically of woman and marriage. Some of these are mentioned by the Wife herself in telling of her fifth husband, Jankyn the clerk. But not one reader in ten, even among special students of Chaucer, has read these many sources or is likely to read them. Most students will rest upon the notes, and these, if taken seriously, almost inevitably lead to the conclusion—so impressive is the list of books they mention—that this famous portrait is purely derivative. And yet, the reading of all these originals—and, I venture to say, of any others in which scholars may subsequently discover parallels or similarities—would only go to prove that in spite of the many strands that have gone into her making, the Wife of Bath is a unique figure. There is no one like her, and she stands out as a great and original character—as one of the greatest and most original in all literature.

Chaucer makes no secret of his indebtedness. On the contrary, he frequently mentions by name the author or authors he is following, and sometimes with obvious pride in their greatness and fame. The Clerk in the *Canterbury Tales* informs the other pilgrims that he will tell them a tale he learned from Francis Petrarch at Padua—a worthy clerk and laureate poet, whose sweet rhetoric and poetry hath illumined all Italy. Chaucer begins the Legend of Dido in the *Legend of Good Women* with lines of praise to Virgil and a modest assertion that he is but a humble follower of the great Roman poet—

> Glory and honour, Virgil Mantuan,
> Be to thy name! and I shal, as I can,
> Folow thy lantern, as thou gost biforn,
> How Eneas to Dido was forsworn.

Likewise, in the Legend of Hypsipyle and Medea he acknowledges his debt to Guido and Ovid; and in the Legend of Lucrece his debt to Ovid and Livy. In *Troilus and Criseyde,* it is true, he makes no mention of Boccaccio, but he refers more than once to "Myn auctour called Lollius," and this seems to be due to his mistaken belief in the existence of a Latin poet so named, who wrote of the Trojan war and was supposedly the source of Boccaccio's story, and also to Chaucer's desire to cite as his authority a Latin author of the greatest possible antiquity.

This readiness of Chaucer's to acknowledge his sources was not only what we should expect of one possessed of his intellectual and artistic modesty, but was entirely in harmony with the practice of his time. The habit of appealing to authority was almost universal in the Middle Ages, and even had Chaucer been capable of wishing to conceal his borrowings, there could have been no point in his attempting to do so, for, in his day, to cite authority was to gain credibility, and to borrow from a writer was to honor him. Little store, it seems, was set by invention—at least by invention of plot. And the writer who in pursuit of originality should avoid all obligation to others would be sacrificing a certain source of popularity and strength for a thing of doubtful worth in the eyes of his contemporaries.

In the Middle Ages no one hesitated to borrow whatever he wanted or needed for his work—least of all a teller of stories. Not only were there no copyright laws, but, as has often been observed, the sense of private property in literary work simply did not exist, and, as I have already said, to borrow from a man, with or without acknowledgment, was not to rob him but to pay him tribute. The Anglo-Norman poet Wace, author of the *Brut,* retold in French the history of the kings of Britain from Geoffrey of Monmouth's Latin. Layamon in turn made his English *Brut* from Wace's, following it closely. Chaucer based his *Troilus and Criseyde* upon Boccaccio's *Filostrato,* but Boccaccio was heavily indebted to Benoit de Sainte Maure. It is true he improved upon Benoit, disengaging the story of Troilus and Criseyde from a poem on the Trojan war, making a separate and independent love story of it, and inventing, it seems, all that part of it that deals with Troilus's falling in love with Criseyde and his wooing and winning of her. But if Boccaccio improved upon Benoit, so did Chaucer improve upon Boccaccio and out of his own invention deepen and enrich and strengthen the narrative, to such an extent indeed that Chaucer's is the best of all tellings of this immortal love story. Chaucer told the tale of the Patient Griselda from Petrarch, but Petrarch got it from Boccaccio—it is the Tenth Story of the Tenth Day in the *Decameron*—and Boccaccio in turn seems to have taken it from a folk-tale.

This freedom in borrowing we are apt to think of as peculiar to the Middle Ages, but in reality it has been characteristic of poets of all ages, except possibly of late modern times—especially of narrative poets. Ovid, as Dryden remarks, "only copied the Grecian fables." Virgil's debt to Homer was immense, and Homer was indebted to we know not what or how many lays, ballads, and other poems and stories before him. Dante, in the *Divine Comedy,* besides his special debt to Virgil, has woven together so many strands from classical and medieval literature, philosophy, and theology that it may be said of him, as Mark Pattison said of Milton, that the task of annotating him is one of the last tests of scholarship. Shakespeare, as we all know, drew heavily upon earlier plays, Italian novelle, Plutarch's *Lives,* and Holinshed's *Chronicles* for plots and characters in his dramas. The history of romance is largely a story of borrowing and influence, and that of Arthurian romance, from the Middle Ages to Tennyson, Binyon, and Robinson, is a tale of variations on a common theme. The reservoir or quarry for narrative poets and story-tellers of all ages has been the great corpus of folk-tales, fables, and myths, and these have always been common property, international common property. A story is most truly his who tells it best. Dryden was of opinion that "the genius of our countrymen in general" is rather to "improve an invention than to invent themselves." But it may well be doubted whether that is any truer of English writers than it is of others.

It must be noted, however, that borrowings and influences are of different kinds and represent different degrees of indebtedness. There are borrowings that amount to little more than translations; borrowings that consist in the retelling of a story with the addition of new elements of plot, character, and setting; borrowings that take the form of numerous influences from a variety of sources skilfully woven together for the adornment and enrichment of an old story. And there are influences that are little more than echoes of a thought or image or phrase in some earlier writer.

These last—echoes, I have called them—are found in lyric poets as well as in others. And they raise the interesting question what exactly a literary influence is, and just when a literary influence amounts to a debt. Wordsworth's lines,

> Have sight of Proteus rising from the sea;
> Or hear old Triton blow his wreathed horn,

are a double echo of Milton's

> . . . and call up unbound
> In various shapes old Proteus from the sea,

and of Spenser's

> Is Triton, blowing loud his wreathed horn.

And Milton's line, in turn, may have within it a memory of "senex . . . Proteus" from Ovid and other classical poets. But neither Milton nor Wordsworth is any the less original on that account. A poet's mind is necessarily stored with images, epithets, and cadences from his reading, and whether or not his verse is original is determined not so much by the presence or absence here and there of suggestions or echoes from others as by its imaginative and musical integrity and its effect upon the reader. Here, in each case, the poet has produced a line of perfect imagery, in perfect harmony with its setting, possessed of an accent and music of its own, and capable of giving the reader true imaginative delight. Though not without some memento of the past, it has sprung, we feel, from the poet's own imagination and brings to us the very tones of his voice. January's exclamation in the *Merchant's Tale*—

How fairer been thy brestes than is wyn—

may show influence of the *Song of Solomon,* as editors of Chaucer tell us it does. But on turning to the *Song of Solomon,* we discover nothing nearer to Chaucer's line than "We will remember thy love more than wine," "How much better is thy love than wine," and "This thy stature is like a palm tree and thy breasts to clusters of grapes." These and one or two similar passages may have supplied certain suggestions which Chaucer's imagination seized upon and fused, but that is all. The line is a new creation, different in thought, figure, and accent from anything that may have contributed to its making. And to imply that it is anything less than original is as uncritical and as false as it would be to assert that Yeats's "I will arise and go now" is derived from "I will rise now, and go about the city in the streets," which also is from the *Song of Solomon.*

Chaucer's favorite line,

For pitee renneth sone in gentil herte,

which with slight variations occurs five times in his works, is said by some scholars to come fram Dante's

Amor, che al cor gentil ratto s'apprende.

And Dante, we are told, took it from Guido Guinicelli.[35] Other scholars[36] derive it from Ovid's

Quo quisque est major, magis est placabilis irae,
Et faciles motus mens generosa capit.

To the frank and disinterested reader—that is, to one who is not bent on discovering influences—it would seem that Chaucer's line is sufficiently different from either, in both thought and expression, to be considered his own. But whatever similarity scholars may insist upon as existing in this

[35] See E. P. Hammond, *Chaucer: a Bibliographical Manual,* N.Y., 1933, p. 253.
[36] See Shannon, *Chaucer and the Roman Poets,* Cambridge, 1929, pp. 178–79.

particular instance between Chaucer and Dante or Chaucer and Ovid, the line is none the less thoroughly Chaucerian.

Echoes such as these are no doubt "influences," in a sense, and some critics may call them "debts." But either of these terms seems greatly to exaggerate the importance of these echoes and to stress unduly the element of indebtedness in them. Echoes are found in every poet; indeed, their occasional appearance seems to be an inevitable consequence of the very act of composition. They involve nothing more than the taking of a hint or suggestion from some older writer, or, it often seems, the using of a thought or phrase or cadence that has floated in the poet's memory more or less unconsciously. And they detract not at all from a poet's originality. On the contrary, for many a reader they add a positive pleasure by the associations they evoke.

Chaucer's indebtedness, however, goes much beyond the presence of mere echoes in his work. He is, as I have said, a prince of borrowers, and his poems afford examples of practically all sorts of borrowing. The *A.B.C. or Prayer to the Virgin,* the *Second Nun's Tale* of St. Cecilia, and the *Tale of Melibeus* are more or less close translations of originals in French or Latin. The *Clerk's Tale* of the Patient Griselda follows a definite source—Petrarch's Latin version of the same story. The *Knight's Tale* and *Troilus and Criseyde* are adaptations of Boccaccio's *Teseide* and *Filostrato* respectively. Like the *Clerk's Tale* they are based upon specific works, but they depart much farther and more freely from their sources than does the *Clerk's Tale* and represent a more original handling of their themes. The *Nun's Priest's Tale,* the *Summoner's Tale,* the *Merchant's Tale,* the *Prioress's Tale* are examples of Chaucer's retelling of stories which were of wide oral and literary currency in the Middle Ages. For them, no definite sources are known and they contain much that seems to be original.

But though in all of these compositions, as well as in most

others, Chaucer is to a greater or less extent a debtor, he is also a creative artist with the gift of invention. Almost without exception he improved upon his originals and produced a work that is truly his own. This is true even of those things which commentators describe as "translations" or "free renderings." One of these is the *A.B.C.,* believed to be one of Chaucer's earliest works. And Chesterton has done real service to Chaucerian criticism in denying that Chaucer's contribution here consists in little or nothing but his improving upon the metre. Chesterton contrasts the first line of the French original—*A toy du monde refin*—with Chaucer's magnificent first line,

> Almighty and al merciable queene,

and remarks, "Chaucer is not expanding his metre; he is expanding himself. He is expanding his lungs and his heart, like a man stretching out his arms in the pattern of the cross." And he adds, "The point that concerns us here is that Chaucer wrote a poem as well as a translation." [37]

The *Clerk's Tale* follows Petrarch closely. But one has only to compare Chaucer's first stanza with the corresponding passage in Petrarch to realize how different and superior it is:

> Ther is, right at the west syde of Itaille,
> Doun at the rote of Vesulus the colde,
> A lusty playne, habundant of vitaille,
> Wher many a tour and toun thou mayst biholde,
> That founded were in tyme of fadres olde,
> And many another delitable sighte,
> And Saluces this noble contree highte.

These lines are the equivalent of a half page of the original, and they illustrate Chaucer's rigorous excision of inessential details, his swift sketching in of a setting, and his power of

[37] Chesterton, *op. cit.,* p. 116–18.

giving to matter borrowed from another a heightened beauty and intensity. Petrarch's prose has been transmuted to golden verse, and at least three of these seven lines—the second, fourth, and fifth—are lines of matchless melody. Further, in the tale as a whole Chaucer makes larger use of dialogue and of homely detail than does Petrarch, and adds little touches here and there that change the characters. Griselda gains in pathos and depth of character, and Walter the Marquis becomes less cold and formal. When, for example, Griselda accepts the conditions set by the Marquis and agrees to marry him, Petrarch has merely *"Satis est," inquit ille.* In Chaucer this becomes

> "This is ynogh, Griselde myn," quod he.

The "Griselde myn" is the added touch, and it makes the Marquis a greater gentleman, a man of truer courtesy and deeper feeling, who though stern to many and capable of cruelty even to those he loves best, is gracious and affectionate too.

The fact is that whatever Chaucer borrowed he adorned. And the adornment consisted not alone in the beauty and melody of his verse but in invention as well. He added vividness by the lavish use of details—of highly specific details—whether in the painting of character or of background. His habitual superiority to Ovid in the matter of concreteness has been noted more than once.[38] But he improves upon Ovid in other ways too. In *Thisbe,* for example, in the *Legend of Good Women,* there is not only more abundant concrete detail than there is in Ovid's version of the story, but the elimination of mythological elements, a surer sense of form or structure, a narrative that is better paced, and an imaginative sympathy more delicate and complete. These are elements of invention, though some of them are perhaps only matters of technique. And similar improvements are

[38] See, for example, Shannon, *op. cit.*, pp. 80, 81, 86, 87.

found in works based upon other sources than Ovid, especially in *Troilus and Criseyde,* the *Knight's Tale,* the *Summoner's Tale,* the *Merchant's Tale,* and the *Nun's Priest's Tale.* In these Chaucer deepens the character interest, giving a more human and more humorous reading of character, adding subtlety and complexity to his characters, and sometimes to such an extent that they are transformed and are so different from the originals as to be distinct creations.

The outstanding example of this is Chaucer's Pandarus in *Troilus and Criseyde* as contrasted with Pandaro in Boccaccio. Chaucer not only makes Pandarus the uncle of Criseyde instead of her more youthful cousin, but gives him a more prominent part in the story. He becomes an infinitely more lively and humorous and interesting character and one of the greatest of comedy characters in all literature. Likewise, Criseyde is different from Boccaccio's Griseida. She is gayer, more various, baffling, and complex; as is apparent, for example, in the scene in Book II in which Pandarus brings her Troilus's first letter. To this Boccaccio gives but six stanzas, Chaucer twenty-nine. All the additional matter is of a kind to add greatly to the liveliness and realism of the characters and to make the scene a bit of life acted before our eyes. Boccaccio's scene in comparison is lifeless and flat. Chaucer's is full of gayety, humor, and the deepest insight into human nature. Criseyde, we perceive, is as good company as Pandarus. She jokes with him, chaffs him about his unsuccessful love-affair. She will not take the letter, but is dying with curiosity to see it. He thrusts it into her bosom, and she of course seizes the first opportunity that offers to read it when she may be thought not to be reading it. It is in such scenes and by the skilful accumulation of details that we are made to realize the fascination of Criseyde, her varying, shifting moods, her hearty laughter, her coquetry, her blend of prudence, modesty, and passion. She is as lively and gay and resourceful in her way as Pandarus is in his, and the success of the scenes between the two is due as much to her vivacity and delightful changes of mood as to Pandarus.

Consider, too, the contrast in the two poems in the way Criseyde finally surrenders to Troilus. In Boccaccio, after Griseida has made up her mind to grant Troilo her love, she simply bides her time till her women are away at some festival and then grants him a rendezvous at her house. Troilo enters secretly and awaits her appearance. In Chaucer the lovers are brought together for their first night only by elaborate maneuvering on the part of Pandarus, who invites Criseyde to his house for supper and is aided in his scheme by a terrific and most opportune downpour. Boccaccio's heroine is won too easily; Chaucer's only with difficulty and after a fascinating and protracted game.

There are differences too between Troilus and Troilo, though not so great as those between Pandarus and Pandaro and Criseyde and Griseida. Chaucer's hero is less sentimental than Boccaccio's. He has more ironical humor—as appears in the account of his scoffing at love and lovers in the scene in the temple just before he discovers Criseyde and falls in love with her. And that he has greater store of philosophy and is more given to thought is shown in all that part of the narrative which follows the decree approving the exchange of Criseyde for Antenor. He is more difficult and complex than Troilo. In the first scene between Pandarus and Troilus, Pandarus visits him in his room, finds him melancholy and ill, and desiring to help him seeks to worm his secret from him. To this Chaucer gives five hundred lines, almost twice as many as Boccaccio, and there are more than three hundred of these before Pandarus succeeds in extracting from Troilus's lips the name of the lady he has fallen in love with. Pandarus must use all his subtlety, diplomacy, and philosophy, together with a little bullying, before he gets what he wants; and the scene not only serves as an admirable introduction of Pandarus, but illustrates the intensity and humility of Troilus's passion and something of the depth of his nature.

The two poems differ in details of plot, in tone, in manner of narration, as well as in their characters. There is much more dialogue in Chaucer, more humor, more homely wisdom, more realism. And these many changes and additions are such as to have brought about the remarkable result that though Chaucer set out merely to retell a story from Boccaccio, he produced a thing utterly new—nothing less, indeed, than what Professor Kittredge has described with perfect accuracy as "the first novel, in the modern sense, that ever was written in the world, and one of the best." [39]

Chaucer's originality is great too in such things as the *Summoner's Tale,* the *Merchant's Tale,* the *Nun's Priest's Tale*—compositions for which analogues have been found, but no direct sources. In these he centers the interest in the character, not the plot. The great feature of the *Summoner's Tale* is the picture it gives of the begging friar, his easy familiarity in the house of the bed-ridden Thomas, his smug preaching, his overweening assurance and hypocrisy; and the picture of the long-suffering Thomas and the hospitable, friendly, credulous wife. This is the real heart of the story. It is the character interest and the vivid portrayal of a phase of contemporary life that make the tale the great thing it is—not the trick played upon the friar.

Much the same is true of the *Nun's Priest's Tale.* The story is an old one, no one can tell how old—the kind of animal story or fable that man has delighted in time out of mind. It belongs to the great body of European folk-lore and Aesopic fable. But given the story, what a masterpiece of narrative art Chaucer makes of it! What subtle characterization of the Cock and the Hen, with their humorous likenesses to man! What gentle and telling satire and happy mock-heroic

[39] G. L. Kittredge, *Chaucer and His Poetry,* Harvard University Press, 1915, p. 109.

style! What grace of language and verse! What gayety in the whole piece! It is a new creation, or re-creation, and one that bears the imprint of Chaucer throughout.

The *Knight's Tale,* the *Nun's Priest's Tale,* the *Merchant's Tale,* the *Summoner's Tale,* the *Clerk's Tale,* and *Troilus and Criseyde* are the best narratives of their respective stories that we have. Though taken from this or that author or paralleled by this or that analogue, they reveal Chaucer's art and originality in the handling of plot and character, in the marvelous effectiveness of the narrative as a whole, and in beauty and grace of language. Though told before, they were never told so well.

The excellence of a work of art is not dependent upon the originality of its subject. A Madonna, a Holy Family, a Crucifixion may be a work of the highest genius though a hundred artists have painted the same subject before. It is a masterpiece not by virtue of its theme so much as by virtue of its treatment of the theme—by the beauty, feeling, and humanity the artist has put into it, by his mastery of technique, by its perfection of form and finish. In viewing a Gothic cathedral, we do not ask where this or that stone came from. Nor do we expect it to be something new. We expect it, in fact, to be something old—simply another Gothic cathedral, conventional in plan and style. What elements of novelty it possesses consist at most in variations of style and plan within the limits of a fixed tradition. It is an old story told anew, and yet a work of creative genius too.

Moreover, a painting, a piece of architecture or sculpture, a poem, is to be judged by its effect, quite apart from questions of sources and influences. By this test, Chaucer's poetry is of the highest excellence. In the *Knight's Tale* or the *Clerk's Tale,* for instance, the telling of the story is without sign of influence or of patching, and without flaw. It is a new and perfect telling, easy and fluent beyond words, with unbroken rhythm, like the undulations of a wave. It is a thing made by the artist from within, a perfect thing by its own law. It satisfies the æsthetic sense as only a flawless work of art can. And as the reader finishes the tale, he is moved by its grave and stately beauty. The question of Chaucer's indebtedness will probably not enter his head, but if it does, he will dismiss it, as Professor Lounsbury did two score years ago, as one that is interesting but not vitally important.

CHAPTER V

Troilus and Criseyde

. . . thou whose dreamy eyes
Beheld the flush to Cressid's cheeks arise,
As Troilus rode up the praising street . . .
William Morris, THE LIFE AND DEATH OF JASON

TO speak justly of *Troilus and Criseyde* is to seem extravagant. Its greatness has largely been obscured by the *Canterbury Tales,* and the popularity of the later work has led many readers to neglect the earlier. Everyone has read the *Canterbury Tales,* at least in part, and that poem is thought of not only as Chaucer's last but his greatest, and as the only one in which his powers are revealed to the full. There are a hundred readers of the *Canterbury Tales,* no doubt, to every two or three who have read *Troilus and Criseyde.* The vivid characters of the *Canterbury Tales,* its many stories, its closeness to the realities of life, its pathos and comedy, its varied drama, have rightly made it the most popular of Chaucer's works. It affords, too, a wider and richer field for research than does any of his other writings, with the result that the industry and enthusiasm of scholars have put an additional emphasis upon it and constituted a further influence in giving it its position of solitary eminence in the popular mind and in establishing the tradition that Chaucer is above all the poet of the *Canterbury Tales.*

And yet there is nothing in the *Canterbury Tales*—not even the *Knight's Tale* or the *Clerk's Tale*—that can compare in grandeur or in sustained perfection of art with *Troilus and Criseyde.* The *Canterbury Tales* is a composite work, consisting of a general Prologue and a series of tales, with links to connect the tales and add variety, life, and realism to the drama of the pilgrimage. The greatness of its design is obvious, and we can imagine with what art Chaucer would have completed that design had he lived. But the work is after all unfinished. It is but a torso—however magnificent—and we cannot judge rightly of its proportions or symmetry or organic unity. Its constituent parts, moreover, are by no means of equal excellence. Some of the tales are earlier works that Chaucer incorporated into the Canterbury scheme and are far from representing the poet at his best.

The *Troilus and Criseyde,* on the other hand, is a masterpiece that is finished. It is a work conceived on a grand scale, executed with consummate art and dramatic realism, and brought to a triumphant conclusion. It demonstrates beyond question that Chaucer as an artist was possessed of the same powers of design as are required in the planning of a great epic, a full-sized drama or novel. And it proves that his art was equal to the task of carrying out his design—that it was an art patient and sustained, as adequate to the demands of the smallest detail as to those of the magnificent whole, to the portrayal of character and of setting or background as to the management of plot. It is a poem with three main characters. All of these are masterpieces of character drawing, and at least two of them rank among the greatest and most memorable of literary portraits. Thus in this difficult phase of the narrator's art Chaucer's score is perfect. And there is no poem in the language in which the background or atmosphere is more vivid or pervasive, or more in harmony with the story and its characters.

To enjoy the poem to the full, and especially to understand its characters aright, one must come to it with mind uncolored. One must forget Boccaccio's and Shakespeare's versions of the story. One must forget the fact that the name of Criseyde has become a byword, a synonym of all that is faithless in women, and that the name of Pandarus has given to our language a noun and a verb of ugly import. Chaucer's Criseyde and Troilus and Pandarus are not Boccaccio's, and they are not Shakespeare's. They are more interesting and complex than Boccaccio's and nobler than Shakespeare's. And one can perceive the fascination and truth of these characters and the comedy, pathos, and tragedy of their story only by coming to them in the first place without prejudice and by following them to the end with the same full sympathy that Chaucer himself bestows upon them.

The poem is a tragedy—but a tragedy blended with a strong element of comedy, supplied chiefly by Pandarus. Chaucer announces his tragic theme in the first stanza, and when invoking the aid of Tisiphone before inditing

> Thise woful vers, that wepen as I wryte

he strikes the note of compassion, of pity for the ill-starred lovers, which runs through the whole poem and is one of its most moving features. It is the tragedy of Troilus—a poem

> In whiche ye may the double sorwes here
> Of Troilus, in loving of Criseyde,
> And how that she forsook him er she deyde.

Troilus is the leading character. But Criseyde is only slightly less prominent than he, and to most readers, it seems, the more interesting of the two. She is given greater prominence than in Boccaccio or Shakespeare. Indeed, she rivals Troilus in the claims she makes upon the reader's attention, and her fate moves one to tragic pity as much as it did Chaucer and only a little less than that of Troilus.

Chaucer's Criseyde is one of the immortal characters of fiction, and this is because she is one of the most fascinating of women, as well as one of the most beautiful. Such is her charm, her gentleness of heart, her depth of passion that the reader easily falls in love with her—as Chaucer himself seems to have done as she developed beneath his pen. And this is not true of Boccaccio's heroine, or of Shakespeare's, or Dryden's—least of all of Shakespeare's. Her elusiveness has given rise to conflicting views of her character. And it is because one can never be sure he has reached to the depths of her nature and understood it rightly that one carries her in memory and dwells upon the ever fascinating problem of her contradictions. For this reason also she is a triumph of Chaucer's art, for he has given her the complexity that we so often find in real life rather than the simplicity that contents a more facile art.

One widely held view of Criseyde conceives of her as an example of betrayed innocence, whose downfall is brought about by the plotting of an unprincipled uncle, Pandarus, and whose faithlessness to Troilus in the end is the result of the corruption of her character following upon her affair with Troilus. At the other extreme she has been described as a "heartless and artful intriguer, most clever in her assumed role of innocent." Both views err on the side of simplicity, and can proceed, I believe, only from a superficial and unsympathetic reading of the poem. To prove the unsoundness of the second view one need do little more than note that in the portrayal of Criseyde, from beginning to end, there is not one touch of that satire, veiled or open, which is so characteristic of Chaucer's method in dealing with characters of whom he did not wholly approve. Neither in his own words nor in the words he puts into the mouths of the other characters of the poem is there any hint of depravity, hardness, or insincerity in her nature. He has for her only words of praise—for her beauty,

> Hir ounded heer, that sonnish was of hewe,

for her wisdom, her golden heart,

A kinges herte semeth by hires a wrecche—

and in the end pity for her weakness and unhappiness.

One must bear in mind Criseyde's estate and her position in Trojan society at the opening of the poem. She is young and beautiful, it is true, but she is neither innocent nor unsophisticated. And this is as it should be. Courtly Love is not founded on innocence; it presupposes sophistication, if not experience. Criseyde is a widow, not a maid. She is the daughter of Calkas,

. . . a lord of greet auctoritee,
A gret devyn.

She is the niece of Pandarus, and Pandarus is not only bosom friend of a prince of the realm but a counselor of the king. In her difficult position as the daughter of a traitor, she has been befriended and protected by Hector. She moves in the highest Trojan society. She is a woman of the world, with a name and an estate to maintain, and possessed, it seems, of considerable wealth. She has her own palace, where, in the "paved parlor," Pandarus finds her and other ladies listening to a maiden reading aloud of the siege of Thebes. Its gardens, with their green alleys, sanded walks, and nightingales, its chambers and dining hall, its "great rout" of servants, point to the luxury, ease, and independence of her existence. Of these things she is absolute mistress, as she is absolute mistress of herself.

The enigma of Criseyde's character is suggested in the first scene in which she appears. She is in the temple, with a throng of people, observing the feast of the Palladium. Though dressed in widow's habit of black, her beauty is such as to gladden all who look upon her. Retiring and alone, she stands near the door, behind other folk, "ay under shames drede," and yet "With ful assured lokyng and manere." When Troilus, the arch-scoffer at love, sees her for the first time he is transfixed:

"O mercy, god!" thoughte he, "wher hastow woned,
That art so fair and goodly to devyse?"

He observes her more closely:

> She nas not with the leste of hir stature,
> But alle hir limes so wel answeringe
> Weren to womanhode, that creature
> Was neuer lasse mannish in seminge.
> And eek the pure wyse of here meninge
> Shewede wel, that men might in hir gesse
> Honour, estat, and wommanly noblesse.
>
> To Troilus right wonder wel withalle
> Gan for to lyke hir mening and hir chere,
> Which somdel deynous was, for she leet falle
> Hir look a lite aside, in swich manere,
> Ascaunces, "what! may I not stonden here?"
> And after that hir loking gan she lighte,
> That never thoughte him seen so good a sighte.

With all her quiet modesty, there is assurance in her manner—a touch of disdain, and something of a challenge. "What? may I not stonden here?" Whether or not she was aware of Troilus's admiration we do not know, nor whether it was for his benefit that "she leet falle Hir look a lite aside." Chaucer does not say. It is possible that he knew as little about it as we do. The suggestion is there, but that is all. But even if we take the passage in its least favorable sense, we can say no more of Criseyde than that she was fully aware of her beauty and not unconcerned with its effect. But that makes her neither a coquette nor "a designing woman" in whom the waters run still and deep. Had she been otherwise, her charm had been the less.

In Book II there is the masterful scene in which Pandarus tells her of Troilus's love. It is a long scene, and Pandarus is most adroit, tactful, and eloquent in broaching the subject and in pleading Troilus's case. After he has gone, Criseyde retires to the privacy of her closet and there turns over in her mind all that he has said. For more than a hundred lines she holds debate with herself, and the subject of her soliloquy is, To love or not to love? Now hot, now cold, her thoughts, Chaucer says, are like a March sky, at times bright and sunny, and again overspread with cloud. She recounts the virtues of Troilus. She dwells upon her position, her youth and beauty, her carefree estate. Shall she jeopardize her freedom and her fair name? She walks all around the situation, surveys the possibilities, weighs the pros and cons, is mindful of the dangers and pitfalls of love. In this self-communion she shows herself to be a wise and experienced woman, a woman of clear vision and knowledge of the world—anything, in fact, but the innocent young beauty that some critics would have her. She does not then and there decide to grant Troilus her love, but as she goes to sleep that night listening to the voice of a nightingale in the moonlit garden beneath her chamber, it is with a heart touched with sentiment and more than half inclined to grant Troilus some easement of his pain—but only "in honestee" and so as to "Kepe alwey myn honour and my name." When finally she enters upon the adventure, she does so with open eyes.

It is in this scene that we have the line

> "It nedeth me ful sleyly for to pleye,"

which some critics have held to be sufficient proof of Criseyde's guile. It occurs in one of her brief soliloquies in the course of her conversation with Pandarus. In well-dissembled rage he has burst out at her hardness, sworn that she will be the death of both Troilus and him, and started up to go. Terrified at such a prospect

> She gan to rewe, and dradde hir wonder sore;
> And thoughte thus, "unhappes fallen thikke
> Alday for love, and in swich maner cas,

As men ben cruel in hemself and wikke;
And if this man slee here himself, allas!
In my presence, it wol be no solas.
What men wolde of hit deme I can nat seye;
It nedeth me ful sleyly for to pleye."

The last line here, taken by itself, seems damaging. But in its context it is nothing more than an expression of Criseyde's recognition of the difficulty of her position. *Sleyly* need not mean "slyly," but only "skilfully," "cautiously," "discreetly." Criseyde is really frightened

. . . she was the ferfulleste wight
That mighte be.

Pandarus has convinced her that the very life of Troilus is in her keeping, has convinced her that he is quite sincere in vowing that he will die if Troilus does. She thinks of the tragedies that happen in love and of the scandal that would fall upon her were she to become the cause of the death of a prince and of a royal counselor. The situation is more serious than she has supposed and one that requires the greatest circumspection and caution if she would successfully steer a middle course and, while saving the life of Troilus, save also her honor and her name.

Pandarus's elaborate intrigues are made necessary not by the fact that Criseyde is an innocent who must be ensnared but by her concern for her honor and by her reluctance to risk her independence for an adventure that may very well bring her more pain than joy.

"... allas! sin I am free,
Sholde I now love, and putte in iupartye
My sikernesse, and thrallen libertee?
Allas! how dorste I thenken that folye?
May I nought wel in other folk aspye
Hir dredful ioye, hir constreynt, and hir peyne?
Ther loveth noon, that she nath why to pleyne."

The struggle is between the promptings of her youthful blood and her native prudence, between the flattering knowledge of her having inspired the love of a man like Troilus and her fear that to return his love might be to plunge from the security and freedom of her present life into the "dreadful joys" and possible scandals of a great passion. With all her sanity and balance, she is a woman of conflicting and changing emotions. After she has apparently decided in her own mind to give Troilus some little encouragement, she at first refuses even to accept a letter from him. Pandarus and Troilus must step warily, and Pandarus especially proceed with infinite caution and ingenuity. But though she speaks of her honor and has genuine misgivings, she is not averse to romance, and we feel that, like Pandarus, she takes such delight in playing the game of love as to be willing to prolong it in order to savor its fascination to the full. She is not deceived by her uncle's subterfuges. She lends herself to his schemes knowingly—but not because she is heartless or calculating. Partly it is because she is amused by Pandarus—as much, perhaps, as we are. She plays perfectly and with zest her rôle of opposite to this master of intrigue. Meanwhile, her sentiment for Troilus changes to love. And she understands the art of love well enough to know that to yield too easily or too soon is to miss much of the romance. She is both modest and passionate, fearful and eager; and along with her womanly dignity and charm, possesses not a little of the spirit of fun. Above all, she has a great instinctive knowledge of the ways of the heart. These things enable her to understand both Troilus and Pandarus, and how best to please each.

Her wisdom in the matter of love is revealed by delightful little touches here and there. At the dinner at Deiphobus's house, when everybody is talking about Troilus's illness and suggesting this and that remedy or charm, Criseyde says nothing, but thinks to herself

"... best coude I yet been his leche."

A little later she goes with Pandarus to speak with him. Troilus, anticipating her coming, has prepared many fine words to address to her and plead his love, but in her presence these have all "thurgh his wit yronne" and for shame and dread he can barely utter a word. Criseyde sees all this and understands—

> Cryseyde al this aspyede wel ynough,
> For she was wys, and lovede him never the lasse.

She knew that his being the very antithesis of glib and bold and self-assured was augury of his worth and truth as a lover.

In Book III Criseyde consents to take supper at Pandarus's house, knowing perfectly well that Troilus is to be there. Of this there can be no doubt. At the first meeting of the lovers, at the house of Deiphobus, Criseyde had agreed to receive Troilus as her lover, beseeching him however to keep always her honor in "trouthe and gentilesse" and warning him that though a king's son he should have no sovereignty over her. Her concluding words had been:

> "And shortly, dere herte and al my knight,
> Beth glad, and draweth yow to lustinesse,
> And I shal trewely, with al my might,
> Your bittre tornen al into swetnesse;
> If I be she that may yow do gladnesse,
> For every wo ye shal recovere a blisse;"
> And him in armes took, and gan him kisse.

Pandarus had then promised to arrange a meeting at his house, where they should have leisure "to speke of love aright." In the meantime, there were letters between them and occasionally Troilus saw his lady and spoke with her, but always briefly and in fear lest some one discover their secret:

She with him spak, whan that she dorste or leste,
And by hir bothe avys, as was the beste,
Apoynteden ful warly in this nede,
So as they dorste, how they wolde procede.

But it was spoken in so short a wyse,
In swich awayt alwey, and in swich fere,
Lest any wyght divynen or devyse
Wolde of hem two, or to it leye an ere,
That al this world so leef to hem ne were
As that Cupido wolde hem grace sende
To maken of hir speche aright an ende.

In spite of these restraints, however, there was a rapid increase of confidence between them—of confidence especially on the part of Criseyde. Troilus in his wisdom understood her so well, Chaucer tells us, that it seemed to her he knew all she thought. He bore himself so honorably that she thanked God twenty thousand times that she had met him. So discreet was he, so submissive and attentive, that she felt he was a wall of steel to her, a shield against every annoyance, and so wise that she was no more afraid.

There is thus a perfect understanding between them, and it is clear that both are anticipating the meeting Pandarus has promised to arrange. Finally, when all is ready, Pandarus comes to invite Criseyde to supper. She laughs and makes excuse, "It rayneth; lo, how sholde I goon?" Whispering in his ear, she asks if Troilus is to be there. Pandarus swears he will not be, that he is out of town, and then adds, "Suppose he were there. What have you to fear? I would die a thousand times rather than anyone should see him." Criseyde then consents to go. But she warns Pandarus

. . . to be war of goosish peples speche,
That dremen thinges whiche that never were,
And wel avyse him whom he broughte there;
And seyde him, "eem, sin I mot on yow triste,
Loke al be wel, and do now as yow liste."

The night is one of profound darkness. There is no moon, and the heavens are pouring rain. When at last the lovers are brought together and Troilus takes her in his arms, Criseyde assures him:

"Ne hadde I er now, my swete herte dere,
Ben yolde, ywis, I were now not here!"

And with these words she endears herself a thousandfold to her lover by proving that she is there not as an innocent who has been trapped, but as his equal in love, who has come of her free consent and because of her passion for him.

That her passion for Troilus was genuine and entirely sincere no one can doubt. There is no sign or hint whatever —in her actions or words or thoughts—that she is anything but loyal and passionately devoted to Troilus, until after she left Troy; and we must remember that at that time their love-affair had already endured more than a year. Her utter loyalty and tenderness are revealed, for instance, in that scene in which, alone in her room after she has got rid of the rout of women who came to commiserate with her on her having to go to her father and the Greeks, she throws herself on her bed and weeps. Again, the oath of eternal fidelity she gives to Troilus as they discuss what they shall do, has the ring of sincerity and truth. Chaucer explicitly tells us that she was sincere in her plan to return in ten days.[40] And when finally she leaves the city she is pictured as being in misery and woe, both on the journey to the Greek camp and after her arrival there. She returns Diomed courteous answers. But her mind and heart are in Troy. She regrets that she did not follow Troilus's advice and escape with him in spite of everything. She determines at all risks to return. Even Diomed says that since first he laid hand on her bridle he has never seen her but in sorrow. When, in the course of his wooing he argues that the city is doomed,

[40] See IV. 1415–21.

her reply is full of loyalty to Troy, of confidence in the Trojans' strength and manhood, and of a touching love for the place of her birth—

> "O Diomede, I love that ilke place
> Ther I was born."

Diomed is no mere lady-killer but much of a gentleman. He believes, it is true, that "He is a fool that wole forgete hymselve," and he has the reputation of being one "that koude his good." But he has tact and delicacy, and the grace to blush and "quake" a little in his speech as he offers his service and loyalty to Criseyde. He gets on wondrously fast from acquaintance to friendship, to love. While escorting her from Troy, he is calling her "my lady deere" and "myn owen lady bright" before the end of his first speech, though she has given him no encouragement and but little audience—has in fact hardly heard what he has said. He is "this sudden Diomed." But Criseyde is won to him only gradually:

> Criseyde, that was in hir peynes stronge
> For love of Troilus, hir owene knight,
> As ferforth as she conning hadde or might,
> Answerde him tho; but, as of his entente,
> It semed not she wiste what he mente.

Again and again she puts him off, even lying to him in saying that she has no lover and has had none since her husband died:

> "Myn herte is now in tribulacioun,
> And ye in armes bisy, day by day.
> Hereafter, whan ye wonnen han the toun,
> Paraunter, thanne so it happen may,
> That whan I see that I never er say,
> Than wole I werke that I never wroughte!
> This word to yow ynough suffysen oughte."

In the end she surrenders to him,[41] but more in sadness than in joy, and only after she has been overborne—by Diomed, by her father, by their confident assertions that the city is doomed, and by her own loneliness and helplessness. Her confident plans to outwit her father and the Greeks and to return to Troy have been frustrated. The scheme that had seemed so easy as she sketched it lightly and optimistically to Troilus she now finds impossible.

> For now is wors than ever yet I wende.

She is helpless, in the midst of a hostile camp,

> —With wommen fewe, among the Grekes stronge—

protected only by her father and, if she would, by this ardent Greek, who, besides being a great warrior

> . . . with sterne vois and myghty lymes square,

lays claim to as good birth "as any wight in Troie." Diomed's terrible words about the certain and entire destruction of the city, together with what she herself has observed in the Greek camp, have made a great impression upon her. And when she goes to her bed in her father's tent that night, she sees the situation of the city and her own situation in their true light and so comes to the decision to remain with the Greeks.

> Retorning in hir soule ay up and doun
> The wordes of this sodein Diomede,
> His greet estat, and peril of the toun,
> And that she was allone and hadde nede
> Of freendes help; and thus bigan to brede

[41] In V. 1086–92 Chaucer says that he knows not how long it was between Criseyde's arrival in the Greek camp and her surrender to Diomed and that

> There is non auctour telleth it, I wene.

But Professor Root has estimated that in Benoit's version of the story in his *Roman de Troie* there is an interval of at least two full years. (R. K. Root, *The Book of Troilus and Criseyde,* Princeton, 1926, pp. 549–50).

The cause why, the sothe for to telle,
That she tok fully purpos for to dwelle.

The next morning Diomed appears again, and so well does he speak for himself

That alle hir sykes sore adoun he leyde.
And fynally, the sothe for to seyne,
He refte hir of the grete of al hir peyne.

Later she gives Diomed a bay steed, a brooch that Troilus has given her, and a piece of her sleeve as a token to wear. When Diomed is injured by Troilus in the war, she weeps over his wounds, and finally

. . . to hele him of his sorwes smerte,
Men seyn, I not, that she yaf him hir herte.

There is nothing heroic about Criseyde, but only softness, tenderness, and charm. With the best will in the world to be true, she is untrue. Loyalty she has, but not the stout-hearted loyalty needed to withstand the pressure of her circumstances. Defenseless, timid, distraught, convinced at last that Troy is to fall, she feels the need of protection, of greater protection than her father is likely to afford. Once before she had sought the aid of a great warrior. When her father turned traitor and fled to the Greeks and the clamor rose against him and his kin, she had sought the protection of Hector. Nigh out of her wits for sorrow and fear, she had fallen on her knees, wept bitterly, and with piteous voice begged his mercy and help.[42] So, now, in her trouble she turns to Diomed. And having once gone that far she is caught and betrayed by her own tenderness of heart, by her compassionate nature, so quickly moved to pity. She is surprised, it seems, at her own inconstancy. No woman was ever in greater woe

[42] See I. 106–12.

Than she, whan that she falsed Troilus.

She is fully aware of her sin against Troilus and against love. She realizes that she has been untrue to one of the gentlest, most faithful, and worthiest of lovers, and that her "name of trouthe in love" is gone forever. And she bursts out weeping. Pathetic indeed is this recognition of her own weakness, and likewise her attempt to salvage something of her self-respect by determining at all costs to be true to Diomed. This unhappiness, this remorse are the basis of Chaucer's compassion for "this sely womman"—this wretched, unhappy woman. He refuses to condemn her and would excuse her out of sheer pity.

Ne me ne list this sely womman chyde
Ferther than the story wol devyse.
Hir name, allas! is publisshed so wyde,
That for hir gilt it oughte ynow suffyse.
And if I mighte excuse hir any wyse,
For she so sory was for hir untrouthe,
Ywis, I wolde excuse hir yet for routhe.

Thus, Chaucer's Criseyde is neither "wanton" nor "fickle." It is true, Chaucer speaks of her as being "slydinge of corage." But this phrase, which has been cited by some as a key to her character, must be read in its context to be properly understood. It no doubt echoes in part Benoit's *"Mais sis corages li chanjot"* and Guido's *"Animi constantiam non servasset,"* as Professor Root notes.[43] But we are studying Chaucer's Criseyde, not Benoit's or Guido's, and it is Chaucer's words that we must consider. They must be taken, moreover, in their context, and not divorced from it.

The phrase occurs in a formal portrait of Criseyde in three stanzas in the middle of Book V. Chaucer describes her

[43] R. K. Root, ed., *The Book of Troilus and Criseyde,* Princeton University Press, 1926, p. 544.

stature, her features, the manner in which she wore her hair, the beauty of her eyes, and thus concludes:

> She sobre was, eek simple, and wys withal,
> The beste ynorisshed eek that mighte be,
> And goodly of hir speche in general,
> Charitable, estatliche, lusty, and free;
> Ne nevermo ne lakkede hir pitee;
> Tendre-herted, slydinge of corage;
> But trewely, I can not telle hir age.

The point is that, save for the fact that her eyebrows were joined, there is in the whole portrait not one detail that is anything but complimentary to Criseyde—to her beauty and her character—unless indeed *slydinge of corage* means that she was fickle of heart. But this is unlikely. *Lusty,* of course, means "joyous," "happy," "vivacious." *Free* means "generous," "gracious." What *slydinge of corage* means is shown by the words that immediately precede it. Emphatically, by using a triple negative, Chaucer tells us she was never lacking in pity. She was tender-hearted, with a heart (*corage*) quick to move (*slydinge*) in sympathy. *Slydinge of corage* means nothing more than "sympathetic," "compassionate," and is thus an additional item of praise, instead of being, as so often interpreted, the one note of blame in a description that is otherwise wholly complimentary. Criseyde, it is clear, is another of the women whom I have already described as characteristically Chaucerian—like Blanche the Duchess, or Emily and Hippolyta in the *Knight's Tale,* or many of the ladies in the *Legend of Good Women,* or the Prioress, who

> . . . wolde wepe, if that she saugh a mous
> Kaught in a trappe, if it were deed or bledde,

or if one of her dogs were dead

> Or if men smoot it with a yerde smerte—

women of tender and compassionate heart and exquisite sensibility. The type, I repeat, is not heroic. It has its weaknesses, as have all other types, and perhaps more than most is exposed to sorrow and danger. But if it is sometimes too soft and yielding, it is never hard, and it makes up for its lack of the heroic virtues by its humanity, graciousness, and charm—at least in Chaucer.

To those who are capable only of rough and ready distinctions, Criseyde is fickle as well as unfaithful, false in intention as in deed, and at bottom no better than a wanton, who, as long as she has to deal with Troilus's inexperience, credulity, and readiness to idealize her, disguises her real nature, only to reveal it when, with a man like Diomed, there is no longer any need for disguise. This, as one would expect and as Criseyde herself anticipated, became the popular view of her, and it was this vulgar, undiscriminating, and cynical conception, hardened to a tradition, that dictated the character of Henryson's and of Shakespeare's Cressida.

But Chaucer was not one to whom all things are either black or white. He was too wise for that. He understood too well the many shadings and nuances of character, the complexities and contradictions of the human heart. Indeed, this fact is demonstrated more fully and completely in the character of Criseyde than anywhere else in his works. So he pities her. But not because he is a sentimentalist. It is because he knows that a woman can be both true and false—as true as steel, if you will, and yet break, even as steel breaks. He knows that Criseyde was entirely sincere in her love for Troilus and that her faithlessness was due in the first place to the momentary weakness of a heart overwrought by grief, fear, and its own excess of tenderness and sensibility, and in the end to a pathetic attempt to mend her battered name and honor by resolving to be true to Diomed.

* * *

Troilus is thought of by many readers as a love-sick youth, as a hero who is not only very young but whose love for Criseyde is the love of "a green-sickness-liver'd boy." Troilus is young, it is true, and his love inexperienced. But he is in no sense a boy, and his passion, when it is aroused, is such as only a mature and profound nature is capable of. He is a great fighter, second only to Hector in prowess and in the popular esteem. Very early in the poem Chaucer refers to him as "this fers and proude knight."

> Ther nas a man of gretter hardinesse
> Than he, ne more desired worthinesse.

Such was his valor that the Greeks feared him like death.

> Fro day to day in armes so he spedde,
> That alle the Grekes as the deeth him dredde.

His greatness as a warrior and his reputation with the people are vividly brought out in the scene in which he rides through the streets victorious from the field and the people shout,

> "A! go we see, caste up the latis wyde!"

To see him, Chaucer says, was like seeing Mars, god of battle.

> This Troilus sat on his baye stede,
> Al armed, save his heed, ful richely,
> And wounded was his hors, and gan to blede,
> On whiche he rood a pas, ful softely;
> But swych a knightly sighte, trewely,
> As was on him, was nought, withouten faile,
> To loke on Mars, that god is of batayle.
>
> . . . .
>
> His helm tohewen was in twenty places,
> That by a tissew heng, his bak bihinde,
> His sheld todasshed was with swerdes and maces,

In which men mighte many an arwe finde
That thirled hadde horn and nerf and rinde;
And ay the peple cryde, "here cometh our ioye,
And, next his brother, holdere up of Troye!"

To think of Troilus as a mere youth is to misread him and to ignore not alone his valor, his heroism, but the strength and depth of his mind. It is to belittle both him and Criseyde. A woman like Criseyde would not have been won by a love-sick boy, king's son though he was. Indeed, Chaucer specifically tells us that Criseyde's liking for Troilus was changed to love by his manhood and his very real suffering.[44] And Criseyde herself informs Troilus that it was not for his royal estate, nor his renown in battle, nor for any pomp, array, or wealth that she loved him, but for his gentle heart, his hatred of all evil, his "moral vertu, grounded upon trouthe,"

"And that your reson brydled your delyt."

Troilus is a great lover as well as a great warrior. Though throughout his youth until he meets Criseyde he is a relentless scoffer at love and all love's servants and refers to love as

Seynt Idiot, lord of thise foles alle,

he becomes a lover whose passion absorbs his whole being. He is one of the world's great lovers, and this not only in the medieval sense or by the standards of Courtly Love, but by any standard.

This is important, for there is a widespread tendency either to laugh outright at Troilus, or to take him seriously only within the limits of what are often considered the highly romantic and fantastic conventions of the Courtly system. It is easy to laugh at Troilus—at his despair of winning his lady when he has apparently done nothing to make

[44] II. 673–79.

her aware that he has so much as seen her; at his taking to his bed and convincing both himself and Pandarus that he is about to die; at his sighs and groans, his tears and swoonings, his sleeplessness and loss of appetite, his melancholy fantasies. It is easy to grow impatient with his helplessness, his inability to further his own suit, his dependence upon Pandarus, his lack of masterfulness. With Pandarus we are tempted to exclaim

> ". . . thou wrecched mouses herte,
> Art thou agast so that she wole thee byte?"

But to laugh at Troilus is unwise. It betrays a superficial reading of his character and raises a doubt as to the reader's having ever been greatly in love himself, or as to his capability of a great passion.

In all these particulars Troilus is showing the symptoms of love as understood by Courtly writers of the Middle Ages. He conforms perfectly to the pattern of the ideal lover as conceived by the code of Courtly Love. But he conforms to the modern ideal of the perfect lover no less than to the medieval, at least as it might be exemplified in a man of his temperament. However conventional Courtly Love came to be, it was for the most part grounded in sound psychology, as is proved by the recurrence of most of its features in many a subsequent poet, dramatist, novelist, and story-teller. The system was not psychologically true to all kinds of love. It was not meant to be. It illustrated only ideal love—the ideal of romantic love between men and women of noble nature, refined manners, and delicate feeling. And such love, though no doubt unusual, still exists. It is perhaps not the present-day ideal. But even in this late day it is possible for a man or a woman to be hit very hard by love, and for a man—and even a grown man—to fall into a love-sickness, to lose appetite and grow lean, to suffer melancholy, and to cry

"Anna, oh Anna!" to the evening star.[45]

It is even possible to contract the malady more than once.

Moreover, if we look closely, we discover that Troilus's actions and reactions are carefully explained by the poet and clearly motivated. Take, for example, his seeming helplessness. It is not so much helplessness as excess of modesty and of thoughtfulness. Between the time of his falling in love with Criseyde and the entrance of Pandarus upon the scene there is a considerable interval—how long, exactly, is not made clear. During that time Troilus has suffered much and alone. Whether or not Criseyde knew anything of Troilus's passion, Chaucer protests he does not know. But he does know that it seemed she recked not at all of him or his pain.[46] Apparently Troilus has done nothing to reveal his love. He fears to do so, lest he be made the butt and laughingstock of all the lovers he has ridiculed. He thinks of the possibility that Criseyde has had some other lover, whom she loved so passionately that she would never take heed of him. Again, he tortures himself by imagining that she is cold in love, "as frost in wynter moone." Having discovered that it is his destiny to love, he is convinced that it is his destiny also to be unsuccessful in love. He wishes for death, for then his languishing in dread would be over. At first he rejects Pandarus's offer to intercede for him and tell Criseyde of his love, because for all that Pandarus might do, she would never be won to such a wretch as he—

"... for al that ever ye conne,
She nil to noon swich wrecche as I be wonne."

And even after he sees his folly and gives Pandarus permission to urge his suit, he is convinced that fortune is his foe. Above all, he fears that Criseyde will be angry,

[45] John Masefield, *The Widow in the Bye Street,* Macmillan, 1916.
[46] I. 491–97.

"Or nil not here or trowen how it is,"

or may think that he meditates harm or villainy against her.

Again, when Pandarus later urges him to write Criseyde a letter, Troilus hesitates to do so and says he is ashamed to write, lest in his innocence he should blunder and lest she refuse to receive it. And even after he has her reply—a discreet but none the less encouraging reply—he is still convinced that his passion is hopeless and that she will refuse to grant him her love.

"So reuleth hir hir hertes goost withinne,
That, though she bende, yet she stant on rote;
What in effect is this unto my bote?"

Troilus has the unhappy faculty of seeing always the several sides of a situation. His impulses are bridled by his reason and by his ability to see at once why a thing should be done and why it should not be done. He sits in rage and despair while the Trojan parliament debates whether or not Criseyde shall be exchanged for Antenor, and he says and does nothing. He can do nothing, without her consent, for, as he argues, she may be angry and accuse him of trumpeting aloud, through his meddling, the secret of their love. So he decides to let the lords do what they will and afterwards to tell his lady, and when he has learned her wishes, to move heaven and earth to carry them out, though all the world oppose it.

This habit of thoughtfulness in Troilus is seen most clearly perhaps in the discussion between him and Pandarus of what can be done in face of the decree that is to send Criseyde to the Greeks. Pandarus, out of patience with Troilus's despair and determination to die, upbraids him sharply and urges him to rise up at once and prove himself a man by carrying her off by main force.

"Artow in Troye, and hast non hardiment
To take a womman which that loveth thee?"

Troilus listens patiently to Pandarus's lengthy and urgent appeal, and then replies, "All this, friend, and much more I have thought of." And he proceeds to give the reasons for his inaction and despair. Some of them are reasons of state, some are concerned with the welfare and reputation of Criseyde. But all of them reveal the nobility of his character, his high-minded selflessness. "All this war," he says, "is due to the abduction of a woman" and therefore

"It sholde nat be suffred me to erre."

"I should be blamed by everybody if I opposed my father's grant, since Criseyde is to be exchanged for the good of Troy. To ask for her, of my father's grace, would be to reveal our love and so accuse her. I cannot buy her ransom, for my father has ratified her exchange in open parliament. Most of all, I fear to disturb her heart with violence, for that would be to slander her name, and I would rather die than defame her. Her honor is dearer to me than life. Thus I am divided between reason and desire. Desire counsels me to carry her off, but reason forbids it."

Pandarus's reply to this is the reply of a forthright and none too scrupulous man of affairs, who knows what he wants and is determined to have it. "Do as you wish," he says to Troilus, "but if I were you and had it so hot and had your estate, she should go with me, though all the town cried out against it. Never yet did wonder last more than nine nights, in any town.

Devyne not in reson ay so depe
Ne curteysly, but help thyself anoon.

It is better that others should weep than you, and it is better to be in despair for a while than die here like a gnat, without a wound. As for your lady, who knows but she may think you too nice if you let her go thus to the Greek host? Suppose she *should* grieve a little, you would soon make your peace with her, and I can't believe she would take it for evil. Has not Paris, your brother, a love? Why should you not have another? Be assured that I and all my kin will back you in the deed, though we lie dead in the street like dogs, with many a wide and bloody wound."

Pressed by such arguments, Troilus finally agrees to take the masterful way, but only if Criseyde consents. "Though I should die," he says, "I will not carry her off, unless she herself wishes it."

Nothing could better illustrate the character of Troilus than this contrast between the resourceful man of action who would ruthlessly pursue his ends, with little or no regard for the consequences to others, and the man whose very virtues, whose "reason" and "courtesy," are the cause of the paralysis and "helplessness" for which he is so often despised.

A somewhat analogous contrast is drawn between Troilus and Criseyde when he goes to discuss the matter with her, and in this case as in the former Troilus shows to advantage. Criseyde is ready with a plan. It has come to her suddenly and she has no doubt of its success. She will go to the Greeks and then return in a week or two. "True," she tells Troilus, "we shall be separated for a time, but there is a truce between the armies and you will hear of me every day; and before the truce is ended, I shall be back—yes, within ten days. My father probably only wants to see me and be assured of my well-being and happiness. Moreover, there is talk of peace, and if peace is made, I shall be free to return. If not, I shall come anyway. Where else should I go? How could I stay among those men of arms, ever in fear? My father is old and covetous. I shall take him all the valuables I have and declare they come from a friend or two of his, who have many more, a huge quantity, which they wish to send, because of the danger the city is in, but which they can send only by me. I shall tell him of the friends I have at court who may soften the king's wrath and reinstate him in the king's grace. I shall declare that he misunderstood the gods, for the gods speak in oracles and for one truth tell twenty lies, and that the city is not doomed. Thus, in one way or another I shall win him round and find a means of escape."

To all this Troilus listens hopefully, but his heart misgives him and he begs her not to go. "Your plans," he says, "are likely to fail altogether. Your father, old as he is, is Argus-eyed and still has such skill and sleight that you will not be able to get round him, for all your womanhood. As for peace, it may never come! But peace or no peace, Calkas will never dare to return to Troy, and to put any trust in that is but folly. You will find, too, that your father will urge you to become a wife and by persuasion or force will marry you to some Greek. He will tell you that Troy is doomed, and you will see so many lusty and worthy Greeks that you will think the less of us wretched Trojans. You must not go! Your father's cunning will get the better of us. I beg of you, do as I say! Let us steal away together and make certain our happiness. I have kin and friends elsewhere, and treasure aplenty, and we can live in honor and happiness the rest of our days. Believe me, this is the best way, if you will but assent."

Criseyde replies, "Yes, dear heart, we may steal away, but we should repent it sorely. God forbid that you should go and leave all your friends, especially when Troy has such need of help. My life and your honor would hang in the balance. If peace came, think how you would grieve that you could never come again to Troy. What would the people say? They would swear that not love but lust and cowardice drove you to the deed. Thus your honor, which now shines so clear, would be gone entirely. Think, too, with what filth my name would be spotted. Be reasonable and patient. Make a virtue of necessity, show a bold front to Fortune, and I swear that unless death assail me, you shall see me here on the tenth day."

Reluctantly Troilus gives in. But once more he begs her to do as he wishes.

"Myn herte seyth that it wol been the beste."

And when he leaves Criseyde at dawn, it is with a mind full of foreboding:

And rewfulliche his lady gan biholde,
As he that felte dethes cares colde.

All through this scene Criseyde is seemingly the more reasonable and practical of the two. But Troilus is really sounder than she—as the event proves—both in practical knowledge of men and affairs among Trojans and Greeks and in that knowledge of the heart which is no more than a conviction from within. Troilus is much of a fatalist. He has debated with himself the problem of foreknowledge and free will. He has experienced the power of the god of love in making him, a scoffer at love, a slave to the passion. And the power of the god of love is but a manifestation of fate or destiny. The sending of Criseyde to the Greeks is another stroke of fate, and he has dark forebodings that she will never return, that she will not be able to return, and even, possibly, that her fate and his are linked with the fate of Troy. His habit of thoughtfulness enables him to see the true complexity of the situation more truly than Criseyde does. She, in her woman's way, touches lightly and confidently on the mere surface of things, is quite sure she can manage her father and the Greeks and return in ten days, as she plans. In spite of her woman's intuition, Troilus is wiser than she.

The day comes when Criseyde must go. Troilus sits on his horse by the gate by which she is to leave, and rages within as he sees Diomed, her escort, prepare to mount. He is helpless to stop her. "Why do I suffer it?" he cries. "Why should I not put all Troy in an uproar, slay this Diomed, and with one or two steal her away?" He dares not, lest Criseyde be slain.

Thus Troilus's inaction and lack of masterfulness result in part from his philosophy and in part from his humility and considerateness as a lover. Like Hamlet he has the habit

> Of thinking too precisely on the event.

But his thought is not, like Hamlet's, "one part wisdom and ever three parts coward." Rather it is one part wisdom and three parts lover. His passion turns inward and gnaws the heart. He has a genius for torturing himself. On one occasion Criseyde urges him to

> "Dryf out the fantasyes yow withinne."

And indeed his nature is of a kind to breed fantasies. Convinced at first that it is his fate to love Criseyde without winning her, he is as certain later that it is his fate to lose her. He has but little of the gift of happiness. The high seriousness of his nature, the depth and intensity of his passion, permit at best a happiness that is fearful and uneasy. Philosophically a fatalist, temperamentally inclined to pessimism and melancholy, he is easily convinced of the malignancy of fate.

> "For al that comth, comth by necessitee;
> Thus to be lorn, it is my destinee."

His rage at the decision of parliament when, retiring to his room, he locks himself in, curses his fate and the day of his birth, and gives vent to his grief, is the very picture of a strong man bound helpless by the weavings of Fortune and by his profound conviction that since Fate is unkind, nothing will avail and his life is futile. So certain is he that he will lose Criseyde that he wishes for death:

> "I, combreworld, that may of nothing serve,
> But ever dye, and never fully sterve?
>
> . . . .
>
> O wery goost, that errest to and fro,
> Why niltow fleen out of the wofulleste
> Body, that ever mighte on grounde go?"

His suffering is very real. Chaucer describes him as

> . . . a man that hurt is sore

and speaks in all seriousness of his "manly sorwe." Pandarus assures Criseyde that Troilus is so gentle and tender of heart

> "That with his deeth he wol his sorwes wreke."

And Troilus himself cries out in his anguish:

> "For I am syk in ernest, doutelees,
> So that wel neigh I sterve for the peyne."

It is in his sufferings more than in his joys that Troilus's character of the passionate and ideal lover is most fully revealed. The nobility and constancy of his love are shown in scene after scene in Books IV and V after the blow has fallen; for example, in his indignant and yet grave and gentle reply to Pandarus's suggestion that since Criseyde must go he should take another love: "Such counsel would be well enough were I a fiend, to turn traitor to one who is true to me. She that I serve shall have me wholly hers till I die. So hold thy peace. Thou slayest me with thy speech." After Criseyde's departure Troilus's days are one long agony of restlessness, suspense, and hope deferred. He rides to his palace and, heedless of all, goes to his chamber. There, "in his throwes frenetyk and madde," he curses the gods, his birth, himself, his fate, nature, and every creature "save his lady." With true lyric cry he utters the exquisite lament beginning

"Wher is myn owene lady lief and dere,
Wher is hir whyte brest, wher is it, where?
Wher ben hir armes and hir eyen clere,
That yesternight this tyme with me were?"

Finally he falls into a slumber, restless and broken, and disordered by dreams. The whole passage reveals in vivid and dramatic way a profound and passionate nature shaken to the depths.

The next morning Pandarus suggests a visit to King Sarpedon, and Troilus reluctantly consents to go. But he cannot endure the ladies at the revels in Sarpedon's palace, because Criseyde is not there. In his fantasy he imagines that because she who bears the key of his heart is not present, "no wight sholde make melodye." He thinks only of her. He reads her letters and dwells upon her image, her womanliness and every word and deed that has passed. At the end of a week Pandarus and he return, and Troilus goes to see her palace, where he had known so many delights, but only to find it closed and desolate. He apostrophizes the empty house—

"O paleys desolat,
O hous, of houses whylom best yhight,
O paleys empty and disconsolat,
O thou lanterne, of which queynt is the light,
O paleys, whylom day, that now art night,
Wel oughtestow to falle, and I to dye,
Sin she is went that wont was us to gye!

O paleys, whylom croune of houses alle,
Enlumined with sonne of alle blisse!
O ring, fro which the ruby is outfalle,

O cause of wo, that cause hast been of lisse!
Yet, sin I may no bet, fayn wolde I kisse
Thy colde dores, dorste I for this route;
And farewel shryne, of which the seynt is oute!"

He visits the temple where he first beheld Criseyde and this and that place where he had seen her dance or heard her laugh. He goes to the gate by which she departed, and to the hill where he took leave of her. He makes a song of his woe. He tells his sorrow to the moon. He imagines the sun has not gone aright, so endless are the days. He mounts the walls and looks toward the Grecian tents (a passage that Shakespeare remembered) and vows that the air coming thence is sweeter because Criseyde is there and that

"It seyth, 'allas! why twinned be we tweyne?' "

The tenth day comes and goes, but without word or sign of Criseyde, and six days later Troilus sees no remedy but to prepare to die. Jealousy enters into his heart. He cannot eat or drink. He grows pale and lean and feeble. When two months are gone he writes Criseyde a letter. It is a letter of noble dignity and grave courtesy, and it breathes a devotion that amounts to worship and that can speak no complaint against the beloved. It is in a style truly elevated, yet with a certain stiffness, as by one unaccustomed to write. It touches the depth of his misery and his devotion in the farewell lines:

"I sey no more, al have I for to seye
To you wel more than I telle may;
But whether that ye do me live or deye,
Yet pray I god, so yeve yow right good day.
And fareth wel, goodly fayre fresshe may,
As ye that lyf or deeth me may comaunde;
And to your trouthe ay I me recomaunde."

Nothing will persuade him that Criseyde is untrue—neither her infrequent and strange letters, nor Cassandra's interpretation of his dream. When, however, he sees his brooch upon Diomed's coat of mail brought in from the field, he at last knows that she is false. But even then, and in spite of all, he cannot find it in his heart to unlove her—not even for "a quarter of a day." In his lament he upbraids her, but in the gentlest of terms. There is no bitterness in him as there is in Pandarus. He loves her to the end and puts the blame for his unhappiness upon his being born in a cursed hour. For him as for Criseyde the tragedy lies in the fact that one who could love so well should prove false.

> "That ye, Criseyde, coude han chaunged so!"

Chaucer's comment upon the irony of it all is

> Swich is this world; whoso it can biholde,
> In eche estat is litel hertes reste.

An outstanding feature of the character of Troilus is the development it undergoes in the course of the story. In his first appearance on the scene he is a debonaire, bantering, boastful young prince, with something of a swagger. He is not only young but a little sophomoric. He is scornful of all love and lovers, immensely superior in his supposed wisdom, and overweening in pride and self-assurance. Then he falls in love, and his self-confidence is gone. He has felt the power of the gods—of the god of love. He has learned that there is something stronger than he and that his wisdom was but ignorance and folly. From gayety he passes to melancholy, and instead of a callous youth becomes a thoughtful, sensitive man, with unsuspected capacities for joy and pain. The change is far-reaching and is the work of love, as several passages in the poem make perfectly clear. In Book I, when Troilus has been roused and reassured by Pandarus and has given Pandarus his consent to speak to Criseyde of his love, he is fired by new zeal against the Greeks. He goes out and plays the lion on the field of battle. And in the town his manner is transformed. Gone are his aloofness and pride, his cruelty and scorn.

> But Troilus lay tho no lenger doun,
> But up anoon upon his stede bay,
> And in the feld he pleyde tho leoun;
> Wo was that Greek that with him mette that day.
> And in the toun his maner tho forth ay
> So goodly was, and gat him so in grace,
> That ech him lovede that loked on his face.
>
> For he bicom the frendlyeste wight,
> The gentileste, and eek the moste free,
> The thriftieste and oon the beste knight,
> That in his tyme was, or mighte be.
> Dede were his iapes and his crueltee,
> His heighe port and his manere estraunge,
> And ech of tho gan for a vertu chaunge.

In the proem of Book III Chaucer sings the praises of love and its power to change men for the better:

> Ye fierse Mars apeysen of his ire,
> And, as yow list, ye maken hertes digne;
> Algates, hem that ye wol sette afyre,
> They dreden shame, and vices they resigne;
> Ye do hem corteys be, fresshe and benigne,
> And hye or lowe, after a wight entendeth;
> The ioyes that he hath, your might him sendeth.

Especially marked is the change in Troilus after his passion is requited.

> And though that he be come of blood royal,
> Him liste of pryde at no wight for to chase;
> Benigne he was to ech in general,

For which he gat him thank in every place.
Thus wolde Love, yheried be his grace,
That Pryde, Envye, Ire, and Avaryce
He gan to flee, and every other vyce.

All this is in accord with the medieval conception of Courtly Love as a power that refines, elevates, deepens, and enriches the mind and character of the lover. Chaucer is following a convention and illustrating an established doctrine. But it is a convention and a doctrine that is true to life, to the facts of human nature, and Chaucer's handling of it is such as to constitute another artistic triumph to the credit of this first of all novels. In the portrayal of Troilus, as in that of Criseyde, he has illustrated brilliantly that law of all great narratives—at least of the longer sort—that the characters should not be static but should unfold, develop, or expand in the course of the story. The contrast between the earlier Troilus, light hearted, shallow, and unfeeling, and the later Troilus, reaching the heights of ecstasy and joy, flung to the depths of sorrow and pain, questioning the gods, probing the problem of necessity and free will, and after death looking from the vantage point of the eighth sphere upon the "erratik sterres" and

This litel spot of erthe, that with the see
Enbraced is—

despising this "wrecched world" and holding that all is vanity in comparison with the full felicity of heaven, is one of the high artistic features of the poem and makes this portrayal of Troilus worthy of comparison with the greatest of character portrayals in subsequent drama and fiction.

* * *

Pandarus has suffered much, at the hands not only of the general reader but of the critic too. He has been called hard names not a few, none of which really fit him, and his own name has undergone one of the worst degradations in the history of word meanings. Whatever he became in subsequent English literature and in popular tradition, in Chaucer he is neither a pander nor a parasite nor a dotard nor a "battered man of the world." He is a man of the world, but he is neither battered nor old. He is perhaps not even middle-aged. He is Criseyde's uncle, it is true, but one need not be old, or even middle-aged, to be an uncle. And though his age is nowhere specifically mentioned, the impression one gets from a careful reading is that he is of much the same age as Troilus, Deiphobus, and Hector. He is great friends with Deiphobus as well as with Troilus—

> Save Troilus, no man he lovede so.

And he is himself still a lover, ardent though unsuccessful in the service of his lady. He touches upon the subject lightly and jokes about it with Criseyde, but he is a bit wistful and pathetic, too—as when he refers to himself as one who has never in all his service of love felt

> A frendly chere or loking of an yë.

The fires of youth are by no means dead in him.

So far from being a parasite, Pandarus is a Trojan aristocrat, a member of the Trojan parliament, a counselor to the king, who on at least one occasion is closeted with the king all day.[47] That he is one who commands a large following is shown by his offering himself and all his kin to back any attempt Troilus may be willing to make to carry off Criseyde from Troy by force. His relations with Troilus are not those of a sycophant but of a friend, and his capacity for friendship is one of his great virtues. Indeed, this friendship between the two men is one of the real beauties of the poem. It is a friendship bluff, hearty, disinterested, whole-souled, and true to death. When in Book I Pandarus is

[47] V. 284.

pleading with Troilus to tell him the secret of his love, he asks,

> "Wostow nought wel that it am I, Pandare?"

And we are reminded of Montaigne's description of his friendship with Etienne de la Boétie, "If a man should importune me to give a reason why I lov'd him; I find it could no otherwise be exprest, than by making answer, because it was he, because it was I."

Pandarus is not a pander, because, for one thing, he is not in the business. What he does, he does for neither covetousness nor gain but for the love and salvation of his friend. And so great is his love for Troilus that on one occasion, before he learns that it is Criseyde with whom Troilus is in love, he vows that

> "Were it for my suster, al thy sorwe,
> By my wil, she sholde al be thyn tomorwe."

This suggestion, however, was not such an offense against morality in ancient Greece, or even in fourteenth-century England, as it is today. Instances of men offering their own sisters to a comrade are not unknown in early literature. Moreover, this readiness to go to such an extreme is not typical of Pandarus. His words here must be taken, I believe, as a rhetorical exaggeration, thrown off in the heat of his eloquence, in his eagerness to discover Troilus's secret and ease his pain. Pandarus is not without conscience, and in one passage—in a conversation with Troilus warning him of the necessity of secrecy in order to guard the fair name of Criseyde—he shows that he understands with perfect clearness what he has done and how it would appear to the world were it known:

> "For thee have I bigonne a gamen pleye
> Which that I never doon shal eft for other,
> Although he were a thousand fold my brother.

That is to seye, for thee am I bicomen,
Bitwixen game and ernest, swich a mene
As maken wommen unto men to comen."

He bemoans the fact that Criseyde is his dear niece, and he her uncle—and her traitor too. "Were it known," he says, "that I had put this fantasy in her head to do all thy desire and be wholly thine, the world would cry out upon it and say that I had done the worst treachery, that was ever done in the world." So he doubly cautions Troilus to secrecy, to avoid all vaunting, and all will be well. And this faith in the sufficiency of secrecy runs through his conversations with Criseyde and is present indeed in Criseyde's mind itself as she weighs the pros and cons of an affair with Troilus. It is, of course, simply an illustration of one of the "laws" of Courtly Love. He protests to Criseyde that in urging her to have pity on Troilus he is not forgetting her honor and that he would rather all three of them should be hanged than that he should be Troilus's bawd or that Troilus should injure her honor. What is "her honor" here? Is Pandarus simply disguising to her his real intent? Or is love, illicit love, consistent with honor, provided it be kept secret? Obviously the latter, in the thought of Pandarus, Troilus, and Criseyde, all three. Pandarus seems to be double-faced —pretending to Criseyde that all he asks is that she make Troilus a little more cheer, while he and Troilus are thinking of her complete surrender. But if our view of Criseyde as a mature woman of the world rather than as an innocent is correct—if she is wise, as Chaucer says she is—there is in reality no double-dealing here at all, for Criseyde understands that "saving her honor" is not a matter of stoping this side of physical surrender but of maintaining perfect secrecy. In any case Pandarus makes it quite clear to her that in his philosophy beauty is given to be used:

"Wo worth the faire gemme vertulees!
Wo worth that herbe also that dooth no bote!
Wo worth that beautee that is routhelees!
Wo worth that wight that tret ech under fote!
And ye, that been of beautee crop and rote,
If therwithal in you ther be no routhe,
Than is it harm ye liven, by my trouthe!"

He reminds her that beauty perisheth ever, and urges her to love before hers is devoured by age. And earlier in the poem, in talk with Troilus, he expresses the opinion that there was never a woman born who did not feel the fires of love—either of love celestial or of love natural—and that though Criseyde, because of her youth and beauty, is not yet ready for love celestial, it would become her well to love and cherish a worthy knight,

"And but she do, I holde it for a vyce."

This again is in harmony with Courtly Love, with the doctrine that love cannot properly be withstood, for "it is a thing so vertuous in kinde."

Thus Pandarus is really neither double-faced nor treacherous. If he is apparently guilty of sophistry it is because he is a servant of Love, who subscribes whole-heartedly to Love's philosophy. There is in his attitude nothing more sinister than the necessary and inevitable conflict between Christian or conventional morality and the morality of Romantic or Courtly Love. Pandarus is a Courtly Lover, Troilus is a Courtly Lover, and Criseyde, a widow, moves in a society that is represented as being given to Courtly Love.

"Swich love of freendes regneth al this toun."

All three are fully aware that Courtly Love, illicit and secret, is more than Platonic and looks forward to possession. Thus Pandarus is not betraying his niece. He is only making possible for her an experience which he believes will be to her as much of a joy and a fulfillment as it will be to Troilus. There is nothing low about Pandarus, and it cannot be justly maintained that his offices bring any harm at all to his fair niece. He is not the author of her ruin—not even indirectly, for his maneuvering and plotting aim simply to bring to a consummation what promises to be a noble, pure, and perfect love. He believes in the sincerity and discretion of Troilus, and is convinced that with secrecy all will go well and Criseyde's honor as well as her name be safe.

Thus Pandarus's motives in playing the rôle he does are mixed. He is serving his friend and prince. He is serving his niece, in a way that by his philosophy and the philosophy of Romantic Love her youth, beauty, and charm demand. And he is serving himself, for, as a lover himself, he takes delight in helping two other lovers to the realization of complete happiness.

Still more, perhaps, Pandarus undertakes his difficult and delicate task because it is one that suits him down to the ground. It is a task such as he came into the world to perform, one that appeals to his native love of intrigue, his genius for management and maneuvering. He is a born strategist and diplomatist. Consider his subtle handling of Troilus in Book I, or of Criseyde in Book II when he goes to tell her of Troilus's love and again to take her Troilus's first letter. He is in his glory in arranging the first meeting of the lovers in the house of Deiphobus, Troilus's brother. All his resources of plotting, stage management, and plausible speech are here called into play. His invention is exhaustless. At dinner there he tells them all a cock-and-bull story of the supposed wrongs a certain Poliphete is plotting against Criseyde.

> He rong hem out a proces lyk a belle,
> Upon hir fo, that highte Poliphete,
> So hëynous, that men mighte on it spete.

Such is his readiness, his mastery of detail, his circumstantial eloquence that he not only persuades them of the truth of the story but engages their support of Criseyde's cause. So convincing is he that they are ready to spit upon Poliphete and his evil designs. Again, consider his busy ingenuity and contrivance in getting the two lovers to bed for the first time —on that night of rain and wind at his house after the supper. He anticipates everything, overlooks nothing. His gusto is enormous, and when he has finally brought them together, he remarks with sly humor

> ". . . for ought I can espyen,
> This light nor I ne serven here of nought;
> Light is not good for syke folkes yën."

Pandarus finds zest in his very sweating. Once he rushes off to his niece's house and finds her just risen from meat. As he sits down he exclaims,

> "O veray god, so have I ronne!
> Lo, nece myn, see ye nought how I swete?"

And he expects his niece to share his gusto in his admirable sweating. Does it not prove his zeal in her behalf?

His energy is boundless, of body no less than of mind. He is full of gayety and animal spirits, as lively as a cricket. His conversation is endless and always interesting, varied, and humorous, well sprinkled with saws, "olde ensamples," and shrewd wisdom. Only once is he speechless—when Troilus tells him of the finding of the brooch on Diomed's coat of mail. But this is only momentarily, for "at the laste thus he spak and seyde." His omniscience is second only to God's —"But god and Pandare wiste al what this mente." His resourcefulness, his agility of mind and tongue, know no hindrance; he shifts and tacks and turns with every wind and tide. He is full of news, of diverting small talk, and at times of sage advice. And Chaucer's reproduction of his conversation has all the vitality, naturalness, and sparkle of life. It is one of the greatest triumphs in the handling of dialogue in all literature.

The keynote of Pandarus's character is struck in the first words he utters, when he comes in and finds Troilus bewailing in the chamber alone. Here you have his lively humor, his animal spirits, his bluff and hearty familiarity, possible only between two very close men friends. And his resourcefulness, his excellent company, his homely old proverbs and thoroughly English humor are revealed in the first long speech he makes.

But Pandarus is not merely a comic figure. A thorough man of the world with a high position in Trojan society, he is possessed of shrewd knowledge of men and women and is most wise and knowing in the ways of love and lovers. He is a man, too, of feeling and of tact and sympathy. Witness his quiet and grief-stricken entry into Troilus's chamber after the Parliament has decreed Criseyde's exchange. Or his gentle sympathy with Criseyde in those words beginning "And thou, my suster, ful of discomfort . . ."[48] But whether serious or gay, his manner has always the ease of the perfectly bred. And this is true of the whole poem. It moves and has its being in high society, courtly society, but the courtliness is tempered with gayety, easy familiarity, and grace. This is seen admirably in Pandarus's first two visits to Criseyde in behalf of Troilus, especially in the second. Pandarus's light jesting, Criseyde's quick responses in the same key and, when they are alone in the garden, his swift change to seriousness—all are in the perfect manner.

Chaucer's Pandarus is not only the greatest of his humorous characters, excelling even the Host and the Wife of Bath as a fully rounded and finished portrait, but the first of the long line of great comic characters in English literature, and one of the greatest. Where did he come from?

[48] IV. 848.

Certainly not from Boccaccio's Pandaro. The suggestion has been made that Chaucer may owe something to Duke Feramonte in Boccaccio's *Filocolo,* or that Chaucer may be sketching some contemporary.[49] But surely he is a product of Chaucer's invention, whatever hints or details the poet may have got from this or that source. If the recorded experiences of the great dramatists and novelists count for anything, we are safe in saying that a creature so thoroughly alive, so convincing at every point, as is Chaucer's Pandarus can be the result only of the creative imagination, of the artist's working from within, not of any process of imitation or copying, however skilful or ingenious.

* * *

Thus the three leading characters of the poem are not only very different one from the other, each possessing an individual complexity and fascination, but are thoroughly alive. This is the result in part of Chaucer's profound knowledge of life and his profound sympathy. But it is due no less to his masterful handling of dialogue and background and to the dramatic quality of his scenes. As one reads the poem again and again—ever coming upon new beauties in it, new strokes of genius and of art—one knows not which to admire the more—the characters themselves and the comedy and tragedy of their story, or the transcendent skill with which they are revealed. There are few poems, outside the realm of lyric, that afford the reader in such full measure the intellectual pleasure that comes from the perfect satisfaction of the sense of form. For one thing, there is the strength of design in the division of the whole action into five books—an arrangement much more subtly in harmony with Chaucer's telling of the story than Boccaccio's division into nine cantos is with his. There is the careful blocking out and spacing of the individual scenes, the skilful indica-

[49] See Robinson, *Works,* N.Y., 1933, p. 451.

tion of the setting and of the passing of time in each scene, so that each is given the right emphasis and made substantial and memorable. The reader is never lost and never forgets where a given part of the action occurred. Chaucer's abundant use of detail, his habit of prolonging the scene for a sufficient time to give it body and significance, to allow it to unfold and develop to a climax, make it seem like a bit of life. It is as if we were sitting at a play, with the setting and the characters before us; or better, as if we ourselves were present in the temple when Troilus first sees Criseyde, or in the hall of Criseyde's palace as Pandarus tells her of Troilus's love.

And it is all Troy; a medievalized Troy in some respects, it is true, but still Troy, and a Troy that to an astonishing degree is classical. In the Deiphobus episode—one of the best in the poem—Chaucer brings together at an imaginary dinner party and conference some of the élite of Trojan society—Troilus, Criseyde, and Pandarus, Deiphobus, Antigone, and Helen—

> Eleyne in al hir goodly softe wyse.

They dine and chat and discuss Troilus's illness and Criseyde's affairs, and in their conversation bring in the names of Antenor and Aeneas, Hector and Paris. The whole thing is most realistic and familiar. Chaucer is at his ease with them all, and so light and sure is his touch, so swift and powerful the pace of his art—like a spirited horse on a dewy morning—that we sense the gayety with which he must have undertaken a scene so ambitious, and the joy he must have felt in seeing it come to life.

This is but one of many great scenes in the poem. Some of the others I have already mentioned: the scenes between Pandarus and Criseyde in Criseyde's palace; the scene in which Criseyde from her windows beholds Troilus riding by in the street, fresh from battle; the scene of the lovers' first night together, as full of the ecstasy and blessedness of love as that other scene, of what proves to be their last night together, is full of anguish and of a passion no longer glad but darkened by the thought of separation and of the possible doom of their love; the scene at the gate as Troilus watches Criseyde depart from the city; and the scene in which Troilus spends the whole day on the walls with Pandarus, expecting Criseyde's return, eagerly scanning the horizon and deluding himself into thinking that every figure and every cart must surely be she. Each of these is dramatic in method and quality, and each has the vividness and realism that we ordinarily think of as existing only in the greatest of dramas. With Sir Philip Sidney we marvel that Chaucer "in that mistie time, could see so clearely."

Chaucer was a great dramatist in all but form. But he did not write dramas. His was not a dramatic age, but an age of story-telling and romance. Drama had not yet been born —anything, that is, worthy of the attention of a great poet. His powers, however, were precisely those possessed by the greatest dramatists. He had the power of structural design, the sense of emphasis, suspense, and climax, the instinct for the dramatic scene, the necessary insight into human character and human motives, the power of putting himself into the lives of others and of following with perfect sympathy and understanding their thoughts and passions. And he had the art of portraying men and women on the stage before us by action and dialogue absolutely in key with the character and the moment.

All this is demonstrated to considerable extent in the *Canterbury Tales,* but it is demonstrated more clearly and fully in the earlier *Troilus and Criseyde.* And the power of *sustained* dramatic composition is revealed in *Troilus and Criseyde* in a way which the very nature of the *Canterbury Tales* made impossible in that work. If the one masterpiece reveals Chaucer's ability to portray in dramatic fashion, in the shorter forms of story and interlude, characters the most diverse, the other shows his power of portraying a smaller and more homogeneous group of characters *in extenso* and in a poem conceived of and wrought on a grand scale and in the grand style.

CHAPTER VI

The Legend of Good Women

THE Prologue of the *Legend of Good Women* is rightly held to be one of Chaucer's most charming and finished works. The list it gives of poems he had previously written, its picture of the poet as a lover of books and of the out-of-doors—of the May morning, "the smale, softe, swote gras," and especially of the daisy—bring us very close to Chaucer himself, even after all necessary allowance is made for the conventional elements the poem contains. It reflects, too, something of the literary tastes and practices of the time and of the way in which the poetry of love and sentiment flourished at the court. We hear in it echoes of the stir caused by *Troilus and Criseyde* among Chaucer's fashionable readers or hearers, particularly, it would seem, among the ladies. It thus reveals a side of the court life of late fourteenth-century England that is seldom mentioned, and it enables us to visualize more clearly the circle in which Chaucer moved. It was an elegant society, much given to the study and practice of Courtly Love, and a society in which, it appears, there was not a little corruption. When in the Prologue Queen Alcestis prescribes the penance Chaucer must do, she commands him to write in his legends not only of women true and unhappy in love, but of men who betray them and do nothing all their lives but try to shame as many women as they can. And she adds,

> "For in your world that is now holde a game."

Besides all this, the Prologue is rich in beauty and in poetry. There is the description of the daisy,

> The emperice and flour of floures alle—

and that of Queen Alcestis,

> So womanly, so benigne, and so meke—

and the Balade sung in praise of her beauty,

> Hyd, Absolon, thy gilte tresses clere—

with its delicate music and its pattern of exquisite names.

But in spite of these excellences one may be excused for preferring the Legends themselves, or at least for choosing to comment upon them rather than upon the Prologue, for this has had full justice at the hands of critics, whereas the Legends have usually been dismissed with scant notice. As we read, we recognize in the Prologue one of the most beautiful and perfect of vision-poems, but we cannot forget that here once more we are in the old world of dream and allegory. And not even Chaucer's great feeling for beauty, nor his mastery of decorative detail, nor his power of rendering these things with so much fidelity and charm, can allay altogether the sense of ennui that seems ever to attend such figures as Danger, Pity, Mercy, Courtesy, or even the "myghty god of Love." But with the Legends it is different. Their matter is classical. Their stories are stories of the passions of men and women of the ancient world; and their characters, though out of books and wholly or in part mythical, mean much more to the modern mind than do the characters of medieval allegory. The Legends are rich in names to conjure with, and they tell some of the world's most famous stories—the story of Antony and Cleopatra, of Aeneas and Dido, Pyramus and Thisbe, Jason and Hypsipyle, Theseus and Ariadne, Phyllis and Demophoön, and others. The work not only deals with classical matter but has the charm of classic story, for Chaucer treats his matter in such way as to cast upon us the spell of its beauty.

The ten Legends are not of equal merit. Here and there they betray evidence of haste and of the fatigue and even boredom of the poet. He gets off to a bad start with the *Cleopatra,* which, though the first of the series, is poorly done. Before he is one-third through it, he shows that already he feels the burden of having undertaken so many stories. He has barely got started when Cleopatra becomes Antony's "wife":

> And, for to maken shortly is the beste,
> She wax his wyf, and hadde him as hir leste.

So few are the lines preceding these that the reader has not had time to get interested in either the heroine or the hero. Contrary to his usual very great art in telling a story, Chaucer proceeds here without the circumstantial detail and careful character portrayal that give most of his narratives so much realism; he is content to present little more than the outline of the story. This is not the way he did the *Troilus,* nor the *Palamon and Arcite,* nor even the *Book of the Duchess.* It is not the way he did the Prologue, for it, as we have seen, is a detailed, rounded, and very beautiful work of art. But in reading the *Cleopatra*—and the same is true of one or two other Legends—we feel that Chaucer's heart is not in it.

Whatever failures must be recorded against the *Legend of Good Women*—including Chaucer's failure to finish it—must in part at least be ascribed to the causes that various critics have urged; namely, the size of the task he had undertaken—the writing of an indefinitely large number of legends of good women, which should take the greater part of his time year by year for the rest of his life; and perhaps the early realization that the scheme was inherently bad because it necessitated his painting all his heroines white and all his heroes black. But another consideration, I believe, was the poet's discovery or growing conviction that he could not do so many stories artistically, especially on the scale he had set; that is, could not tell them fully and with all the detail and proportion that good story-telling demands. The ten Legends he wrote vary in length from one hundred to 444 lines. The *Medea* is the shortest, the *Dido* the longest, and the average is slightly over two hundred lines. Before undertaking the *Legend of Good Women* Chaucer had, we believe, told two great love stories—the *Palamon and Arcite* and the *Troilus and Criseyde*. And in these he had used all the breadth of canvas needed for full and circumstantial narration. In the *Troilus and Criseyde* he had spread his wings to the widest and had had ample room in which to spend all his art on details of scene and character. But in the *Legend of Good Women* this was impossible, except in a very restricted way. And after writing the *Troilus and Criseyde* he must have found the small canvases of the individual Legends extremely cramping. There were to be so many that he had to be brief, or comparatively brief. Again and again he must omit things because, as he says, it would take too long to tell them. So he omits all account of the winning of Cleopatra by Antony, and of the wedding and the feast. He says merely, "She wax his wife, and hadde hym as hire leste." Again, in the story of Hypsipyle he wishes to God that he had leisure and time to tell in detail of Jason's wooing of her; and when Jason deserts her, Chaucer mentions a letter she wrote reproving him for his falseness but says it is too long to give. Chaucer, it is clear, was a story-teller who needed a fairly large canvas to get his effects. This is true even in the *Canterbury Tales*. And he was so good a story-teller that he understood the necessity of circumstantial detail, of interesting the reader in the character, and in these Legends, of making the heroines as beautiful and charming as possible. But he could not do these things in such brief compass as the plan of the work dictated. So he gave it up. This does not mean, however, that the Legends are failures. Some of them are very fine, and even in those which as wholes are not particularly impressive are to be found exquisite things.

The *Cleopatra,* for example, though disappointing, brings into English poetry the magical names of Antony and Caesar and Cleopatra and something of the aura of that great and tragic love story. In telling us that Antony was so enslaved by the love of Cleopatra

> That al the world he sette at no value

it strikes the note of "All for Love, or the World Well Lost." There is the suggestion, too, of the might and majesty of Rome in the line that tells us it was the ambition and custom of the Romans

> To have the world unto her obeisaunce;

and something of the glamor and royalty of Egypt lies in the line describing the Queen's flight after Actium:

> Fleeth eek the queen, with al her purpre sail.

There is a vivid account of the battle of Actium, rendered in terms of a medieval sea fight. And the death of the Queen is told with true pathos and tragedy. After building a shrine of precious stones and filling it with spicery, she has the body of Antony embalmed and sealed within it. Beside the shrine she has a pit dug and into this she puts all the serpents she has. Then, calling to mind the oath she had taken ever to be one with Antony—to be one in thought and feeling, in weal and woe, life and death, with the lover who has never been out of her heart's remembrance, she casts herself naked into the pit of serpents, where "she ches to have hire buryinge." In this way Chaucer reveals at once the greatness and humility of her passion, and something of its pagan quality too.

The *Thisbe* is done well, with full sympathy and detail.

It is a gem of narrative art and tells this old story out of Ovid with the utmost delicacy and grace. Especially notable is Chaucer's success in rendering the innocence of the youthful lovers and the pathos of their untimely end. How well this story gives the spirit of innocence and youth and takes us back to a simplicity of feeling almost Arcadian is seen in Chaucer's description of the wall that separates the lovers and yet permits them to whisper through its narrow cleft. To Chaucer, as to the lovers, the wall is a living presence, sentient of their woes and envious of their joys. In Ovid there is much the same thing, but nothing can equal the delicate, intimate touches by which Chaucer gets his effect. It is beyond analysis and beyond praise, and one can only quote the whole passage:

> This wal, which that bitwix hem bothe stood,
> Was cloven a-two, right fro the toppe adoun,
> Of olde tyme of his fundacioun;
> But yit this clifte was so narwe and lyte,
> It nas nat sene, dere y-nogh a myte.
> But what is that, that love can nat espye?
> Ye lovers two, if that I shal nat lye,
> Ye founden first this litel narwe clifte;
> And, with a soun as softe as any shrifte,
> They lete hir wordes through the clifte pace,
> And tolden, whyl that they stode in the place,
> Al hir compleynt of love, and al hir wo,
> At every tyme whan they dorste so.
> Upon that o syde of the wal stood he,
> And on that other syde stood Tisbe,
> The swote soun of other to receyve,
> And thus hir wardeins wolde they deceyve.
> And every day this wal they wolde threte,
> And wisshe to god, that it were doun y-bete.
> Thus wolde they seyn—"allas! thou wikked wal,
> Through thyn envye thou us lettest al!
> Why nilt thou cleve, or fallen al a-two?

Or, at the leste, but thou woldest so,
Yit woldestow but ones lete us mete,
Or ones that we mighte kissen swete,
Than were we covered of our cares colde.
But natheles, yit be we to thee holde
In as muche as thou suffrest for to goon
Our wordes through thy lyme and eek thy stoon.
Yit oghte we with thee ben wel apayd."
  And whan thise ydel wordes weren sayd,
The colde wal they wolden kisse of stoon,
And take hir leve, and forth they wolden goon.

The success of this, I suppose, is to be ascribed to Chaucer's sympathy and insight, combined with a tenderness almost womanly—a tenderness never excelled by English poet, not by Shakespeare or Landor.

Greatly to be admired, too, is the scene in which Thisbe finds Pyramus dying. Thinking he may come and not find her and thus believe her false or unkind, she leaves the cave in which she has taken refuge from the lioness and searches for him

Bothe with her herte and with her yën,
And thoghte, "I wol him tellen of my drede
Bothe of the leonesse and al my dede."

At last she discovers him, slain by his own hand,

Beting with his heles on the grounde.

Deadly pale and with quaking heart she casts herself upon him, mingles her tears with his blood, and clasps his dying form—

How doth this woful Tisbe in this cas!
How kisseth she his frosty mouth so cold!
"Who hath doon this, and who hath been so bold
To sleen my leef? O spek, my Piramus!
I am thy Tisbe, that thee calleth thus!"
And therwithal she lifteth up his heed.

This woful man, that was nat fully deed,
Whan that he herde the name of Tisbe cryen,
On her he caste his hevy deedly yën
And doun again, and yeldeth up the gost.

The picture here of the dying youth—in his agony beating his heels upon the ground, beyond the power of speech, able only to lift "his hevy dedly yën" to his love—is a perfect foil to that of the passionate and anguished Thisbe, and the two are woven together with such art as to make a scene tragic and unforgettable.

The *Dido* is perhaps the best of the Legends. It opens magnificently, as with a trumpet note, heralding the fame and greatness of Virgil:

Glory and honour, Virgil Mantuan,
Be to thy name! and I shal, as I can,
Folow thy lantern, as thou gost biforn,
How Eneas to Dido was forsworn.

It is a marvelous piece of condensation—of the story of Troy, the wanderings of Aeneas, and his sojourn and love-affair with Dido. Chaucer's narrative art is working well here. The story moves swiftly from point to point. It is done with great gusto, with a firm sense of structure throughout, and in a perfectly flexible and finished style.

The center of interest, of course, is the character of Dido. She is one of Chaucer's lovely heroines. He succeeds in making her fascinating, as he fails to do with Cleopatra—especially in her warm, generous nature, her womanly heart, her graciousness and pity. He gives us her portrait in four lines as Aeneas first saw her, standing in the temple, as was Criseyde when first seen by Troilus:

This fresshe lady, of the citee quene,
Stood in the temple, in her estat royal,
So richely, and eek so fair withal,
So yong, so lusty, with her eyen glade . . .

She delights in "all these newe lusty folk of Troye." Indeed, this whole ancient world, as Chaucer paints it—both here in the *Dido* and in other Legends—is a lusty world, a brave young world of beautiful ladies, young, fresh, and amorous, and of lusty knights, as youthful and handsome as they are vigorous. Dido is "this amerous queene," "this lusty freshe queene." When she goes hunting with Aeneas she is surrounded by "al hir lusty folk," "hire yonge knyghtes," and "of hire women ek an huge route." They are mounted "upon coursers, swift as any thought." Dido, "as fair as is the bryghte morwe," rides a stout palfrey as white as paper, and Aeneas, like Phoebus, "So was he fressh arayed in his wyse," sits upon "a courser stertlynge as the fyr." In the *Legend of Hypsipyle* Jason is "yong and lusty of corage," and Hypsipyle herself is

> The faire yonge Isiphilee, the shene.

And in the *Ariadne* Theseus is a king's son and a seemly knight

> And yong, but of a twenty yeer and three.

Dido's welcome and hospitality to Aeneas and his men are not merely those of a queen, but of a woman lovely and generous and warm-hearted. She is moved by pity for their hard case, but also by the renown of Aeneas, the honor which all his followers pay him, his manner, which is that of "a verray gentil man," and his gift of speech. "Have ye nat herd him telle his adventure?" she later asks her sister. She is also taken with his physical beauty, his "noble visage," his figure, "formed wel of braunes and of bones," and his fairness, which he had from his mother Venus. When she takes her sister into her confidence and confesses her passion for Aeneas, she remarks that he seems so well made

> And eek so lykly for to be a man

that all her love and life are in his care. She has such desire

> With Eneas, her newe gest, to dele

that she loses both color and health. Chaucer is never one to balk at the physical side of love, whether it be in the fabliaux of the *Canterbury Tales* or in tales of romantic love between great ladies and gentlemen, as in *Troilus and Criseyde* or here in the *Legend of Good Women.* Dido passes from pity to love, to consuming passion. Hers is a tender and impressionable heart, and her romantic nature is seen in her love of the new and strange:

> And, for he was a straunger, somewhat she
> Lyked him the bet, as, god do bote,
> To som folk ofte newe thing is swote.

These things—her pity and love and "gentilesse"—lead her to entertain her guest with a magnificence truly regal. In "hire frendly speche," with "many a gentil word," she gives him welcome and promises him all worship and succor. She sends food and wine to the ships. She prepares a feast in her royal palace, with music, song, and dancing, and after the spices and the wine she escorts Aeneas and his men to their chambers, with rich beds and ornaments. She combs her realm for gifts worthy of her guest—noble coursers, steeds, and palfreys, falcons and hounds, rich jewels, and cups and sacks of gold. She sends to the ships for Ascanius that for the father's sake she may honor and cheer the son. And yet, in spite of all this, one thinks not of her queenliness and wealth so much as her gentle and compassionate womanhood. For the time being at least, the queen is submerged in the woman.

The picture of Aeneas meanwhile is that of a man suddenly come to paradise, and the contrast between his estate when he landed on Dido's shores and his life in the midst of all this luxury and delight is admirably brought out.

So longe he sailed in the salte see

. . . .

So was he with the tempest al to-shake

that the ministrations of Dido are doubly sweet, and he passes suddenly from storm, shipwreck, and despair to perfect comfort and ease. At the banquet

He never beter at ese was in his lyve;

and when he is led to his chamber, it is

To take his ese and for to have his reste.

What spacious and heartfelt content is here! Nothing could suggest better the perfect tact and success of the queen's hospitality.

Dido's generosity, of course, makes Aeneas's desertion of her all the more base. Chaucer represents him simply as a false lover who has tired of a mistress:

This Eneas, that hath so depe yswore,
Is wery of his craft within a throwe;
The hote ernest is al overblowe.

And the dream of his father's ghost warning him to go on to Italy is merely a convenient fiction. In a lengthy and eloquent apostrophe to women on their fondness and blindness—

O sely wemen, ful of innocence,
Ful of pitee, of trouthe, and conscience,
What maketh yow to men to trusten so?
Have ye swich routhe upon hir feined wo,
And han swich olde ensamples yow beforn?—

the poet bids his hearers note how this hero and great gentleman, seemingly so true and secret, so point device in all the requirements of chivalric love, repaid his lady's trust.

At the end the despair and self-abasement of Dido are

pitiable indeed. When, in reply to a question, Aeneas tells her that his "destine is sone for to sayle," she cries "Is that in ernest? Will ye so?" She reminds him that he has sworn to make her his wife, that she is a gentle woman and a queen. She falls on her knees and offers to be

> His thral, his servant in the leste gree.

She swoons at his feet

> Dischevele, with her brighte gilte here—

and begs him to marry her and slay her with his sword that night

> "For than yit shal I dyen as your wyf."

And she ends her plea with

> "Mercy, lord! have pite in your thoght!"

But to no avail. Aeneas leaves her, sleeping, in the night. And when she awakes and finds him gone, Chaucer has such pity for her, he protests, that he cannot write of the complaint she made to her sister Anne. He feels for Dido, it seems, much the same as he did for Criseyde, and was perhaps in both cases not a little in love with the heroine he had portrayed.

The *Hypsipyle* and the *Medea* are really a double legend, with Jason as the common hero or villain. In him we have another great gentleman, perfect in all the outward observances of knighthood and Courtly Love. A lord of great renown, in his look as royal as a lion, famous above all other knights for "gentelesse," freedom, strength, and lustiness, he is goodly in speech and knows all the art and craft of love. But he is false to the core, and Chaucer reserves for him some of his bitterest invective; in fact, he devotes a special introduction or proem of some twenty-five lines to condemning this "root of false lovers," this

. . . sly devourer and confusioun
Of gentil wommen, tender creatures . . .

this traitor to love, whose only desire was

To doon with gentil wommen his delyt,
This is his lust and his felicitee.

Chaucer vows that he will put his name in English that his kind may be known, and he proceeds to the attack with right good will:

Have at thee, Iasoun! now thyn horn is blowe!

Both heroines, Hypsipyle and Medea, are queens, young and fair, and though Hypsipyle's portrait is the more clearly drawn, we are given enough of the character of Medea to know that both are, like Dido, women of tender and generous heart. Hypsipyle is another queen who succors sea-worn mariners—

Of veray bountee and of curtesye,

and nothing in her Legend is finer than the scene where

The faire yonge Isiphilee, the shene,

roaming on the cliffs of the sea with her attendants, watches the ship of Jason and Hercules come to harbor in the isle of Lemnos. She sends a messenger to meet them as they row to land in a cog

Hem to refresshen and to take the eyr.
The morwening atempre was and fair . . .

and to find out

Yif they were broken, or oght wo begoon,
Or hadde nede of lodesmen or vitaile;
For of socour they shulde nothing faile,
For hit was utterly the quenes wille.

Jason sends her courteous thanks and the assurance that they need nothing

> . . . but that we wery be,
> And come for to pleye, out of the see,
> Til that the wind be better in our weye.

It is a delightful picture—the ship under the bank, the two heroes going ashore after their long voyage and the many travails

> That they han suffred in the salte see,

the fair young queen "with hire meyne" playing along the cliffs and the strand—a picture that breathes of the fresh clear air of that fair morning and takes us back to a simpler and more gracious and leisurely world.

Chaucer's Medea is a much softer, more pitying and pitiable woman than Ovid's. Ovid's Medea is a stronger character, full of righteous wrath as well as passionate grief, capable of terrible deeds and vengeance, a more heroic and primitive type. The *Legend of Medea* is very brief—the shortest of them all—and the single noteworthy passage in it is the brief excerpt from the letter Medea wrote to Jason upbraiding him for his falseness:

> "Why lyked me thy yelow heer to see
> More then the boundes of myn honestee,
> Why lyked me thy youthe and thy fairnesse,
> And of thy tonge the infinit graciousnesse?"

This is based upon Ovid, but how great and exquisite an improvement it is!

> Cur mihi plus aequo flavi placuere capilli
> et decor et linguae gratia ficta tuae?

It is one more example of Chaucer's originality even when telling a story from another, and of his power of exalting what he borrowed.

The *Legend of Lucrece* is told briefly and effectively. It is only slightly more than two hundred lines long, and yet its tragic story is in some ways more impressive than Gower's version in close to four hundred lines and than Shakespeare's in more than eighteen hundred. Three scenes are especially good. The first is the picture of Lucrece as Tarquin and her husband Collatine see her from her chamber door. She is sitting by the bed, working the soft wool and wishing for the siege to end that her husband may return:

This noble wyf sat by her beddes syde
Dischevele, for no malice she ne thoghte;
And softe wolle our book seith that she wroghte
To kepen her fro slouthe and ydelnesse;
And bad her servants doon hir businesse,
And axeth hem, "what tydings heren ye?
How seith men of the sege, how shal hit be?
God wolde the walles weren falle adoun;
Myn husbond is so longe out of this toun,
For which the dreed doth me so sore smerte,
Right as a swerd hit stingeth to myn herte
Whan I think on the sege or of that place;
God save my lord, I preye him for his grace:"—
And therwithal ful tenderly she weep,
And of her werk she took no more keep,
But mekely she leet her eyen falle;
And thilke semblant sat her wel withalle.
And eek her teres, ful of honestee,
Embelisshed her wyfly chastitee;
Her countenaunce is to her herte digne,
For they acordeden in dede and signe.
And with that word her husbond Colatyn,
Or she of him was war, com sterting in,
And seide, "dreed thee noght, for I am here!"
And she anoon up roos, with blisful chere,
And kiste him, as of wyves is the wone.

Lucrece is a woman to whom "wyfly chastitee" and the love of her husband are everything, a lady entirely simple and natural—

> And by no crafte her beautee nas nat feyned.

The effect of her beauty upon Tarquin is immediate. In the early morning he returns to the siege, and the description of his actions that day is terse and dramatic. He walks about restlessly and alone, brooding upon her image and the dark design that is shaping in his mind—

> Thimage of her recording alwey newe;
> "Thus lay her heer, and thus fresh was her hewe;
> Thus sat, thus spak, thus span; this was her chere,
> Thus fair she was, and this was her manere."

His passion is like the waves of the sea after a storm. Suddenly he resolves to act, whatever the cost:

> "For, maugre her, she shal my lemman be;
> Hap helpeth hardy man alday," quod he;
> "What ende that I make, hit shal be so."

He girds on his sword, mounts his horse, and rides straight to Rome and the house of Collatine:

> Doun was the sonne, and day hath lost his light;
> And in he com unto a privy halke,
> And in the night ful theefly gan he stalke,
> Whan every wight was to his reste broght,
> Ne no wight had of tresoun swich a thoght.

In the narration of the actual rape, Gower has rather the better of Chaucer. He makes the helplessness of Lucrece more probable and gives greater sense of suspense just before

> The horrible deed of her oppressioun.

And with how much simplicity and restraint the medieval poet—whether Chaucer or Gower—can tell a tragic story is shown in their management of the scene after Tarquin is gone. Either poet's account is superior to Shakespeare's. In Chaucer, Lucrece sends for her father, mother, husband, and friends. In habit of mourning she sits ever weeping, and is almost dumb with grief and shame:

> A word for shame ne may she forth outbringe,
> Ne upon hem she dorste nat beholde.

Shakespeare's Lucrece is more eloquent than tragic. She bewails her fate for three hundred lines, complaining against Night, Time, and Opportunity with the most ingenious figures, images, and conceits. After a brief pause, she continues for eighty-seven lines more. Finally she calls her maid, writes a note to Collatine and dispatches it by a groom. Then she searches "for means to mourn some newer way." She discovers a great painting of the siege of Troy, and in it finds suggestions that keep her going for fifty-six additional lines. This is not tragedy. It is not great poetry. It is embroidery. And the result is that we are not greatly impressed by Shakespeare's Lucrece or her tragedy. She doth protest too much. We feel nothing of the awfulness of her experience, nor of her shame or pathos. She talks too glibly to be pitiable or tragic. She is too much interested in what she shall say, in what she *can* say. And we suspect that she might even be willing to go through the experience again for the chance to compose another such series of elaborate complaints. In dramatic truth and effectiveness, Chaucer sometimes excels Shakespeare.

The *Legend of Ariadne* is the second longest in the series, and here again we have a hero and great gentleman whose treachery is made doubly base by the debt he owes his lady. Chaucer turns aside from the narrative and in an apostrophe reminds him of his plight—in prison, in fetters, and about to be devoured by the Minotaur—and of his need of truth and loyalty to any woman who should help him now:

Wel maystow wepe, O woful Theseus,
That art a kinges sone, and dampned thus.
Me thinketh this, that thou were depe yholde
To whom that saved thee fro cares colde!
And now, if any woman helpe thee,
Wel oughtestow her servant for to be,
And been her trewe lover yeer by yere!

Ariadne and her sister Phaedra, daughters of King Minos, are two very romantic young ladies. As

Hem leste nat to go to bedde sone,

they are standing on the wall looking at the moon, when they hear Theseus complaining in the dungeon below. They are moved to compassion at once, and Phaedra is ready with a fully thought-out plan to save his life. They summon the jailor and Theseus and lay their scheme before him. When in gratitude he offers to be Ariadne's slave and serve her for nought but meat and drink, she resents the idea that a king's son and a knight should fall so low, and she insists that he take her to wife and swear to betroth her sister to his son when they arrive in Athens. Theseus consents gladly, and the two girls—they are little more—relish the prospect of being duchesses, and mayhap queens, and glory in the thought that they will have saved a king's son from death—

As ever of gentil women is the wone
To save a gentil man.

The escape is carried through without a hitch. The Minotaur is slain, and the three romantic young people, taking the friendly jailor with them, steal out of the land by night in a barge laden with Ariadne's treasure.

But the last scene is the best—that of Ariadne's desertion. Awaking at dawn, she turns in bed to find that Theseus has gone. She rends her hair, and barefoot hastens to the shore, crying aloud her husband's name—

The holwe rokkes answerde her again;
No man she saw, and yit shyned the mone,
And hye upon a rokke she wente sone,
And saw his barge sailing in the see.

She raises her kerchief aloft on a pole,

But al for noght; his wey he is ygoon.

And as Chaucer thinks of her awaking there alone, in an island inhabited only by wild beasts, abandoned by Theseus for her fairer sister, he exclaims

Allas! for thee my herte hath now pite!

Most of the details here are found in Ovid's parallel scene in the *Heroides,* but Chaucer's account is briefer and superior in its power of suggestion, and there is nothing in Ovid's version to equal the line with which this part of Chaucer's narration opens:

And in an yle, amid the wilde see—

And it would be difficult to find anything better than this in Chaucer himself.

The remaining three Legends are not particularly outstanding, and yet each has at least one noteworthy passage or scene. In the *Philomena* there is the old father of Philomena and Procne at Athens, King Pandion, reluctantly giving up his younger and only remaining daughter that she may cross the sea to visit her sister. He is a gracious and touching figure in his grief at parting with her and in the strength and weakness of his love. In a few lines Chaucer contrives to reveal the whole man and make him memorable, though but a minor character in a brief story. He is a more pathetic figure than King Pandion in Ovid—older and feebler, it seems, and more dependent on this last prop of his old age.

In the *Legend of Phyllis* there is an excellent description of Demophoön sailing home toward Athens after the fall of Troy. With him are

> . . . many a ship and many a barge
> Ful of his folk, of which ful many oon
> Is wounded sore, and seek, and wo begoon.
> And they han at the sege longe ylain.

A tempest of wind and rain overtakes them and hunts them "to and fro." The darkness, the broken helm, the deep rent in the ship's side, the sea burning in the night as fiercely "as any torche," bring them to despair—weak and famished as they are. But the gods have compassion

> And maden him upon a lond to falle,
> Wherof that Phillis lady was and quene.

The scene is not epic in quality, but it paints vividly a bit of the antique world and has about it the romance of the far away and long ago. Demophoön is another sea-worn warrior succored by a fair queen.

The last of the Legends, *Hypermnestra,* is not successful. For once in Chaucer the story is not told with that crystal clearness which is usual with him. And the characters are faint. But there is one memorable scene—that in which the timid bride rises in the night to slay her husband, as her father had commanded, and cannot do it:

> The night is wasted, and he fel aslepe;
> Ful tenderly beginneth she to wepe.
> She rist her up, and dredfully she quaketh,
> As doth the braunche that Zephirus shaketh,
> And husht were alle in Argon that citee.
> As cold as any frost now wexeth she;
> For pite by the herte her streyneth so,
> And dreed of death doth her so moche wo,
> That thryes doun she fil in swiche a were.
> She rist her up, and stakereth here and there,

And on her handes faste loketh she.
"Allas! and shul my handes blody be?"

This is not the whole scene, but it will serve to show that here again, drawing details from Ovid, Chaucer produces an original and striking effect. Not only is he briefer but more concentrated, vivid, and dramatic. His lines have more of the intensity of great poetry. Consider the dramatic value and economy of that last line! One inevitably thinks of Lady Macbeth.

Scenes such as these—and there are many of them in the Legends—illustrate Chaucer's great art in doing perfectly the little thing—the little thing like a miniature or an episode.

The Legends as a whole, then, are delightful reading, in spite of the familiarity of the stories and the way they are associated in our minds with the work of later English poets. To understand their appeal to readers of Chaucer's time we must remember that they were less well-worn than they are today. They had much more freshness of appeal, more of the charm of novelty. Indeed, the work is important, in one way, as being the first considerable collection or body of classical story in English poetry, unless Gower's *Confessio Amantis* is earlier, which is unlikely. Even if Gower's poem did come first, it is none the less to Chaucer that we must turn to find the beginning of the great tradition of classical story in English poetry, because of his greater popularity and the higher poetic quality of his work. As we have seen, Chaucer had told classical stories before this, but here he gathered together ten such stories—ten of the most famous in the whole corpus of classical legend—and established them in what was to be the great tradition of English poetry. One evidence of this is the beauty of his heroic couplets, used in this work for the first time in English.

But quite apart from their historical significance, the Legends are full of interest for the reader of today. They are concerned with great ladies and great gentlemen, with queens, princesses, and daughters of great lords—all of them beautiful, tender-hearted, and true; and with kings and kings' sons, lords, and knights, who are great lovers, though so often false. The work is rich in beauty and poetry, a romantic and lovely beauty, and it contains some of the best examples of Chaucer's pathos. Though not without touches of humor, it possesses too a realism different from the realism of the *Prologue* to the *Canterbury Tales*—a realism that is not sly and satirical and wedded chiefly to truth, but one allied to beauty and romance. And however familiar we may be with these old stories as we come to read them, we find in them that happy combination of freshness, simplicity, and charm which only Chaucer is master of in equal degree.

CHAPTER VII

Chauncer, the Classics, and the Renaissance

CHAUCER'S extensive use of classical story and allusion in *Troilus and Criseyde* and the *Legend of Good Women* is the culmination of a practice which he began early—in the *Book of the Duchess* at least. The subject of that poem is not one that would particularly encourage the introduction of classical references, and yet there are in it fifty or more such allusions. The *House of Fame,* as we have seen, is likewise rich in them. *Anelida and Arcite* and the *Parliament of Fowls* contain not a few. And the *Troilus and Criseyde* and the *Legend of Good Women* are shot through with them, as the nature of the stories would lead us to expect. In the *Canterbury Tales,* on the other hand, there are relatively few classical allusions. The *Prologue* and the Links and such tales as the Miller's, the Reeve's, the Friar's, the Summoner's, the Clerk's, the Pardoner's, etc., contain practically none. Others, like the *Wife of Bath's Prologue and Tale,* the *Merchant's Tale,* the *Franklin's Tale,* the *Nun's Priest's Tale,* have some; and of course the *Knight's Tale* has many. In general it may be said that in the *Canterbury Tales* Chaucer has restricted his use of classical allusion, as compared with his earlier practice. But even here there is enough to warrant our speaking of Chaucer as a poet whose habit and delight it was to adorn his work with references to Greek and Roman myth and story similar to those which became so characteristic and admired a feature of much subsequent English poetry, at least from the sixteenth century on.

It is not merely that Chaucer retells classical stories, as he does that of Ceyx and Alcyone in the *Book of the Duchess* and the story of Dido and Aeneas in the *House of Fame* and the *Legend of Good Women,* but that he draws upon classical myth and story for similes, parallel examples, and illustrative instances, serious or humorous. If he sees a flowery path, he imagines that Flora and Zephyrus must have made their dwelling there. In the *Book of the Duchess* the grief of the Knight in Black is so great that neither Ovid with all his remedies of love, nor Orpheus, nor "Dedalus with his playes slye," can dispel it. His Lady is as good as Penelope or the noble wife Lucrece. And in the *Nun's Priest's Tale,* when Renart runs off to the woods with Chanticleer in his mouth, the cry and lamentation raised by the hens in the yard is greater than was that of the noble ladies of Troy when Ilium fell and King Priam, seized by the beard, was slain by the sword of Pyrrhus; it was like the cries of the Senators' wives when Nero burned Rome. And Pertelote's shrieks were louder than those of Hasdrubal's wife when she lost her husband at the burning of Carthage. Chaucer's use of such allusions is so frequent and so happy, he weaves them into the texture of his narrative with so much ease and skill, that it is clear his mind was full of them. He seems to have lived imaginatively in the classical world as much as in the medieval, and to have been as much at home there. His marvelous use of local color in his great story of Troy, *Troilus and Criseyde,* is alone sufficient proof of this. And if at times in his earlier work he is overpunctilious in explaining an allusion—as he is in the *House of Fame,* when in mentioning iron as the metal of Mars and lead as the metal of Saturn, he adds that Mars is god of battle and Saturn "hath a ful large whel to turne"—we must remember that he was educating his public, as perhaps he was also at that time educating himself.

So accustomed are we to the presence of classical names

and stories in English poetry that we take them for granted and imagine it must always have been so. But the fact is that before Chaucer there are surprisingly few such allusions in the English poets. In the early thirteenth-century *Love Rune* by Thomas of Hales the reference to Paris and Helen, Hector and Caesar, is conspicuous as one of the very few instances of graceful and lyrical classical allusion in all English poetry before Chaucer:

> Hwer is Paris and Heleyne
> That weren so bryht and feyre on bleo
>
> . . . .
>
> Hector with his scharpe meyne
> And Cesar riche of wordes feo?

In *Havelock the Dane* and the *Owl and the Nightingale* there are no classical allusions, and in *Floris and Blaunche-fleur* there are but five or six, consisting of incidental mention of Paris and Helen, Aeneas at Troy, Lavinia, and Caesar. In the fourteenth century, even in the Age of Chaucer, we find much the same state of affairs. The whole of *Piers Plowman* contains but a half-dozen classical names—Cato, Aristotle, Hippocrates, Virgil, Alexander, and Trajan. The *Pearl* has but one, and *Cleanness* none. In *Sir Gawain and the Green Knight* the first few lines make mention of Troy and Aeneas, Rome and Romulus, but in the rest of the poem there is not one classical reference, not even in those scenes between Gawain and the fair Lady of the castle, though the subject of their conversations is love. Later, in speaking of men deceived by women, the poet mentions Adam and Eve, Samson and Delilah, David and Bathsheba, but no classical instances. Was the Gawain poet unfamiliar with classical story, or did he disapprove of it as being unchristian?

It is difficult to believe that this poverty of classical allusion in English poetry before Chaucer, and even in some outstanding poets of Chaucer's time, was in general due to ignorance, for, as has often been pointed out, there was a constant infiltration of classical story into literature of one kind or another all through the Middle Ages. Boethius, for example, makes reference to Nero, Orpheus and Eurydice, Circe and Ulysses, Agamemnon, Polyphemus, Hercules, etc., as well as to various ancient philosophers and other writers. The abundant and varied Latin literature of the later Middle Ages is rich in classical matter.[50] John of Salisbury, it has been observed, quotes from the classical authors "as spontaneously and aptly as he quotes from Scripture."[51] Virgil and Ovid were widely known and read and were allegorized, moralized, and imitated. Ovid was especially popular. His *Metamorphoses* was "a great storehouse of myth and legend, from which both clergy and laity, ascetics and lovers drew material."[52] In French, such works as the *Roman de Troie,* the *Roman d'Enéas,* the *Roman de Thèbes,* and the *Ovide Moralisé* introduced many of the old stories in a guise suited to medieval tastes in history, romance, or morality. In the thirteenth-century *Roman de la Rose* appear the stories of Narcissus and Echo, Appius and Virginia, Lucrece, Jason and the Golden Fleece, Jason and Medea, Dido and Aeneas, Phyllis and Demophoön, Paris and Oenone, Vulcan, Mars and Venus, Venus and Adonis, Pygmalion and the Image, Deucalion and Pyrrha, etc.—most of these occurring in that part of the poem composed by Jean de Meun.

De Meun, indeed, is much given to the use of classical matter. He not only retells classical stories but makes frequent use of incidental classical allusions. And in this respect his practice differs remarkably from that of William de Lorris. In the four thousand and odd lines which constitute de Lorris's part of the *Roman de la Rose* there are only six

[50] See C. H. Haskins, *The Renaissance of the Twelfth Century,* Cambridge, 1927, 104ff. and 154ff.

[51] Taylor, *Medieval Mind,* Macmillan, 1919, vol. II, p. 114.

[52] W. H. Schofield, *History of English Literature from the Norman Conquest to Chaucer,* Macmillan, 1906, p. 297.

or seven classical names—Venus, Cupid, Narcissus, Echo, Boreas, and Cerberus. But the eighteen thousand lines by de Meun contain roughly a hundred and fifty such names, some of them used several times. Are we to believe that this difference in the practice of two poets of successive generations, writing on the same subject—the one, indeed, continuing a poem left unfinished by the other—is due to the difference of forty or fifty years in the time in which they wrote? Hardly, though the interval fell in the thirteenth century. It seems rather to be the result of a difference in the equipment, taste, and temperament of the two men. De Meun was clearly the more widely read. His was the more eager, curious, and restless intellect. More worldly in temperament—broader, more receptive and critical—he seized with avidity upon the old yet new thought of the classics; and with no misgiving apparently as to the safety of his immortal soul, lived at ease and with enormous gusto in a world that to most men of his time must have seemed utterly pagan and godless. De Lorris, on the other hand—gentle, unworldly, devout—appears to have found little that was congenial in classic story, though the theme of his poem was love and though he himself was so great a lover of beauty.

In this use of classic story and allusion in Latin and French writers of the Middle Ages a distinction must be made between those authors and those instances in which the allusion is employed for moral and didactic purposes and those in which the interest is chiefly aesthetic. When Boethius, for example, tells the story of Circe and Ulysses, he does so in some detail, but not for the story's sake, nor for the delight that he or his readers may take in it. He is interested in pointing his moral—to the effect that though vices are more powerful than the poisons of Circe, man's reason may withstand them if it be sufficiently strong. Likewise with his story of Orpheus and Eurydice, which he tells with greater fullness and considerable feeling; it is prefaced and concluded with the obvious moral. In both instances the story is slight. It is surrounded, though not submerged, by moral and philosophical matter. Not the story but the philosophy and the morality are the thing. And this is the case in the great majority of writers in the Middle Ages who make use of classical story.

In a poet like Jean de Meun, however, we note a difference. The doctrine is still present, but it is less serious. It is light and satirical. And the stories told are calculated not so much to point out the ways of salvation as to make us wiser in the ways of the world. They are part of a criticism of life and thus come within the purlieus of literature. In de Meun's poem the story of Lucrece is told by Friend in the course of his denunciation of woman, the stories of Dido, Phyllis, and Oenone are told by the Duenna to illustrate the danger of a woman's setting her heart on one lover only, and the story of Vulcan, Mars, and Venus is introduced as a comment on the folly of jealousy. In all these instances the narrative is very brief. But in two others we have an example of that process by which the story emerges, as it were, from its background of doctrinal matter and takes on independent significance and interest, the moral or doctrine meanwhile receding and losing emphasis and importance. The first of these, the story of Venus and Adonis, is told at greater length than the other stories I have mentioned and is brought in as an item of interest, so to speak, in connection with the Isle of Cythera, to which Cupid has sent his messengers to solicit the aid of Venus. Though at the end de Meun tacks on a moral, to the effect that from the fate of Adonis men may learn not to ignore their sweethearts' advice, the story is far more important than the moral. Finally, in Pygmalion and the Image, which is the longest and most detailed of all these classical stories in the *Roman de la Rose,* as it is the last, the story has emerged completely and exists for itself as a thing of beauty. The poet gives it his undivided interest. He is the moralist and satirist no longer, but the artist pure and simple, and he tells it with full imaginative freedom and sympathy.

The French poets of the fourteenth century whom Chaucer studied with such profit—Machaut, Deschamps, and Froissart—made frequent use of classical allusion, though their practice varied in different poems. Froissart, for example, introduced a score of classical names into his *Paradys d'Amours* and none at all into *Li Orloge Amoureus;* Deschamps wrote many a ballade without one such name, and then again in a single ballade would introduce a dozen or more. All three poets, however, were familiar with classical story and made frequent use of it in their works, sometimes in the form of little narratives, but oftener in mere allusions.

From all this it is clear that if English poetry before Chaucer was almost altogether lacking in classical allusion, it was not because the practice of drawing upon classical story was not well established in contemporary Latin and French poetry. The example was there, and if English poets for the most part failed to follow it, this must have been due either to ignorance of classical story and of its use in Latin and French poetry or to a seriousness of temper which looked upon it with suspicion or distaste. The greater part of English poetry before Chaucer, at least of that which has come down to us, was either historical, pseudo-historical, or religious. It was conceived in moral earnestness and begotten of fact, or the supposed fact, and it thus had but slight interest in fiction—least of all in the pagan fictions of Greece and Rome. If, on the other hand, Chaucer made much of classical story, it was because he was thoroughly familiar with the tradition of its use, especially in French, and was in entire sympathy with it. This is perhaps another of his debts to the French poets, and in particular to Jean de Meun. Moreover, his worldly, cosmopolitan mind, unburdened by any religious or moral conceptions of the function of literature, his love of beauty, his delight in stories as stories, were precisely the things to enable him to appreciate the classics and to use them as had no English poet before him.

Next to Chaucer, the English poet of the Middle Ages who makes most extensive use of classical story is Gower, and Gower's practice is one of the best possible examples of the medieval habit of enlisting the classics in the service of morality and philosophy. The many classical stories he tells in the *Confessio Amantis,* for instance, vary greatly in excellence. Some are long drawn out, matter of fact, and almost totally pedestrian, while others—such as his *Lucrece* and his *Jason and Medea*—possess not a little art and succeed in stirring us with the sense of pity and tragedy. But whether ill told or well told, the moral is really never lost sight of. Inevitably it is dragged in by the Priest or the Lover. And Gower uses these stories of Greece and Rome merely as illustrations of morality, as exempla in a didactic discourse. He treats them not as things of beauty, but as means of instruction and edification. He introduces them in great numbers, but by the back door. His attitude toward them is at bottom apologetic and in the last analysis partakes more of the spirit of the Middle Ages than of the Renaissance.

This use of classical matter—whether in the twelfth century or the fourteenth; whether in Jean de Meun or a Goliardic poet, or Gower or Chaucer; and whether for moral or aesthetic purposes—is in itself a Renaissance thing. It is a Renaissance thing because it is part of that turning to the literature of Greece and Rome which constituted, or was to constitute, the "new learning." It is part of that process by which culture came to have a broader basis than the Bible and the Christian writers alone, and by which men acquired an interest in all things human, and not merely in those that pertained to medieval Christianity.

Now it is the peculiar distinction of Chaucer, among English poets down to and including his time, that he not only makes extensive use of classical stories, but that his attitude toward them is one of frank and joyous acceptance. He has no compunctions about them. Untroubled by the fact that they are pagan, he delights in their human interest and their beauty, and these things are to him a sufficient justification for their use. He is a teller of stories, not a moralist or philosopher, and he sees that these are among the best stories in the world. A student of human nature in its many phases, he finds here illustrations of human nature that are at once profoundly true and profoundly beautiful. An artist and lover of beauty, he is able to perceive that these gifts of the pagan world of Greece and Rome are their own excuse for being and a treasure-trove to the artist who has the breadth and power to comprehend their true value and make artistic use of them.

More than this, Chaucer succeeds in treating his classical matter with something of the classic spirit. The congeniality of his temperament with Ovid's has been noted by more than one critic. Both he and Gower went to Ovid for their stories of Theseus and Ariadne, but while in Gower we have only the story, without the charm, in Chaucer there is much of the charm of the original. Chaucer's version is not without its characteristic medieval touches, but it possesses also true classical feeling. Gower's is a classical story in name only, not in effect. And the difference is due not alone to the fact that Chaucer is a greater poet, but to his greater sympathy with the classical ideal. There was indeed something of the classicist in him, a sensitiveness to classical beauty and to the charm of classic story. His feeling for these things was so vivid and delicate that he was able to reproduce them, in no small measure, in his writings on classical themes. Instances of this have already been cited from the *House of Fame* and the *Legend of Good Women.* The most numerous are those in the individual legends of the latter poem. But other instances of classical and Renaissance feeling are to be found in *Troilus and Criseyde* and in parts of the *Canterbury Tales*. In other words, Chaucer must be placed in the list—and in point of time, first in the list—of those English poets who, like Landor and Keats, possessed not only an exquisite feeling for antique beauty but the power of giving to certain of their poems something of what Professor Saintsbury once called "the magical air of Hellenic quality."

What exactly the Renaissance movement was, in its many-sided development, and when precisely it began, are matters of divided opinion, but the characteristics of the Renaissance spirit, of the Renaissance way of looking at life, in contrast with the typical medieval attitude, are fairly well agreed upon. Certainly the spirit of the Renaissance owed much to the spirit of the classics. Pater, indeed, defined the Renaissance movement, the beginnings of which he traced far back in the Middle Ages, as an attempt to revive the Hellenic ideal. He described it as "a many-sided but yet united movement, in which the love of the things of the intellect and the imagination for their own sake, the desire for a more liberal and comely way of conceiving life, make themselves felt." To him the Renaissance was an "outbreak of the human spirit" against that "tendency of medieval religion to depreciate man's nature, to sacrifice this or that element in it, to make it ashamed of itself, to keep the degrading or painful accidents of it always in view." And he speaks of "that rehabilitation of man's nature, the body, the senses, the heart, the intelligence, which the Renaissance fulfils." Its motives are "the care for physical beauty, the worship of the body, the breaking down of those limits which the religious system of the Middle Age imposed upon the heart and the imagination." To the rude strength of the Middle Ages was added something of the beauty and sweetness of Greek thought and

Greek art. "The taste for sweetness . . . becomes the seed of the classical revival" and men are led more and more to "seek after the springs of perfect sweetness in the Hellenic world." In his essay on Winckelmann, Pater finds the characteristics of the Hellenic ideal to be blitheness, repose, serenity, generality or breadth, and sensuousness. It is the ideal "in which man is at unity with himself, with his physical nature, with the outward world." And in his essay on Coleridge he holds that the "essence of classical feeling" lies in the power "to forget the distant horizon . . . to be content with what is here and now," in contrast with "that inexhaustible discontent, languor, and homesickness, that endless regret," which marks the romantic element in literature.

Much the same view was held by John Addington Symonds. The history of the Renaissance is "the history of the attainment of self-conscious freedom by the human spirit." Symonds notes the "reawakening faith in human reason," the "reawakening belief in the dignity of man," "the desire for beauty," "the liberty, audacity, and passion of the Renaissance." "Men began to conceive that the human body is noble in itself and worthy of patient study"; "the Renaissance wrought for the modern world a real resurrection of the body." And Symonds, like Pater, found Renaissance beginnings deep in the Middle Ages and linked always with the spirit of the classics. "A certain breath of paganism, wafting perfumes from the old mythology, whispering of gods in exile, encouraging men to accept their life on earth with genial enjoyment, was never wholly absent during the darkest periods of the Middle Ages." In certain medieval Latin poems, especially the Goliardic, he detected "the note of humanity conscious of its Graeco-Roman pagan past." In the fourteenth century, Petrarch opens a new era. Unsatisfied with medieval beliefs and intellectual conceptions, he found a more fascinating ideal in antiquity. In him "toleration took the place of earnestness"; he felt "none of the unsatisfied cravings after the infinite." Boccaccio, with a temperament "unburdened by asceticism," conceived of human existence as "a joy to be accepted with thanksgiving"; he "proclaimed the beauty of the world, the goodliness of youth and strength and love and life, unterrified by hell, unappalled by the shadow of impending death."

These features of the Renaissance spirit as outlined by Pater and Symonds are found, almost all of them, in greater or less degree in the temperament and the poetry of Chaucer. But for the moment let us concern ourselves with but one, "the care for physical beauty, the worship of the body." This is less prominent in Chaucer than are certain other Renaissance characteristics, but it is present and is worth noting.

The late M. Jusserand, in his valuable book *English Wayfaring Life,* noting that a sculptor worked from the nude in the first half of the fourteenth century in England, remarks that the incident "ought to be remembered . . . as one of the precursors of the Renaissance in this country." Chaucer does not exactly paint from the nude, but there are passages in his poems that suggest at least an approximation to that method and bespeak something of that frank and full delight in womanly beauty which was so marked a characteristic of the high Renaissance. This is the case in certain parts of his description of Blanche the Duchess; and that they may have been suggested in whole or in part by similar passages in medieval love poems does not alter the fact that here in English we have an example of that care for the beauty of the body which was to become a more and more marked feature of the Renaissance. In the *House of Fame* a single line, giving us a picture of Venus

> Naked fletinge in a see,

is a Renaissance painting done in words—a Botticelli. The line in the *Merchant's Tale,*

"How fairer been thy brestes than is wyn!"

occurs in a passage intended, at least by the Merchant who tells the tale, to add to the ridicule heaped upon January, the amorous old bridegroom. This is shown by the Merchant's comment, "Swiche olde lewed wordes used he." But to a temperament more aesthetic than the Merchant's, the passage suggests poetic passion of a high order rather than the "lewd words" of an old roué and doting bridegroom. And the line quoted is an excellent example of "the care for physical beauty, the worship of the body," the expression of which in poetry and art we associate much more with classical and Renaissance times than with any other. Moreover, this instance of the delight in physical beauty occurs in a Renaissance setting. January is more than a dotard making a fool of himself over a young wife. He is an Italian nobleman, typical of the Renaissance in his love of luxury and splendor.

> This noble Ianuarie, with al his might,
> In honest wyse, as longeth to a knight,
> Shoop him to live ful deliciously.
> His housinge, his array, as honestly
> To his degree was maked as a kinges.

He is a Sybarite, a lover of wine, women, and lovely gardens. Close by his palace he has built for himself a princely garden, walled with stone, and there he delights to walk and play. The key of its wicket, which he will allow no one to carry but himself, is of silver. He is something of a poet and is fond of music and song. His generosity is magnificent—to his wife, to his squire Damian, and to his guests. The feast he provides on the occasion of his marriage—he and his bride and other worthy folk sitting on the dais in the great hall—is in lordly style. The palace is full of joy and bliss, with all manner of musical instruments, and viands of many sorts,

The moste deyntevous of al Itaille.

And in Chaucer's description of the festivities there is the characteristic Renaissance blending of the classical pagan world with the medieval Christian world. There is the priest who has married them in church

And made al siker ynogh with holinesse,

and who will shortly bless the bridal bed; and there is Bacchus, who pours the wine for all, and Venus, who

. . . laugheth upon every wight.

. . . .

And with hir fyrbrond in hir hand aboute
Daunceth biforn the bryde and al the route.

The scene is full of the Renaissance joy of life. And the whole description of January and his ménage is a noteworthy feature of this elaboration by Chaucer of what is sometimes rather contemptuously called the Pear Tree Story. To a story that is fundamentally humorous, witty, satirical, cynical, and cruel it adds an element of beauty, and that beauty is certainly of the Renaissance.

In the *Knight's Tale* a further example of typical Renaissance blending of the medieval and the classical is found in the description of the theatre erected by Theseus for the great tournament, and in the account of Arcite's funeral. The gates of white marble at the eastern and western ends of the theatre, surmounted by temples to Venus and Mars; the temple to Diana in a turret on the north wall, built of white alabaster and red coral; the statues of the three gods and the noble carvings and paintings of figures and scenes out of classic story; the prayers and sacrifices made by Palamon, Arcite, and Emily; and the resulting strife among the gods in heaven—all these are out of the ancient pagan world and are introduced to give local color to a story whose setting is Athens. The tournament itself is thoroughly medieval and true to actual practice in fourteenth-century England and France. But the theatre and its decorations are classical, the chief characters are pagans praying to pagan gods, and the outcome of the contest and the resolution of the plot are determined, as in Homer or Virgil, by the intervention of the gods. Likewise, Arcite's funeral in almost all its details is pagan. The three warriors mounted on white steeds and carrying Arcite's shield, spear, and bow; the bier borne on the shoulders of the noblest Greeks; Egeus and Theseus bearing golden vessels of honey, milk, blood, and wine, and Emily carrying the fires for the funeral office; the building of the pyre in the grove; the felling of many kinds of trees for the purpose; the nymphs, fauns, and hamadryads dispossessed of their homes; the garlands, spices, jewels, arms, vestments, wine, milk, and blood cast into the flames; the Greeks riding thrice about the pyre, with shouts and clattering spears; the games played after the body is consumed and the ashes are cold; the wrestlers, naked and anointed with oil—all these features are of the ancient world, derived through Boccaccio from Statius. Introduced into a romance of chivalry as elements of splendor and magnificence, they are harmonized in an astonishingly successful way with a tale of medieval knights and courtly love, and are a perfect illustration of that turning to the beauty of Greece and Rome which was so characteristic of the Renaissance.

But to return to Chaucer's care for physical beauty. The most striking instance of it occurs in *Troilus and Criseyde,* in that scene in Book III which describes the lovers' first night together. I refer not merely to the passage describing Criseyde's body,

> Hir armes smale, hir streyghte bak and softe,
> Hir sydes longe, fleshly, smothe, and whyte—

a stanza that Hazlitt thought "divine," but to the whole scene, the climax of which alone runs to 356 lines. It is one of the finest things of its kind in all literature. In intimacy and sensuousness it is unexcelled by anything in Spenser or the other Elizabethans. And its Renaissance daring and passion are equaled only by its truth to life and its entire delicacy of handling.

But, after all, the instances in which Chaucer paints from the nude are few. It was his habitual practice, however—at least in his mature work—to paint from life, and often, it seems, from a living model. And his interest was not confined to the beautiful. Like any great painter he delighted in the ugly, too; or rather in whatever had salience and character. His marvelous portraiture in *Troilus and Criseyde* and in the *Prologue* and tales of the *Canterbury Tales* proclaims him to be of the Renaissance. It is work done from life, by an artist with his eye on the object. Chaucer the realist is a Renaissance figure, not to say a modern figure.

And Chaucer is of the Renaissance in still other ways. Certain aspects of his work illustrate the critical spirit of the Renaissance. His use of classical material, for example, is almost always a critical use. He often rejects the supernatural and miraculous features of classical stories he retells; he is skeptical whether Venus really made Aeneas invisible, or substituted Cupid for Ascanius. His numerous criticisms of the clergy, though they are possibly merely dramatic and in no sense personal, are full of the daring and independence of Renaissance thought. The opinions of the Wife of Bath on the subject of marriage, though they may be only hers and not Chaucer's, constitute a revolt against established doctrine and represent that "awakening faith in human reason" which was one of the definite notes of the Renaissance.

But above all Chaucer partakes of the Renaissance spirit in his hearty and robust acceptance of life, and in the fact that he is always the artist, not the moralist. Like Boccaccio, he was "unburdened by asceticism"; he tells us himself that his "abstinence is lite." Like Boccaccio he "proclaimed the beauty of the world, the goodliness of youth and strength and love and life." In him, as in Petrarch, there was toleration rather than earnestness, and, so far as we can see, no "unsatisfied cravings after the infinite." "Standing upon earth, not wrapt above the pole," his interest is in the here and now. He accepts life with a semi-pagan gladness, its joys and pleasures, its good and evil; and it is contrary to his nature to gloss life with any problematical spiritual or mystical symbolism. He is interested in the heart and the imagination for their own sake, in men and women for their humanity. To him a character is a character, however vicious—or saintly. His tolerance is more than toleration; it is enjoyment and zest. All men and all sides of man's nature engage his interest. He will forego nothing of the pageant of life, least of all perhaps its rascalities and knaveries. For all is human. And having come in contact with Renaissance thought and absorbed its spirit, he has acquired the necessary freedom and breadth to accept what is human—what is of human interest to men here and now—as a worthy and sufficient basis for his art.

CHAPTER VIII

The Canterbury Tales: I

I

THE PROLOGUE

THE *Prologue* to the *Canterbury Tales* is one of the greatest pieces of descriptive verse in existence, and perhaps the greatest and most extended devoted to the delineation of men and manners. It is the first thing of its kind in all literature, and there is nothing comparable to it in subsequent writers except in Chaucer's avowed imitators, as in Part I of Mr. Masefield's *Reynard the Fox.*

The "character" as a literary type seems to have originated with Theophrastus. But quite apart from the fact that Chaucer knew nothing of Theophrastus, the "characters" of Theophrastus and those of Chaucer's *Prologue* are very different artistic forms. In Theophrastus we have sketches of types rather than individuals; in a word "characters," not portraits. And the method is at bottom expository rather than descriptive. This is true likewise of the "characters" of many English writers from Sir Thomas Overbury and John Earle in the seventeenth century to Lamb and Leigh Hunt in the nineteenth century. Leigh Hunt's *The Old Gentleman, The Old Lady, Seamen on Shore,* and Lamb's *Poor Relations* are sketches that are purely typical and represent the Theophrastian tradition.

Chaucer's sketches in the *Prologue* are largely typical, it is true. The Host, for instance, is in many ways typical of hosts or innkeepers in general, at least of the old England of Chaucer's day, and perhaps of England down to the eighteenth or early nineteenth century. The same is true of the Yeoman, the Prioress, the Merchant, and others of the pilgrims. But the portrait of the Host is highly particularized too, and it seems probable that Chaucer was sketching an actual innkeeper of Southwark of that day and even of that name, whom he knew well. And this may be the case with several, or even many, of the other pilgrims. So vivid are these portraits and so full of highly significant details that scholars have sought to find their originals in certain of Chaucer's contemporaries.[53]

The uniqueness of Chaucer's *Prologue* consists in its being a series of portraits, and in there being so many of these and of such variety that they constitute a gallery—a gallery of portraits of men and women of different callings and different estates, and covering practically the whole of English life of the time. Before this there had been a series of sketches or of characters in a single work, as in Theophrastus. But these were not portraits. There had been portraits before this, and even portraits of great vividness, as those of the Duenna and of False-Seeming in the *Roman de la Rose*. And there had been at least one attempt at giving a series of portraits. In Benoit de Sainte Maure's *Roman de Troie* (ll. 5073–5568), the author introduces sketches of the Greek and Trojan warriors and of the Trojan princesses to the number of thirty. Most of these are very short, a few fairly long, as that of Hector, which runs to sixty-seven lines. But the characters here are all of much the same rank and occupation, and their portraits lack variety and are deficient in differentiating details. They cannot compare with Chaucer's in vividness or in the qualities that convince us that the artist is working from life.

The *Prologue* is a triumph of realism, and Chaucer's realistic method here is essentially descriptive, not dramatic.

[53] For the most ambitious attempts in this kind, see John M. Manly, *Some New Light on Chaucer*, N.Y., 1926, pp. 70–264.

There is no use of dialogue or of direct discourse until the very end, when the Host proposes that the pilgrims tell tales while they ride. The portraits are descriptive, and if we examine them closely we find that each consists in the skilful building up, in greater or smaller number, of a series of details, of highly specific details, as to the dress and equipment, the physical appearance, the accomplishments, and sometimes the opinions and ideas, the peccadillos and even the crimes, of the several pilgrims. A good brief example is the portrait of the Squire:

> With him ther was his sone, a yong Squyer,
> A lovyere, and a lusty bacheler,
> With lokkes crulle, as they were leyd in presse.
> Of twenty yeer of age he was, I gesse.
> Of his stature he was of evene lengthe,
> And wonderly deliver, and greet of strengthe.
> And he had been somtyme in chivachye,
> In Flaundres, in Artoys, and Picardye,
> And born him wel, as of so litel space,
> In hope to stonden in his lady grace.
> Embrouded was he, as it were a mede
> Al ful of fresshe floures, whyte and rede.
> Singinge he was, or floytinge, al the day;
> He was as fresh as is the month of May.
> Short was his goune, with sleves longe and wyde.
> Wel coude he sitte on hors, and faire ryde.
> He coude songes make and wel endyte,
> Iuste and eek daunce, and wel purtreye and wryte.
> So hote he lovede, that by nightertale
> He sleep namore than dooth a nightingale.
> Curteys he was, lowly, and servisable,
> And carf biforn his fader at the table.

This is one of the most delightful things of its kind ever done, and yet it is really nothing but a series of facts, of facts moreover that are closely packed. The same is true of portrait after portrait—from the homely sketches of the

Yeoman and the Plowman to the charming and slightly malicious picture of the Prioress; or to the portrait of the Monk, which is as full of easy tolerance and hearty, unaffected admiration as it is of sly satire. They are facts, nothing but facts. In some cases, moreover, the facts are largely technical, as in the description of the Doctor of Physic or the Sergeant of the Law, and so technical as to necessitate a whole battery of explanatory notes for the modern reader. And not content with this piling up of fact on fact, Chaucer sometimes goes further and gives us facts about facts, the details of a detail. The Pardoner, he tells us, had hair as yellow as wax, and he adds that it hung smooth like a hank of flax and that what locks he had hung in bunches and overspread his shoulders. To the one line Chaucer adds three more, going into particulars about the yellow hair. The Miller, he says, had a wart on the top of his nose, and on this wart was a tuft of hairs, and these were redder than the bristles of a sow's ears. Was there ever a writer with such an eye for detail, or such a gusto in running down and noting the minute differences of things? Or with such an understanding of the force of the particular? Why the sow's *ears?* Are the bristles there redder than other bristles? I do not know, but I do know that the simile is incomparably forceful.

The truth is, the *Prologue* is one of the most matter-of-fact compositions in the world. It is one of the supreme illustrations of what can be accomplished in literature by the sense of fact; and it is one of the supreme examples of intensity in art. It is distinguished by these things more than by imagination. And it is a high tribute to Chaucer's powers to be able to say that the poem carries its load of fact admirably. Such is the strength and solidity of this matter, that the facts, so far from being a burden, are the chief source of the power and effectiveness of the work. The facts are of the very stuff of life, and they illustrate Chaucer's genius of selection, his instinct for selecting, from all the facts available, precisely the right sort of facts to give us a sense of life in all its color and fascinating variety. The portraits of the Prioress, the Monk, the Friar, the Parson, the Summoner, the Pardoner, to mention only a few, are so many miracles of telling details, of details fresh and vivid, lively and colorful, beyond words. The Summoner loved garlic, onions, and leeks,

> And for to drinken strong wyn, reed as blood.

The Friar knew the taverns in every town, and every innkeeper and barmaid. The Reeve's legs were full long and lean,

> Ylyk a staf, ther was no calf ysene.

The Pardoner sang "Com hider, love, to me!" and the Summoner bore him

> "a stiff burdoun
> Was never trompe of half so greet a soun.

They are facts that come straight out of life and not from the poet's invention or reading, though his reading gave him hints here and there. They are Chaucer's facts, harvested by his ever alert and discriminating eye and ear from the living, motley throng of his own day. The matter of the *Prologue* is classical matter—in the sense in which Pater used the word—homely, familiar, here-and-now matter. And this in itself goes far toward explaining the *Prologue's* success—the strength and freshness of its details. It is still fresh and vivid after five hundred years, and it retains its power to surprise and delight us after the tenth or the hundredth reading.

But in addition to his genius for choosing the right sort of facts, there is the way in which Chaucer uses his facts—his power of imbuing them with his own spirit. They are shot through with his tolerance, sympathy, humor, satire, and zest—above all with his zest. Here is a poet, we say, to whom life is never dull, who cannot get too much of life, who delights in the world of men and women and no less in the world of beasts and flowers and trees. To him no detail, however slight or homely, is insipid. The wart on the Miller's nose, the nut head and "brown visage" of the Yeoman, are as interesting as the Prioress's smile that "was ful symple and coy" or as the fact that the Knight through all his life

> . . . loved chivalrye,
> Trouthe and honour, fredom and curteisye.

The "smale houndes" of the Prioress claim his attention as well as the greyhounds of the Monk, which were "as swift as fowel in flight"; and the horse of the Clerk, lean as a rake, is as worthy of mention as the Monk's palfrey, that "was as broun as is a berye." Chaucer says of the Squire

> Embrouded was he, as it were a mede
> Al ful of fresshe floures, whyte and rede,

and again,

> So hote he lovede, that by nightertale
> He sleep namore than dooth a nightingale.

Such touches of poetry in passages that are fundamentally realistic and humorous prove the humorist a poet and the poet a humorist. When the Monk rode,

> . . . men mighte his brydel here
> Ginglen in a whistling wind as clere,
> And eek as loude as dooth the chapel-belle.

The eyes of the Friar twinkled in his head

> As doon the sterres in the frosty night.

And such was the appearance of the Summoner that

> Of his visage children were aferd.

Lines of sheer beauty such as these are all the more striking in the contrast of their surroundings, and they are one of the means by which the massing of facts is saved from becoming monotonous.

Another is the introduction of those sly touches of satire which Chaucer slips in parenthetically and as an afterthought, as it were, following some word of praise. The most famous instance of this, perhaps, is the reference to the Prioress's French.

> And Frensh she spak ful faire and fetisly,
> After the scole of Stratford atte Bowe,
> For Frensh of Paris was to hir unknowe.

What could be better? What more seemingly innocent? Or more tellingly satirical? "And French she spoke, full fair and gracefully, but, if she only knew, it was the provincial French of an English nunnery, the French of Paris was unknown to her." But Chaucer, in his charity (and in his art), omits the "but." Other instances occur in the description of the Friar,

> He was an esy man to yeve penaunce
> Ther as he wiste to han a good pitaunce;

in the description of the Merchant,

> His resons he spak ful solempnely,
> Souninge alway thencrees of his winning.

and in that of the Sergeant of the Law,

> No wher so bisy a man as he ther nas,
> And yet he semed bisier than he was.

Of the Wife of Bath Chaucer says

> She was a worthy womman al hir lyve,
> Housbondes at chirche dore she hadde fyve,
> Withouten other companye in youthe . . .

and of the Host, that after supper he began to play

> And spak of mirthe amonges othere thinges,
> Whan that we hadde maad our rekeninges . . .

In all these instances the sting, if sting it is, is in the tail. Usually it is the most innocent looking tail in the world, but in reality the most deadly. And yet, from another point of view—from Chaucer's point of view—not deadly at all, but only brilliantly illuminating, like the tail of a firefly. For, to Chaucer, and I hope to us, the Prioress is all the dearer for being mistaken about her French, and the Wife of Bath all the more admirable for having had five husbands,

> Withouten other companye in youthe.

The amount of information Chaucer possesses concerning the pilgrims is prodigious. What are we to suppose was the source of it? Ostensibly the poet, as one of them, is telling us only what he learned by observation and conversation, either at the Tabard on the night of their assembling or on the road during the three or four days of the journey. He undertakes to tell us

> . . . al the condicioun
> Of ech of hem, so as it semed me,

and he does so. One or two of the portraits contain nothing but what might have been learned by the eye. This is true of that of the Yeoman, save in the one detail that he knew all the usage of woodcraft. And this might easily have come out in conversation. That the Squire was

> A lovyere, and a lusty bacheler

and could make songs, joust and dance and draw and write, would naturally appear in his talk, for he was a young blade, effervescing and bubbling over with gayety and energy. The

Merchant would inevitably boast about his shady dealings in exchange, for he was that kind of man,

> Souninge alway thencrees of his winning.

The Miller would brag of his always winning the ram at wrestling matches and of the fact that there was no door he couldn't heave off its hinges,

> Or breke it, at a renning, with his heed;

and in a drunken moment he might even confess that

> Wel coude he stelen corn, and tollen thryes.

The pilgrimage was not only a pilgrimage but a holiday, and apparently we are to suppose that under the circumstances most of the pilgrims were outspoken and self-revealing to a degree. Such knaves as the Summoner and the Pardoner would be frank and boastful to the point of recklessness. The Shipman might well have held forth on his skill in navigation and his knowing all the havens from Gotland to Finisterre and every creek in Brittany and Spain. He might even have boasted of his smuggling. But would he have confessed to the murders he committed at sea?

> If that he faught, and hadde the hyer hond,
> By water he sente hem hoom to every lond.

The Reeve must have been indiscreet indeed to reveal in his talk how he swindled his lord and how

> Ful riche he was astored prively.

The Parson can hardly be supposed to have expatiated on his own virtues, for he was not the man to indulge in self-praise. Nor was the Plowman likely to talk about himself. As for the Knight, Chaucer gives us not only "al the condicioun" of the man, "so as it semed me," but all his history

> . . . fro the tyme that he first bigan
> To ryden out . . .

and is able to inform us that

> He never yet no vileinye ne sayde
> In al his lyf, unto no maner wight.

Now Chaucer was undoubtedly possessed of extraordinary powers of observation. He seems also to have been one who, like George Borrow, had the gift of meeting people easily, engaging them in conversation, and extracting pretty much the whole story of their lives in the first five minutes of talk. He tells us himself that "when the sonne was to reste" on the evening the pilgrims gathered at the Tabard,

> So hadde I spoken with hem everichon,
> That I was of hir felawshipe anon.

And we can well believe it. We can believe, too, that such a person, in the intimacies and relaxations of such a group on such a journey, would glean an enormous amount of information, all sorts of curious and out-of-the-way facts, about his fellows. But allowing all this, we must note that in some of these descriptions there are details that could be known only to one familiar with the whole history of the man, with the opinions of him held by his neighbors, to one who knew him on his native heath—at home, in his parish, or on his land—and not alone on this pilgrimage. This is true of the descriptions of the Parson, the Plowman, and the Doctor of Physic. It is true of certain details in that of the Wife of Bath; for example, that the head-coverings she wore on a Sunday must have weighed ten pounds. It is true also of numerous items in the account of the Friar —that he was well beloved and familiar

> With frankeleyns over al in his contree,
> And eek with worthy wommen of the toun

and that

> In love-dayes ther coude he muchel helpe.
> For there he was nat lyk a cloisterer,
> With a thredbar cope, as is a povre scoler,
> But he was lyk a maister or a pope.

On the other hand, in the sketch of the Monk there is nothing but what might have been gleaned by observation and conversation in the course of a brief acquaintance.

In a word, these portraits of the *Prologue* are to a certain extent idealized. In some of their details they ignore or break down the fiction that everything here springs from the pilgrimage itself and represents the notings by eye and ear of one of the pilgrims. But that is to say no more than that occasionally Chaucer falls back upon the omniscience which convention has allowed story-tellers time out of mind.

The *Prologue* is great in itself, considered as a self-contained work of art. But it is greater still as a part of the larger whole, the *Canterbury Tales,* than it is by itself. The *Prologue* is static. The portraits are still-life. And it gains its chief interest and importance from what follows, from the tales and links which put the pilgrims in action.

II

THE LINKS

The realism of the *Prologue* is of a high order, but that of the Links is of a higher and more remarkable order. Some of the pilgrims appear only in the *Prologue,* as is true of the Yeoman and the Plowman. The Prioress is revealed chiefly in her matchless portrait in the *Prologue,* and we learn nothing more of her subsequently save indirectly through the Host's elaborately courteous address to her when he calls upon her for a tale and through the tale she tells of the martyred boy, which reveals her feeling for pathos and for childhood. But most of the pilgrims, and even those that are described at length in the *Prologue,* appear again and more vividly in the Links. The Host, as sketched in the *Prologue,* is an interesting and lively character. But the Host in the Links is infinitely more lifelike and memorable. It is only there that he becomes one of Chaucer's great comic characters. The Wife of Bath in the general *Prologue* is merely a picture; in the Prologue to her tale she is a living woman, alive to her finger tips as she airs her views on marriage and with delightful and disarming frankness and garrulity tells of her life with her five husbands. The Friar, the Summoner, the Pardoner are drawn in the *Prologue* with what one will think the utmost vividness until one sees them in the Links, quarreling, drinking, and breaking in on each other's stories.

The reason for this is not that the Links give the artist a larger canvas to work on—not that the Wife of Bath's Prologue is so much longer than the description of her in the general *Prologue.* It is due to the difference of method. In the Links Chaucer is the dramatist, putting the characters upon the stage and making them act and speak before our eyes. The Wife of Bath's Prologue is a long dramatic monologue five hundred years before Browning.

The Links—Head Links and Tail Links—are in some ways the most interesting part of the *Canterbury Tales.* There are between twenty and thirty of them, and each is a little scene in itself—sometimes a scene of high comedy. Not only do they bring the characters of the *Prologue* to life, enabling us to see the Wife of Bath, the Pardoner, and the Host in all their glory, but they give the work continuity and unity, connecting tale to tale. By them we are kept aware that this is a pilgrimage, with its diverting incidents along the way, and that each tale is being told by a living and a different narrator to a living audience. By them the work gains tremendously in liveliness and diversity of interest and becomes a drama, with play and interplay of character, and not merely a collection of stories.

The Host starts the ball rolling in the last part of the *Prologue,* when, after the pilgrims have had supper and have made their "rekenynges," he proposes in his downright hearty way that as they ride they shall disport themselves by telling tales. He offers,

> ". . . for to make yow the more mery,"

to go with them and be their guide. On the morrow they get an early start, and when they have ridden as far as the Watering of St. Thomas, he halts them, reminds them of their agreement, and insists that they draw lots to see who shall tell the first tale. The truly dramatic nature of the work is revealed for the first time in the words with which he rallies the pilgrims—words that indicate the presence, and even something of the station and manner, of others:

> "Sire knight," quod he, "my maister and my lord
> Now draweth cut, for that is myn acord.
> Cometh neer," quod he, "my lady prioresse;
> And ye, sir clerk, lat be your shamfastnesse,
> Ne studieth noght; ley hond to, every man!"

The cut falls to the Knight and he proceeds to tell the tale of Palamon and Arcite and their love for the fair Emily.

How full of drama the Links often are is illustrated by the first of them, that between the *Knight's Tale* and the *Miller's Tale.* The "noble storie" told by the Knight has impressed everyone, especially "the gentils." The Host is delighted. He laughs and swears

> "So moọt I goon,
> This gooth aright; unbokeled is the male;
> Lat see now who shal telle another tale:
> For trewely, the game is wel bigonne."

And he requests the Monk to tell

"Sumwhat to quyte with the Knightes tale."

But as it happens, the Miller is drunk and insists that he shall tell the next tale. In a loud voice he cries,

"By armes and by blood and bones,
I can a noble tale for the nones,"

The Host, with gentle words, tries to put him off:

"Abyd, Robin, my leve brother,
Som bettre man shal telle us first another:
Abyd, and lat us werken thriftily."

But the Miller is determined.

"By goddes soul," quod he, "that wol nat I;
For I wol speke, or elles go my wey."

So, for the sake of peace, the Host gives in,

"Tel on, a devel wey!
Thou art a fool, thy wit is overcome."

And with that the Miller proceeds to address the company:

"Now herkneth," quod the Miller, "alle and some!
But first I make a protestacioun
That I am dronke, I knowe it by my soun;
And therfore, if that I misspeke or seye,
Wyte it the ale of Southwerk, I yow preye;
For I wol telle a legende and a lyf
Bothe of a Carpenter, and of his wyf,
How that a clerk hath set the wrightes cappe."

Hearing this, the Reeve, who happens to be a carpenter as well as a reeve, breaks out angrily,

"Stint thy clappe,
Lat be thy lewed dronken harlotrye.
It is a sinne and eek a greet folye

To apeiren any man, or him diffame,
And eek to bringen wyves in swich fame."

The Miller may be drunk, but he has all his wits about him, and in his retort he manages both to silence the Reeve and to be sententious on the subject of husbands, wives, and cuckolds:

"Leve brother Osewold,
Who hath no wyfe, he is no cokewold.
But I sey nat therfore that thou art oon;
Ther been ful gode wyves many oon,
And ever a thousand gode ayeyns oon badde,
That knowestow wel thyself, but if thou madde.
Why artow angry with my tale now?
I have a wyf, pardee, as well as thou,
Yet nolde I, for the oxen in my plogh,
Taken upon me more than ynogh,
As demen of myself that I were oon;
I wol beleve wel that I am noon.
An housbond shal nat been inquisitif
Of goddes privetee, nor of his wyf.
So he may finde goddes foyson there,
Of the remenant nedeth nat enquere."

In this little interlude of fifty-some lines we learn much about the Host and the Miller and something of the Reeve. We hear their rough, downright speech, racy, angry, witty, and profane. We are granted some comic relief after the long and grave story told by the Knight. And we are prepared for what is to come in the tales told by the Miller and the Reeve.

A still more realistic bit of low life is found in the Prologue of the *Manciple's Tale.* Here the comedy is supplied by the Host, the Cook, and the Manciple. The Host, who once before in the course of the journey has taunted the Cook, calls the attention of the company to him now, nodding on his horse.

"See how he nappeth! see, for cokkes bones,
As he wol falle from his hors at ones.
Is that a cook of Londoun, with meschaunce?
Do him come forth, he knoweth his penaunce,
For he shal telle a tale, by my fey!
Although it be nat worth a botel hey.
Awake, thou cook," quod he, "god yeve thee sorwe,
What eyleth thee to slepe by the morwe?
Hastow had fleen al night, or artow dronke,
Or hastow with some quene al night yswonke,
So that thou mayst nat holden up thyn heed?"

Without anger, but with much astonishment at his own heaviness, the Cook replies

"So god my soule blesse,
As ther is falle on me swich hevinesse,
Noot I nat why, that me were lever slepe
Than the beste galoun wyn in Chepe."

The Manciple, to carry on the game, offers to tell a tale in the Cook's stead,

"For, in good feith, thy visage is ful pale,
Thy yën daswen eek, as that me thinketh,
And wel I woot, thy breeth ful soure stinketh,
That sheweth wel thou art not wel disposed;
Of me, certein, thou shalt nat been yglosed.
Se how he ganeth, lo, this dronken wight,
As though he wolde us swolwe anonright.
Hold cloos thy mouth, man, by thy fader kin!
The devel of helle sette his foot therin!
Thy cursed breeth infecte wol us alle;
Fy, stinking swyn, fy! foule moot thee falle!"

This is more than the Cook can stand. He nods angrily at the Manciple, but so heavy is he with drink that he falls off his horse. And there is much ado before he is got up again—

So unweldy was this sory palled gost.

The Host fears that the Manciple has gone too far, thus openly to reprove the Cook of his vice, and that some day he may suffer for it. The Manciple agrees with him, protests that he spoke only in jest, and says that he will give the Cook to drink of some excellent grape wine he has in a gourd. The Cook drinks eagerly and is delighted, and he thanks the Manciple "in swich wyse as he coude."

Than gan our host to laughen wonder loude,
And seyde, "I see wel, it is necessarie,
Wher that we goon, good drink we with us carie;
For that wol turne rancour and disese
Tacord and love, and many a wrong apese."

And after praising Bacchus—

"That so canst turnen ernest into game"—

he calls upon the Manciple to proceed with his tale.

In both of these instances we are reminded of nothing so much as of the realistic comedy of Elizabethan times. Most of the Links indeed are devoted to comedy, and to comedy of a realistic kind. But in one or two the matter is serious. In the Parson's Prologue, when the Host calls upon him for a tale and asks specifically for a fable, the Parson replies, "You will get no fable from me." He disapproves of "swich wrecchednesse" and asks why he should sow chaff when he can sow wheat. He will tell them of

"Moralitee and vertuous matere,"

and endeavor to show them the way of that glorious pilgrimage to Jerusalem the celestial. Again, in the Link between the *Squire's Tale* and the *Franklin's Tale* we have a touch of tragedy—in the words with which the Franklin praises the Squire and wishes that his own ne'er-do-well son were like him.

"I have a sone, and, by the Trinitee,
I hadde lever than twenty pound worth lond,
Though it right now were fallen in myn hond,
He were a man of swich discrecioun
As that ye been! fy on possessioun
But if a man be vertuous withal.
I have my sone snibbed, and yet shal,
For he to vertu listeth nat entende;
But for to pleye at dees, and to despende,
And lese al that he hath, is his usage.
And he hath lever talken with a page
Than to comune with any gentil wight
Ther he mighte lerne gentillesse aright."

How admirably these little prologues and epilogues serve to keep the action moving is seen in the three successive Links that deal with the quarrel between the Friar and the Summoner. When the Wife of Bath has finished her Prologue and is about to tell her Tale, she is interrupted by the Friar:

"Now, dame," quod he, "so have I ioye or blis,
This is a long preamble of a tale!"

This uncalled-for comment is seized upon by the Summoner as an excuse to attack his enemy the Friar and to put him in his place. The Summoner tells the company that friars are ever meddlesome—

"Lo, gode men, a flye and eek a frere
Wol falle in every dish and eek matere.
What spekestow of preambulacioun?
What! amble, or trotte, or pees, or go sit doun;
Thou lettest our disport in this manere."

In angry reply the Friar swears that he will tell a tale or two of a summoner that will make everyone laugh. The Summoner, in return, vows that before they get to Sittingbourne he will tell two or three tales of friars that will make the Friar's heart grieve. The Host calls for peace—

"Ye fare as folk that dronken been of ale—"

and bids the Wife tell her story.

Thus the way is prepared for a tale by the Friar about a summoner, and for "tales two or thre" by the Summoner about friars. And when the Wife has ended her tale, the Friar proceeds to carry out his threat. He announces that he will tell a jest about a summoner. And he adds, you all know by the name that no good may be said of a summoner, for

"A somnour is a renner up and doun
With mandements for fornicacioun,
And is ybet at every tounes ende."

The Host, fearing a quarrel, intervenes, but the Summoner tells him to let the Friar say what he will, for

". . . whan it comth to my lot,
By god, I shal him quyten every grot."

The Friar then tells a story that not only reveals the corrupt practices of a particular summoner but damns pretty much the whole fraternity. And he concludes with a pious prayer that these summoners may repent of their misdeeds before the fiend carries them off to hell. The Summoner by this time is so enraged that he is shaking like an aspen leaf. He rises in his stirrups and asks the company, inasmuch as they have listened to the lies of this false Friar, to hear him next. And in his Prologue he tells the scandalous and highly amusing anecdote of the friar who was carried to hell in a dream and shown there the particular place reserved for friars. Then, in his Tale, he tells of a begging, preaching, hypocritical friar and of the trick played upon him by a long-suffering victim.

Thus tales and links are woven together to make a unified and living drama, the tales growing out of the links, and the links out of the tales, and both springing from the characters of the various pilgrims. And the realism of the thing is heightened still further by the occasional interruption of a story of this or that pilgrim, and by the way in which a narrator will sometimes turn to and address one of the pilgrims or the whole company of pilgrims. There is the well-known instance of the Host breaking in on Chaucer's *Sir Thopas;* and of the Knight stopping the Monk's seemingly endless series of "tragedies." The Pardoner interrupts the Wife of Bath in the middle of her Prologue, and Chaucer uses this colloquy of twenty-five lines between the Wife and the Pardoner as an interlude marking the division between the two main topics of her discourse. The Summoner interrupts the Friar's tale, and the Friar the Summoner's, and in both cases the Host calls them to order. The Clerk, at the end of his tale of the patient Griselda, addresses the company, makes satirical reference to the Wife of Bath, her life and opinions, and ends by singing them a song, "with lusty herte, fressh and grene." And, most remarkable instance of all, the Pardoner, after finishing his tale illustrating the text that avarice is the root of all evil, turns to the pilgrims as if they were a congregation in a village church, calls their attention to the relics and pardons he carries, urges them to come forth, make their offerings, kneel down, and receive pardon. Or, he suggests, they may be pardoned at every mile's end,

> "So that ye offren alwey newe and newe
> Nobles and pens, which that be gode and trewe."

It is an honor to everyone here, he says, to have a sufficient pardoner in the company,

> "Tassoille yow, in contree as ye ryde,
> For aventures which that may bityde.
> Peraventure ther may falle oon or two
> Doun of his hors, and breke his nekke atwo."

And with crowning impudence and malice he bids the Host step forth first—

> "For he is most envoluped in sinne—"

to make offering and kiss the relics each one. The Host, furious, replies in words that are a model of foul and effective speech, with the result that the Knight intervenes and bids them kiss and make up.

The Pardoner is one of the three characters best served by the Links—the other two being the Wife of Bath and the Host. In the End-Link to which I have just referred, and in the Head-Link or Prologue which precedes his tale, we see the Pardoner in full action, revealing with gusto and eloquence all the tricks of his trade and all the greed, humbug, and rascality of his nature. He is as unblushing in self-portrayal as is the Wife of Bath, and as delighted with his own depravity. In his Prologue he describes his procedure when he preaches in churches. His text is always one and the same:

> Radix malorum est Cupiditas.

He takes pains to have a haughty speech

> "And ringe it out as round as gooth a belle"

and he knows by rote all that he says. First he announces whence he comes, then shows his bulls and his liege lord's seal on his patent, and bulls of popes, cardinals, patriarchs, and bishops. He speaks a few words of Latin, to color his discourse and stir folk to devotion. Then he shows his relics—long crystal stones,

> "Ycrammed ful of cloutes and of bones,"

a shoulder-bone of a holy Jew's sheep, with all manner of curative properties, a magical mitten, guaranteed to insure fine crops when worn on the hand of the sower. He warns his hearers that the man or woman guilty of horrible sin, such as dare not, for shame, be confessed, shall have no power or grace to offer to his relics, but that whoever is free of such sin will come up and offer in God's name and be absolved. By this trick, he says, he has won a hundred marks a year since he became a pardoner. Most amusing is his description of his manner in the pulpit:

> "I stonde lyk a clerk in my pulpet,
> And whan the lewed peple is doun yset,
> I preche, so as ye han herd bifore,
> And telle an hundred false iapes more.
> Than peyne I me to strecche forth the nekke,
> And est and west upon the peple I bekke,
> As doth a dowve sitting on a berne.
> Myn hondes and my tonge goon so yerne,
> That it is ioye to see my bisinesse."

Four times he assures the pilgrims that his only aim is to win money—

> "For my entente is nat but for to winne,
> And nothing for correccioun of sinne."

He does not labor with his hands. Why should he so long as he can win gold and silver by preaching?

> "I wol non of the apostles counterfete."

He will have money, wool, cheese, and wheat, though it be from the poorest page or a poor widow with starving children. He will drink liquor of the vine and have a jolly wench in every town. And after all this, after describing himself as "a ful vicious man," after telling a story to illustrate the sin of avarice, gluttony, and lechery, and in that story giving a little sermon on the same theme, he has the effrontery and insolence to invite the pilgrims to kiss his relics, buy his pardons, and be absolved, and to remind them how fortunate they are in having such a pardoner in the company. Nothing could reveal better the depth of his cynicism.

The Head-Link of the *Wife of Bath's Tale,* otherwise known as the Wife of Bath's Prologue, is beyond all praise. It is a dramatic monologue more than eight hundred lines long, and there is no portrait in literature that is contrived with greater art. Nor is there any that is richer in humor or that succeeds better in giving to a creature of the imagination the semblance of life.

The Wife of Bath is a realist and a pragmatist. "Experience," she says, in the first words she utters, "is right enough for me." And a little later she clinches her argument against the view that the generative organs are only for purgation and for the purpose of distinguishing male and female, by remarking pithily,

> "The experience woot wel it is noght so."

It is to experience that she appeals—and to common sense, too—in dealing with the question of marriage and virginity. And it is her experience with her five husbands that forms the basis of her claim that in marriage sovereignty should rest with the wife. She speaks from experience and hence with authority and conviction. Even when she is quoting or referring to Scripture or St. Jerome, her opinions are her own. They are opinions she has worked out for herself or put to the test of her thought and experience, and not mere hearsay. At least, so it seems. She is not parroting others or speaking at second-hand. Hers is an independent mind and an original and forceful habit of speech. Witness her explanation of the fact that women, and especially wives, are so often defamed in books—because books are written by clerks. If women had written stories, they would have written more wickedness about men than all the sons of Adam could redress.

> "The clerk, whan he is old, and may noght do
> Of Venus werkes worth his olde sho,
> Than sit he doun, and writ in his dotage
> That wommen can nat kepe hir mariage!"

On the subject of marriage her point of view is, for her time, a revolutionary one. And she has been won to it by the demands of her nature, by the intensity of her ruling passion.

By these she has been led to seize upon and emphasize those incidents and arguments in scriptural story and doctrine that serve her end and give her leave not only to marry but to marry five times, and to

> "Welcome the sixte, whan that ever he shal."

She has a firm grasp on the distinction between a command or precept and a mere counsel of perfection, and she expounds it fully and effectively in her argument in favor of marriage. Men may counsel a woman to remain a virgin,

> "But conseilling is no comandement."

If God had commanded virginity, he would, by the same token, have damned matrimony;

> "And certes, if ther were no seed ysowe,
> Virginitee, wherof than sholde it growe?"

St. Paul held only that virginity is more perfect than marriage. And here the Wife of Bath is entirely liberal, as well as realistic. She does not condemn virginity; she even grants that it may be a higher and holier state than matrimony.

> "The dart is set up for virginitee;
> Cacche who so may, who renneth best lat see."

Let those who will be virgins

> "Hem lyketh to be clene, body and goost."

But not she. She makes no boast of her estate. A lord, in his household, has not every vessel of gold. Some are of wood and do him good service. Christ did not urge everyone to sell all he had and give to the poor. He spoke to those who would live perfectly,

> "And lordinges, by your leve, that am nat I."

Virgins are pure white bread; we wives only barley bread.

"And yet with barly-breed, Mark telle can,
Our lord Iesu refresshed many a man.
In swich estaat as god hath cleped us
I wol persevere, I nam nat precious.

. . . .

If I be daungerous, god yeve me sorwe!"

What could be franker or fairer? What more perfect example could be found of sweet reasonableness and Christian humility? She will make no claim to perfection or to an exalted place in the hierarchy of God's world, but she refuses to be read out of the Christian dispensation because she has seen fit to marry, to marry five times. She will serve God in the place to which He has called her and with the powers with which He has so superbly endowed her. In all this she may seem to be guilty of sophistry. But in reality she is doing no other than protestants of all ages have done. She is simply interpreting Scripture in the light of her philosophy, and as with most of us, her philosophy is the product of her character. Why were such powers given her if not that she might use them

"In the actes and in fruit of mariage"?

In the same pragmatic way she argues that because she ruled it over her five husbands and found sovereignty good, the wife should always be the whip and the husband the thrall and debtor. And in the second and longer part of her discourse she proceeds to enlighten the pilgrims as to her technique. It is in this narrative of her marital adventures that she is most truly and magnificently herself. She is highly specific. For example, she treats the pilgrims to a lengthy specimen of the curtain lectures she administered to her first three husbands—who were good and rich and old—showing how by continual murmuring, grumbling, chiding, and lying she made them miserable and brought them to heel.

"O lord, the peyne I dide hem and the wo,
Ful giltelees, by goddes swete pyne!
For as an hors I coude byte and whyne."

She is of opinion that

". . . half so boldely can ther no man
Swere and lyen as a womman can."

And she confesses she was as stubborn as a lioness

"And of my tonge a verray iangleresse."

There can be no doubt about it. She demonstrates it to the satisfaction of all. Her husbands were no match for her in quickness of wit or sharpness of tongue:

"For thogh the pope had seten hem biside,
I wolde nat spare hem at hir owene bord.
For by my trouthe, I quitte hem word for word.
As help me verray god omnipotent,
Thogh I right now sholde make my testament,
I ne owe hem nat a word that it nis quit.
I broghte it so aboute by my wit,
That they moste yeve it up, as for the beste;
Or elles hadde we never been in reste.
For thogh he loked as a wood leoun,
Yet sholde he faille of his conclusioun."

To be provided against the death of a husband by choosing her next well in advance was with her a matter of principle.

"I holde a mouses herte nat worth a leek,
That hath but oon hole for to sterte to."

She dallied with "Jankyn our Clerk" while her fourth husband was still alive, and upon his death, she covered her head and face

"As wyves moten, for it is usage,"

but as she followed the corpse to the church, her eyes were upon Jankyn:

"As help me god, whan that I saugh him go
After the bere, me thoughte he hadde a paire
Of legges and of feet so clene and faire,
That al myn herte I yaf unto his hold."

And at the month's end she married him. Jankyn was but twenty, while she was forty. And though he was more nearly her match in wit and tongue than any of the other husbands, she loved him best, because

". . . in our bed he was so fresh and gay"

and in love a bit difficult and distant, and because at times he beat her. But in the end she conquered even him and won

"By maistrie, al the soveraynetee,"

and

"After that day we hadden never debaat."

The Wife of Bath continues to be true to herself, to act, think, and speak "in character" in her Tale as well as in her Prologue. In the Tale she cannot resist the temptation to turn aside and tell the story of Midas to prove that women "kan no conseil hyde." This is in keeping with her earlier confession that it was her habit to reveal all her husband's secrets to her gossip, Alisoun,—

"To hir, and to another worthy wyf,
And to my nece, which that I loved weel."

And the prayer with which she ends is a masterpiece—

". . . and Iesu Crist us sende
Housbondes meke, yonge, and fresshe abedde,
And grace toverbyde hem that we wedde.
And eek I preye Iesu shorte hir lyves
That wol nat be governed by hir wyves;
And olde and angry nigardes of dispence,
God sende hem sone verray pestilence."

One of the great features of this portrait of the Wife of Bath is its naturalistic method. Her life and character are brought out in the most natural way in the world—gradually, and by means of the opinions, memories, and stored bits of wisdom that come to her in the course of her narrative. It is apparently without premeditation, on either Chaucer's part or hers. The Wife of Bath is greatest in her parentheses and digressions, and in her outbursts of pure lyric. Her talk is coherent, but not too much so. It is loosely jointed, as real talk always is; and it is so full of exclamations, repetitions, and happy departures from the strict narrative that she is almost garrulous. Once she loses herself momentarily, and here we have one of Chaucer's greatest strokes of art. Something she has said recalls a memory that she dallies with in her thought but says nothing of, and so she hesitates and falters. But only for a second.

> "But now sir, lat me see, what I shal seyn?
> A! ha! by god, I have my tale ageyn."

And she is off for three pages more. In another place she says she will now tell of her fourth husband. But no sooner has she started to do so than she is diverted by memories of her youth when she was

> ". . . ful of ragerye,
> Stiborn and strong, and ioly as a pye,"

and could dance and sing, especially when she "had dronke a draughte of swete wyn." And then she breaks out in that fervid paean to the goodness and fullness of life and youth which is the very antithesis of all asceticism and implies repentance for nothing—

> "But, lord Crist! whan that it remembreth me
> Upon my yowthe, and on my iolitee,
> It tikleth me aboute myn herte rote.
> Unto this day it dooth myn herte bote
> That I have had my world as in my tyme."

She has missed nothing, and she thanks God. The inevitable lament at the ravages of age follows—of age that

> "Hath me biraft my beautee and my pith."

But the spirit in which she accepts the inevitable shows that her old pagan heart is as stout as ever:

> "Lat go, farewel, the devel go therwith!
> The flour is goon, ther is namore to telle,
> The bren, as I best can, now moste I selle."

And we are sure she will find zest even in selling the bran. After all this—a digression of twenty-odd lines—she comes back to her theme and announces a second time

> "Now wol I tellen of my fourthe housbonde."

In still another digression she expatiates for twenty-five lines on her aptness for love and her admirable equipment for it. Her frankness here is equaled only by her pride in her perfections, and she explains her temperament and her appetite on astrological grounds—

> "I folwed ay myn inclinacioun
> By vertu of my constellacioun."

It is in this passage that she strikes out the immortal line

> "Allas! allas! that ever love was sinne!"

a line that stands alone—a single exclamation in the midst of narrative and explanation. And it comes with tremendous dramatic effectiveness. It is a sigh from the depths, and one which shows that the Wife of Bath, though nine parts pagan, is Christian too and has her moments of doubt as to the welfare of her immortal soul. But such moments are brief. The depths are not profound. She is still lusty and strong, and healthy enough in spirit to brush aside such morbid misgivings and to rejoice

"That I have had my world as in my tyme."

We love the Wife of Bath for her utter frankness, for her downright opinions—as when she says

> "I hate him that my vices telleth me,
> And so do mo, god woot! of us than I"—

for her humor, for her very outrageousness. And we love her no less for her forthright, vigorous, picturesque speech. Chaucer had a definite genius for portraying great talkers. The Eagle in the *House of Fame,* Pandarus, the Host, the Pardoner, the Wife of Bath, Madame Pertelote, Chanticleer, the Canon's Yeoman, all are "tall men of their tongues," who talk with tremendous gusto and fluency. And the best of them are Pandarus and the Wife of Bath, with the palm going to the Wife of Bath for what is usually called "masculine" force and directness. No one, not even the Host, knows better than she how to call a spade a spade or does so more consistently. Nowhere will one find better examples of speech that is salty, racy, homely. She is as full of proverbs as is Pandarus. She has at her command as many and as various oaths, curses, and choice, reviling names as has the Host. Her description of her fight with her fifth husband, in which she got the blow that made her "somdel deef," is noble in its rightness and simplicity

> "I with my fist so took him on the cheke,
> That in our fyr he fil bakward adoun."

What could be better? She did not *hit* him on the cheek, she *took* him on the cheek—in the swift fury of her rage. But just before, in telling of her husband's endless stories against women and of her suffering from them, she has spoken in tone and accent very different—

> "Who wolde wenen, or who wolde suppose
> The wo that in myn herte was, and pyne?"

And it is one of the triumphs of Chaucer's art that he is able in this way to give the living voice of this dynamic woman and to follow in swift, sure verse the nervous energy and sudden turnings of a mind and spirit so keen and active.

The Host is as quick of wit and tongue as the Wife of Bath and equally the master of forceful, vivid speech. But his forte lies rather in the give and take of dialogue than in lengthy monologue.

The Host is the chief character of the Links, the hero and protagonist of their drama, as he is of the whole work. He appears in almost all of them and in many rôles. He is host, guide, master of ceremonies and of the revels, patcher-up of quarrels and keeper of the peace, diplomatist, literary critic, jester-in-chief, occasional philosopher and commentator on life, henpecked husband, and master of profanity. And in spite of his versatility, a consistent and convincing character.

We must not think of the Host as a low person. In spite of his swearing and his "rude speche and boold," he has the respect and admiration of Chaucer and of the Knight, as well as of most of the other pilgrims. Chaucer describes him as a seemly man, worthy

> For to han been a marshal in an halle;
>
> . . . .
>
> Bold of his speche, and wys, and wel ytaught,
> And of manhod him lakkede right naught.

The Knight on one occasion addresses him with words of affection—

> "And ye, sir host, that been to me so dere"—

and this right after what is perhaps the foulest and most indecent of his speeches. Of course, none of the pilgrims, not even the Knight, was given to squeamishness; in fact, Chaucer tells us that all the people laughed at the Host's retort to the Pardoner. Even so, the Knight's words are the more remarkable, coming when they do, and must be taken as evidence of his true affection and respect. As for the Host's swearing, to which only the Parson makes objection, it is a harmless sort of thing—a phase really of his heartiness and of his delight in forceful and picturesque speech, and not in any sense a sign of viciousness.

If at times he stoops to billingsgate, at others he can "speke as lordly as a kyng." He addresses the Prioress with elaborate and studied courtesy. He is deferential to the Knight. To the Monk he is both respectful and what would be offensively personal, save that

> This worthy monk took al in pacience.

In short, he is equal to the occasion, is the spokesman for the company, and "hadde the wordes for us alle." He can quote Scripture and Seneca. In speaking to the Clerk he makes reference to the terms, colors, and figures of rhetoric, and offers sound advice on the subject of style. And he lards his speech to the Physician with such technical terms as the Physician himself would use.

The Host's curiosity and his habit of sizing up the people he sees and uttering bluntly his opinion of them are shown again and again. He has a shrewd eye for physical features. The only portrait we have of Chaucer in the *Canterbury Tales* is that given by the words of the Host, and this is true also of the Nun's Priest, who tells the jolly tale of Chanticleer and Pertelote. The Host looks at Chaucer and asks, "What man art thou?"

> "Thou lokest as thou woldest finde an hare,
> For ever upon the ground I see thee stare.
> Approche neer, and loke up merily.
> Now war yow, sirs, and lat this man have place;
> He in the waast is shape as wel as I;
> This were a popet in an arm tenbrace
> For any womman, smal and fair of face.

He semeth elvish by his contenaunce,
For unto no wight dooth he daliaunce."

He notes the Clerk's silence and abstracted manner.

"Ye ryde as coy and stille as dooth a mayde,
Were newe spoused, sitting at the bord;
This day ne herde I of your tonge a word.
I trowe ye studie aboute som sophyme."

He is curious about the Canon and the Monk. He wants to know the Monk's name, the house to which he belongs. He judges him to be a master in his monastery—

"No povre cloisterer, ne no novys,
But a governour, wyly and wys."

He comments upon the Monk's size and strength and fitness for marriage, as he does later with the Nun's Priest, and curses those who first brought such men "into religioun." They should be married and help to improve the human race.

The Host has an excellent heart and is moved by a pathetic or tragic story. At the end of the Physician's tale of the martyred Virginia, he curses all false judges and their advocates and bemoans the fate of the young girl.

"Algate this sely mayde is slayn, allas!
Allas! to dere boghte she beautee!

. . . .

Hir beautee was hir deeth, I dar wel sayn;
Allas! so pitously as she was slayn!"

But he is not comfortable with the pathetic or tragic. He must have "a draughte of moyste and corny ale" or hear a merry story, or his heart is lost for pity of this maid. His taste is for "a tale of mirth," or "some dainty thing," or at least a tale that will "make us nat to slepe," "som murie thyng of aventures." He hates "sermonyng" and angrily asks the Reeve

"... What amounteth al this wit?
What shul we speke alday of holy writ?"

He prays the Clerk not to preach,

"... as freres doon in Lente,
To make us for our olde sinnes wepe."

But on one occasion he himself gives in to the weakness of preaching, and edifies the company with a sermon on the folly of wasting time. His soundness as a literary critic is seen in his outspoken words on the Monk's "tragedies" and on Chaucer's *Sir Thopas*. It is painful, he tells the Monk, to "here of hevinesse."

"Your tale anoyeth al this companye;
Swich talking is nat worth a boterflye;
For therein is ther no desport ne game."

In this he is taking his cue from the Knight. But in stopping Chaucer's rime of *Sir Thopas* he acts upon his own initiative. And when Chaucer protests and asks why he may not tell his tale like anyone else, the Host replies with a finality of judgment from which there is no appeal, and with a certainty of his own rightness that is worthy of a literary dictator—which he is.

"By God," quod he, "for pleynly, at a word,
Thy drasty ryming is nat worth a tord;
Thou doost nought elles but despendest tyme,
Sir, at o word, thou shalt no lenger ryme."

Nothing better illustrates the Host's masterful way.

He is masterful, it seems, everywhere but at home. His wife is a shrew and "hath a heep of vices mo." But of these he will not speak, lest some of the company should report it to her. In confidence, however, he will say that he sorely regrets being tied to her. He is led to go this far by hearing the Merchant's tale of January and the false May, and by his sympathy with the Merchant, who is worse off even than he, for the

Merchant has a wife who is "the worste that may be" and who would overmatch the devil himself were he wedded to her. But after Chaucer has told his tale of Melibeus and the faithful and wise Prudence, the Host returns to the subject of his wife and her shrewish tongue. He tells in detail how "she rampeth" in his face, goes into tantrums, and nags him from day to night. And he confesses that though a parlous man with a knife, he dare not withstand her,

"For she is big in armes, by my feith,"

and there is nothing for him to do but to run out of the house. Such and so little is the mastery of this masterful man.

The Host is the embodiment of the holiday spirit of the pilgrimage. It is he who proposes the telling of stories by the way, and it is he who, by his energy, humor, shrewd sense, unfailing heartiness and high spirits, keeps the fun going. He knits the pilgrims together and makes of them, for the time being, a fellowship. He is their common denominator, and as he rides in their midst, he becomes, by virtue of his obvious delight in this "so myrie a compaignye" and his relish in all they do and say, the symbol of the varied and abounding life they represent, and the symbol too of the poet who made them and whose love of life was so intense and complete.

III

THE KNIGHT'S TALE

The *Knight's Tale* is the most ambitious of the *Canterbury Tales,* as, with the exception of the *Parson's Tale* and the *Tale of Melibeus*—both of which are in prose—it is the longest. It is indeed the longest of Chaucer's poems, save the *Troilus and Criseyde* and the *Legend of Good Women.* And of all his stories it is perhaps the best known and most widely admired.

The *Knight's Tale* is a romance—the finest metrical romance we have in English. It is a tale of chivalry and romantic love, of "two noble kinsmen" of the royal family of Thebes, born of two sisters—cousins by blood relationship, and sworn brothers in war and love—who fall in love with the same lady, the fair Emily, young sister of a queen and sister-in-law of Theseus, lord and duke of Athens and their mortal enemy. The young knights are mad with love for a lady they have only seen, and that at a distance—as she walks in the garden beneath the high window of their prison in the tower. In the fierce and bitter rivalry that springs up between them they forget ties of blood and oaths of brotherhood. Seven years they pine for her. They are ready to slay each other and actually seek to do so in the duel in the woods. And all for a lady they have never spoken to. Neither, so far as we are told, has had so much as a word with her or from her. In some respects, a fantastic tale!

And yet, it is a tale that holds for the modern reader all the glamour of the romantic past. In it are illustrated the splendor and pageantry of chivalry, the feasting, minstrelsy, and dancing in the hall, the magnificence of medieval dress and armor in the palace and on the field, and the glory of the tournament. Its characters are knights and ladies who maintain the ideals and practices of romantic love. In honor of May they wander in the woods, sing roundels, and weave garlands of woodbine and hawthorn. Love is a species of worship, in which the lady is idealized and almost deified. And the true knight holds life cheap in her service. One and all, from lords and ladies to churls and wenches, are ready to exclaim

> "To fighte for a lady, *benedicte!*
> It were a lusty sighte for to see."

The poem is out-and-out romantic—at least so it appears to us. But it must seem more completely and thoroughly romantic to the modern reader than it did to the reader of Chaucer's day. Many a passage which to us is romantic, because of the vivid way in which it takes us back to the distant and romantic past, must have held for Chaucer and his courtly readers nothing more than matter of familiar experience. To them castles and dungeons, knights and tournaments, were elements of realism, not of romance. Take the following passage as illustration:

> The minstralcye, the service at the feste,
> The grete yiftes to the moste and leste,
> The riche array of Theseus paleys,
> Ne who sat first ne last upon the deys,
> What ladies fairest been or best daunsinge,
> Or which of hem can dauncen best and singe,
> Ne who most felingly speketh of love:
> What haukes sitten on the perche above,
> What houndes liggen on the floor adoun:
> Of al this make I now no mencioun . . .

Here the details are what we ordinarily think of as the very stuff of romance, the kind of thing that many a modern writer depends upon to give background and color to his historical romance. But to the knights and ladies of Chaucer's time such details were familiar matter of every festal courtly occasion, and the dancing and singing of fair ladies, the discoursing feelingly upon love by ladies and knights, were items no less familiar than the hawks sitting on the perch or the hounds lying on the floor.

The same is true of those parts of the poem that pertain to battle, duel, and tournament. Scholars have shown that the accounts of Theseus's siege and capture of the city of Thebes, of the single combat between Palamon and Arcite in the forest, and of the great tournament decreed by Theseus to decide which of the lovers shall have Emily, are paralleled by things found in the chroniclers of the time, especially Froissart, and are true to the medieval spirit of history "as distinguished from the medieval spirit of fiction." "The actual course of the tournament," it has been declared, "is pure realism." The idea of deciding by battle the issue between Palamon and Arcite, the enthusiasm of Theseus for the tournament and the lavish preparations he makes for it, the assembling of knights from many countries, the magnificence of the Duke's entertainment, the feasting, dancing, and singing before and after the event, the showering of gifts upon his guests—these and many other details were undoubtedly matters of familiar experience to the Knight who is telling the tale, to Chaucer, and to the courtly readers of the time. The realism of the poem extends even to the character of Theseus, which has been found to possess "many points of resemblance" to that of Edward III.[54]

Nothing in the poem is more realistic, in one sense, than the description of Athens on the morning of the tournament. The city is full of the bustle of preparation, of the noise and clatter of horses and harness. Lords in rich array ride to the palace on steed and palfrey. Knights, squires, armorers, yeomen, and commons crowd the hostelries and streets—

> Knightes of retenue, and eek squyeres
> Nailinge the speres, and helmes bokelinge,
> Gigginge of sheeldes, with layneres lacinge;
> Ther as need is, they weren nothing ydel;
> The fomy stedes on the golden brydel
> Gnawinge, and faste the armurers also
> With fyle and hamer prikinge to and fro;
> Yemen on fote, and communes many oon
> With shorte staves, thikke as they may goon . . .

The palace is crowded with people, here three, there ten, discussing the warriors of the two parties and the chances of the combat. The Duke, waked from his sleep by the minstrelsy

[54] See Stuart Robertson, "Elements of Realism in the Knight's Tale," *Journal of English and Germanic Philology,* vol. 14 (1915), pp. 226–55, and H. Cummings, *Indebtedness of Chaucer's Works to the Italian Works of Boccaccio,* Menasha, Wisconsin, 1916, pp. 144–146.

and the noise, formally receives Palamon and Arcite before the battle. The herald, mounting a scaffold, proclaims the rules of the contest, the people shouting their approval. And the whole procession rides from the palace to the lists through streets hung with cloth of gold. It is a lively scene, and the details that go to its making are not "trappings of romance"; they are the actual doings of fourteenth-century lords, knights, and commons on an occasion of high holiday and sport. For Chaucer's Knight and his hearers they had the fascination not of the strange and unknown, but of the present and familiar, of the present and familiar in one of its bravest and most glorious aspects.

The *Knight's Tale,* then, is entirely romantic only to us. To Chaucer and his contemporaries it was largely realistic. And yet even for them it would possess many of the elements of romance and have a romantic appeal. For one thing, it is a story of Athens and Thebes, with incidental mention of Scythia, Thrace, and India, and thus it would have that "remoteness of scene" which is one of the essentials of romance. Though to the Knight and to many of his class it may not have seemed remote in point of space—for the Knight had fought in many a distant land—it would be remote in time, since it belongs to ancient Greece and to a pagan rather than a Christian world. It would thus have for most readers the appeal of the far away and long ago. The theatre with its gates of white marble and its temples of Venus, Mars, and Diana, the prayers and sacrifices made to the gods by Palamon and Arcite and Emily, the fatal accident to Arcite wrought by the magic of Saturn and Pluto, the funeral of Arcite with its pagan rites and ceremonies—these would constitute elements of the strange and the marvelous.

There is, too, the scale on which things are done, the size and magnificence of the tournament. Never was there such a noble theatre in the world,

For in the lond ther nas no crafty man,
That geometrie or arsmetrik can,
Ne purtreyour, ne kerver of images,
That Theseus ne yaf him mete and wages
The theatre for to maken and devyse.

The contending knights, numbering a hundred on each side, were a larger company, so far as we know, than was ever seen in an historic tournament, even the greatest. The leaders of the two parties—Lycurgus, the great King of Thrace, and Emetrius, King of India—in their barbaric splendor and display seem to represent the accumulated memories of a thousand fierce and proud warriors, from Greek heroes and Roman conquerors to feudal champions of England and France. Lycurgus, clad in a coal-black bearskin, stands high upon a golden chariot drawn by four white bulls and surrounded by a score or more of white wolfhounds.

Blak was his berd, and manly was his face.
The cercles of his eyen in his heed,
They gloweden bitwixe yelow and reed;
And lyk a griffon loked he aboute,
With kempe heres on his browes stoute;
His limes grete, his braunes harde and stronge,
His shuldres brode, his armes rounde and longe.

. . . .

His longe heer was kembd bihinde his bak,
As any ravenes fether it shoon forblak:
A wrethe of gold arm-greet, of huge wighte,
Upon his heed, set ful of stones brighte,
Of fyne rubies and of dyamaunts.

Emetrius, on his bay steed trapped in steel, covered with cloth of gold,

Cam ryding lyk the god of armes, Mars.

In his hand is a tame eagle, and about his horse runs many a tame lion and leopard.

> His cote-armure was of cloth of Tars,
> Couched with perles whyte and rounde and grete.
> His sadel was of brend gold newe ybete;
> A mantelet upon his shuldre hanginge
> Bret-ful of rubies rede, as fyr sparklinge.
> His crispe heer lyk ringes was yronne,
> And that was yelow, and glitered as the sonne.

His look is that of a lion, and his voice thunders like a trumpet. The heightened glory and magnificence of these portraits, the exotic details such as the white bulls and white wolfhounds, lions and leopards, would strike the note of romance at once and give to the Knight's audience a greater or at least a different thrill than that caused by the realistic description of the fight itself——vivid, swift, and glorious though it is.

As is to be expected in a romance, the characters of the *Knight's Tale* are less clearly drawn than are those of the other Tales. They are subordinated to the action and the setting. Of the four principal figures, Theseus is really the most prominent and most vividly seen. Palamon and Arcite and Emily pale beside him, and he and his wars, his alliances, his passion for arms, whether on the field or in the lists, nearly steal the show from the lovers and their tragic story. Palamon and Arcite and Emily are pawns in the game of statecraft and war he plays, and the story celebrates his greatness as a ruler and a conqueror, a lover of sport and a princely host, as much as it does the bitter rivalry of the two cousins.

Theseus is typical of the feudal lord at his mightiest and best—proud, autocratic, prompt to move against an enemy, swift and ruthless in avenging a wrong. His oaths are worthy of William the Conqueror. He swears "By mighty Mars!" and "By mighty Mars the Red!" And yet, terrible as is his quick wrath and stern justice, he is accessible to pleas for mercy, especially if they are accompanied by the plaints and tears of noble ladies. Beneath a haughty manner he has a heart almost womanly in its capacity for pity.

> This gentil duk doun from his courser sterte
> With herte pitous, whan he herde hem speke.
> Him thoughte that his herte wolde breke,
> Whan he saugh hem so pitous and so mat,
> That whylom weren of so greet estat.
> And in his armes he hem alle up hente,
> And hem conforteth in ful good entente . . .

At the request of his old friend, Duke Protheus, he frees Arcite from prison without ransom, but only to banish him for life, upon pain of losing his head by the sword. His generosity is tempered by his iron will and realistic statecraft. When he finds his erstwhile prisoners fighting in the woods, he fairly quakes with ire and swears they shall both die. But the gentler side of his nature, his compassion for suffering women, and a certain sweet reasonableness that is his, get the better of his wrath. Every man, he argues, will help himself in love and also seek to escape from prison:

> And softe unto himself he seyde: "fy
> Upon a lord that wol have no mercy,
> But been a leoun, bothe in word and dede,
> To hem that been in repentaunce and drede
> As wel as to a proud despitous man
> That wol maynteyne that he first bigan!
> That lord hath litel of discrecioun,
> That in swich cas can no divisioun,
> But weyeth pryde and humblesse after oon."

And so he forgives Palamon and Arcite, and in doing so shows his sense of humor in a vivid satirical speech on love and lovers, beginning:

> "The god of love, a! *benedicite,*
> How mighty and how greet a lord is he!"

He reminds the cousins that after all Emily cannot marry both at once.

"That oon of yow, al be him looth or leef,
He moot go pypen in an ivy leef;
This is to seyn, she may nat now han bothe,
Al be ye never so ielous, ne so wrothe."

The magnificence of the Duke's nature is seen in the grandeur of the tournament he gives, in his royal entertainment of his guests, in his riding home from the lists

With alle blisse and greet solempnitee,

notwithstanding the accident to Arcite—

He nolde noght disconforten hem alle;

in the pains he takes to see that the conflict should leave no rancor or envy, in his grief at the death of Arcite, in the noble funeral he provides for the dead hero, and lastly in his sending to Thebes for Palamon after certain years and, with grave and wise speech and due reverence for the memory of Arcite and the grief of them all, arranging for the marriage of Emily and Palamon. With Theseus the story begins and ends, and we leave him with the sense of having met a feudal lord as noble and generous as he was strong.

Palamon and Arcite are a bit blurred. They are not like the vivid, individualized characters of Chaucer's more realistic stories. They are conventional knightly lovers of medieval romance. They act and think much alike, and yet one is distinguishable from the other. Palamon, who sees Emily first and in the end wins her as his bride in spite of his being vanquished in the lists, is the gentler, more honorable and straightforward of the two. His love, one feels, runs deeper than Arcite's. Possibly he is more subtle too, for while Arcite prays to Mars and asks only for victory, Palamon worships in the temple of Venus and pleads that he may win Emily. Their characters are revealed best in the dispute that arises between them immediately after they first see the lady and discover they are both in love with her. Arcite is the hotter-headed, harder, and more aggressive. His answer to Palamon and his defense of his loving the lady in spite of Palamon's having seen her first and having first declared his love, is full of sophistry. To him all is fair in love. His honor as a knight and his sworn oath to Palamon suffer complete eclipse before his sudden passion. By means of a quibble he seeks to put Palamon in the wrong and to prove him the false one and the traitor to their oath. He asks, "Who shall give a lover any law?"

> "Love is a gretter lawe, by my pan,
> Than may be yeve to any erthly man.
>
> . . . .
>
> A man moot nedes love, maugree his heed."

And he concludes, "Love her if you like. But I love her too and always shall. Let it be each man for himself." In this he is supported by the well-known law of Courtly Love that love is irresistible, but at the same time he is damned by the law of knighthood which declares that a knight must always keep his oath. Herein is the conflict, and the reason that

> Greet was the stryf and long bitwixe hem tweye.

Both young knights are ardent, spirited, and generous; and if in some respects Arcite seems a little less admirable than Palamon, he reveals the heights to which he is capable of rising when, just before he dies, he tells Emily, as she holds him in her arms, of his great love for her and urges her, if she shall ever be a wife, to think of Palamon. There is no one in this world, he says, so worthy to be loved as Palamon, "Palamon the gentil man." This scene of the death of Arcite is one of the most affecting in all Chaucer. Hurt in the hour of his triumph, with the full cup of his bliss at his lips, he can only die. "What," he asks,

> "What is this world? what asketh men to have?
> Now with his love, now in his colde grave
> Allone, withouten any companye."

But he dies with words of forgiveness and of love upon his tongue. The rancor and the strife are over, and his last thoughts are of his cousin and brother-at-arms, so lately his mortal foe, and of his beloved.

> The vital strengthe is lost, and al ago.
> Only the intellect, withouten more,
> That dwelled in his herte syk and sore,
> Gan faillen, when the herte felte deeth,
> Dusked his eyen two, and failled breeth.
> But on his lady yet caste he his yë;
> His laste word was, "mercy, Emelye!"

Emily is a negative character, who in spite of her importance and necessity to the plot stands shadowy in the background. The Duke's sister-in-law, she is also his ward, to be married by him to whom he sees fit. Only once in the story does she speak—in praying to Diana in the temple before the tournament. And then her only words are in praise of the goddess of chastity and in supplication that she may be granted her dearest wish—to remain ever a maiden, to be neither love nor wife to anyone. Her heart is set on hunting and on walking in the wild woods. She prays that peace may come between Palamon and Arcite, and that their love for her may be quenched or turned elsewhere; or, if it is her destiny to wed one of the two, that she may marry him who desires her most.

From this we are not to suppose that Emily is cold and unworthy of such passion as that of the two knights. The modern reader finds it difficult to warm to her as a heroine of romance, but she must be thought of as being the more desirable because of her youth and innocence and her having as yet been untouched by love. She goes in maiden meditation, fancy free. No doubt she overdoes it. She walks in the garden quite unaware of the ardent eyes of Palamon and Arcite in the tower window above. She is hunting with the Duke and his Duchess when they come upon the knights fighting to the death. She sits at the tournament and watches the great contest for her hand. She holds the dying Arcite in her arms, shrieks and weeps at his death, and weeps and swoons at his funeral. And finally she accepts Palamon at the hands of the Duke with apparently nothing more than passive obedience. Through all this she utters no word to either of her lovers, gives them no sign that she is aware of their passion, not so much as a friendly look, save on the one occasion when Arcite, as victor in the tournament, rides on his courser beneath her box, doffs his helmet, and looks up at her—

> And she agayn him caste a freendlich yë.

But in spite of this coldness and indifference to love, this maidenly shamefastness, Chaucer contrives to make her winsome and desirable. He does so indirectly, by little touches here and there, by describing her beauty and charm, and especially by revealing its effects upon Palamon and Arcite. Wandering in the garden at sunrise on that May morning, gathering flowers to make a garland for her head, she has all the freshness of the springtime and the dawn.

> And as an aungel hevenly she song.

Palamon sees her,

> And therwithal he bleynte, and cryde "a!"
> As though he stongen were unto the herte.

Upon Arcite the effect is likewise instantaneous:

> "The fresshe beautee sleeth me sodeynly
> Of hir that rometh in the yonder place."

And later in the story there is that exquisite cry from the heart—

"Ye sleen me with your eyen, Emelye"—

uttered by Arcite when, on another May morning, he is in the woods plaining of his love and his fate.

Such a method may be less to our taste than that the poet uses in portraying the Prioress or the Wife of Bath or Criseyde, but it is effective. It leaves much to the imagination and therefore is all the more in harmony with the spirit of romance and has the greater appeal to the romantic temperament. The reader believes in Emily's beauty and charm if for no other reason than that they play such havoc with the hearts of Palamon and Arcite. It is a beauty fresh and cool and flower-like—like that of the young green of the woods in spring.

Thus, into the *Knight's Tale,* which belongs to a literary type that is usually relatively deficient in realism and in character portrayal, Chaucer has succeeded in introducing a great deal of realism and not a little character interest without sacrificing its essentially romantic atmosphere. It is a poem full of pageantry and action, and it moves with a grave and stately beauty. It is one of the great descriptive and narrative poems in the language. Most famous are the descriptions of the theatre, of the temples with their elaborate decoration, of the warriors and the great tournament in which they do battle, of Arcite's death, and of the burning of his body. But the scene in which Arcite goes to celebrate the May should be remembered too. It is a scene full of fresh air and lusty spirits. There is the early morning, the bright sunshine drying the dew,

The bisy larke, messager of day,

the spirited horse, "startling as the fire," the woodbine and hawthorn. It is a true bit of English countryside, of Chaucer's

England and the English May, and of Chaucer's out-of-door heartiness.

The *Knight's Tale* was Dryden's favorite. "I prefer," he said, "far above all his other stories, the noble poem of *Palamon and Arcite,* which is of the Epique kind, and perhaps not much inferior to the Ilias and the Aeneis." This is high praise, which to some may seem exaggerated. But it is eloquent of the greatness of the poem, and "noble" is the right word to apply to it. The pilgrims, one and all, declared it to be a "noble storie," and it is a noble story today.

CHAPTER IX

The Canterbury Tales: II

I

HUMOROUS TALES

THAT Chaucer is one of the greatest of humorists all critics agree. And most critics agree in ignoring or slighting some of the finest examples of his humor. Of the humorous tales in the *Canterbury Tales,* only one—the *Nun's Priest's Tale* of Chanticleer and Pertelote—receives adequate notice. The others—the *Miller's Tale,* the *Reeve's Tale,* the *Summoner's Tale,* the *Merchant's Tale,* etc.—are for the most part dismissed briefly and curtly—sometimes with pious reprobation and regret—as "churls' tales" or tales of harlotry.[55] And yet, these fabliaux are masterpieces not alone of humor but of narrative and characterization. They are among the greatest of Chaucer's achievements. The conclusion is inescapable that in spite of latter-day claims to breadth and emancipation, criticism is still capable of confounding morality with art and of accepting as its guide a conception of art in which there is a good deal of puritanical narrowness. Criticism, it seems, is not sufficiently robust to deal with the robust humor of Chaucer.

One of the best of the books on Chaucer makes no mention whatever of the fabliaux. One of the most recent, whose author, incidentally, considers that Chaucer is not one of the greatest poets and that the *Canterbury Tales* is prose "to be

[55] Professor Lowes's enthusiastic observations on the *Miller's Tale* and the *Reeve's Tale* constitute a refreshing exception to the prevailing blindness, not to say hypocrisy, in this phase of Chaucerian criticism. See his *Geoffrey Chaucer,* Houghton Mifflin Co., 1934, pp. 216–24.

approached by the path of prose," touches briefly upon one or two of the "churls' tales," but with censure and reproach, and with no perception apparently of their excellence. A third book describes the fabliaux as tales which "no sophistry can elevate into true art"; they are "by their nature not true art."

One wonders what "true art" is. And one wonders what justification a critic can have in thus setting up a purely personal and *a priori* definition of art only to rule out of the category of masterpieces some of the greatest masterpieces of humorous narrative that we have. Are we here face to face with a second instance of the prejudice against humor which, as we have seen, Matthew Arnold entertained? Is a humorous subject prejudicial to the highest art? Or are we dealing here with nothing more than a moral objection to ribaldry and a certain squeamishness of taste cloaking itself in the mantle of criticism? A critic worthy of the name will never allow the presence of certain offensive details in a humorous piece to blind him to its general artistic excellence. And in the determination of what is offensive and what inoffensive he will rise above the limitations of his personal taste and even of the taste of his age.

In the *Merchant's Tale* Chaucer alludes to "precious folk" who might be wroth with him if he told all the ways of January with May. Well, we have "precious folk" with us always, whether in the fourteenth century or the nineteenth or the twentieth. But we do not expect the critic to be of their number. The business of the critic is to perceive and proclaim truth and beauty and artistic excellence wherever they exist. To deserve our applause he must be able to see in, let us say, even the "worst" of Boccaccio's stories the very great art with which they are told. And in the case of Chaucer the important thing to note, for the critic and the reader alike, is not that some of the *Canterbury Tales* are "churls' tales" containing offensive and ribald details, but that in spite of these details they are perfect examples of story-telling—in particular, of the fabliau as a literary type, and unequaled by any other fabliaux in the art of their handling. In management of plot, in handling of character, and in rendering of background or setting, they are the work of one of the world's great story-tellers. But besides perfection of technique and wealth of realistic and satiric detail, they possess elements of pathos and touches of poetry. And above all they are rich in humorous character portrayal.

* * *

The *Miller's Tale* has four characters of note. There is John, the old carpenter; Alisoun, his young wife,

> Which that he lovede more than his lyf;

Nicholas, the jolly clerk who boards with them and is in love with Alisoun; and Absolon, the young clerk of the parish, also in love with Alisoun and thus a rival of Nicholas. All four are done with great care, though the three gay young folks stand out more prominently than the elderly John.

Alisoun is the most widely remembered. She is a country girl, it seems, and of Oxfordshire. In some respects no better than she should be, she is none the less sweet and wholesome. She smacks of the countryside and the open air. The poet compares her with flowers, fruits, birds, and beasts of farm and field. Her body is as slender and graceful as a weasel's. Her eyebrows, though plucked, are as black as any sloe. She is softer than the wool of a wether, and more blissful to look upon than an early pear-tree in bloom. Her mouth is sweet as ale or mead,

> Or hord of apples leyd in hey or heeth.

Her song is as loud and lively

> As any swalwe sittinge on a berne.

She is as skittish as a colt and skips and plays

> As any kide or calf folwinge his dame.

Nicholas matches her in youth and gayety. He is a poor scholar, intent on learning astrology, but not to the exclusion of amorous dalliance. He knows much of love. He is sly and artful, though in appearance as meek as a maid. On shelves at his bed's head are his books, his astrolabe, and other things pertaining to his art. He has, too, a psaltery on which at nights he makes melody—

So swetely, that al the chambre rong.

He sings a hymn to the Virgin, and after that "The King's Note." His chamber is scented with herbs, and he himself is as sweet as licorice root or zedoary. In love, as his actions show, he is master of the attack direct, and his technique is that of the country, not of the court.

Absolon, though the parish clerk, is in no wise clerkly. Even on Sundays his mind runs on the ladies. He casts many a lovely look at the parish wives as he swings the censer before them. Such is his courtesy that he will take no offering from a wife. His golden hair is curled and spreads about his ruddy face like a fan. His clothes are gay and of the latest fashion. In his shoes are cut designs of the window of St. Paul's. His hose are red. His kirtle, with points set fair and thick, is a light blue. And his gay surplice is as white as a spray of blossoms.

A mery child he was, so god me save.

He can trip and dance in a score of ways—after the school of Oxford—and play the guitar and the fiddle, and sing songs. There is no brewhouse or tavern in the town that he does not visit, especially if there is a gay barmaid there. At night he sallies forth with his guitar in search of adventure, or to serenade some lady of his fancy. He woos her with presents of spiced wine and ale and mead, and piping hot cakes, as well as songs. And at times, to show his lightness and mastery, he plays the part of Herod in a mystery play on a high stage.

These three young people, in their gayety and high spirits, belong to a brighter and better day. They all dance and play and sing. They are thoroughly English, and they go far toward convincing us that in olden times there was veritably a Merry England. The young clerks are to be compared with the young squires found elsewhere in the *Canterbury Tales*—with the Squire in the *Prologue;* with Damian, squire to January, in the *Merchant's Tale;* and with Aurelius in the *Franklin's Tale*. The squires are of higher social rank than these young clerks, and they move in a very different sphere. But all are much alike in their love of fine clothes, of song and dance and gallantry. All are "lusty bachelors"

. . . as fresh as is the month of May.

John, the elderly husband of Alisoun, is one of Chaucer's minor characters, but he is thoroughly individualized and is an excellent illustration of the poet's practice of drawing his minor characters with the same care and perfection of finish as he gives his major characters. Our hearts go out to John—but not because he is hoodwinked and cuckolded and made the butt and laughingstock of the whole town, and has, to boot, a broken arm as a result of the practical joke played upon him. In accordance with the tradition of the old literature of the *Senex Amans* he deserves to be cuckolded and has invited his fate by the very act of marrying a young and attractive wife. We love him for his honest-going stupidity and gullibility, his large-hearted humanity, his real concern for the health and safety of Nicholas, his prompt, energetic action, his praise of ignorance—a subject that philosophers have written upon—his large, generous way of doing things, as when he seizes Nicholas mightily by the shoulders to shake him out of his lethargy, or when he brings for Nicholas and himself "of myghty ale a large quart." And we love him for his love of his wife. It is the proud, simple, whole-hearted love of a simple, right-hearted man. And his thinking first of her when Nicholas tells him of the coming flood is one of the most human touches in all Chaucer—

"allas, my wyf!
And shal she drenche? allas! myn Alisoun!"

In this, as in all these humorous tales, the setting is made so vivid that as we read, we feel that we know this house well and all its inmates, including Robyn, John's prentice. He is a lusty knave, who, when sent to find out what has happened to Nicholas, goes up the stairs "ful sturdily," knocks at the chamber door, and cries out like mad:

"What! how! what do ye, maister Nicholay?
How may ye slepen al the longe day?"

We see the heavy roof-beams in which John hangs the kneading-tubs; the gable

Unto the gardin-ward, over the stable,

the little shot-window low down in the bower wall, where jolly Absolon comes to serenade Alisoun; and, most homely touch of all, the hole

. . . ful lowe upon a bord,
Ther as the cat was wont in for to crepe.

* * *

The *Reeve's Tale* opens with four lines that place the scene of the action with utter precision. At Trumpington, not far from Cambridge, there goes a brook, and over that a bridge, and on the brook there stands a mill,

And this is verray soth that I yow telle.

We believe it absolutely and are prepared to believe all the subsequent details the story gives us—of the mill, of the miller, and of his wife and daughter. Such is his command of explicit detail that the story-teller, whether Chaucer or the Reeve, convinces us once and for all that all he says is "verray soth."

The *Reeve's Tale* is perhaps less rich in character interest than the *Miller's Tale,* and yet it too makes vivid and real a whole ménage. There is Symkyn himself, as proud and gay as any peacock, who besides being a thriving miller, regularly given to stealing corn and meal, is a man of parts. He can play on the pipe, fish, mend nets, turn cups in a lathe, and wrestle and shoot. He is proud of his estate as a yeoman. He is proud of his wife as the daughter of the parson—though but the illegitimate daughter, to marry whom the parson gave him "ful many a panne of bras." He is proud of her gentle fostering in a nunnery, and jealous of her station and her dues as his wife. On Sundays it is a fair sight to see them walking to church, he going before with his tippet bound round his head and in red hose, she in a red mantle.

> Ther dorste no wight clepen hir but "dame."

No one is so hardy as to dally or play with her, unless he would be slain by Symkyn. To show the world he is a parlous man, Symkyn carries a long knife or cutlass in his belt, and a sword with a sharp blade. In his pocket he has a dagger and in his hose a Sheffield knife.

The wife, too, is proud, as proud "as water in a ditch," and as pert "as is a pye." She is full of scorn and mockery and thinks that because of her kindred and the learning she imbibed at the nunnery, any lady should be delighted to honor her.

The daughter is a stout, well-grown girl of twenty years, with fair hair and eyes as gray as glass, and

> With buttokes brode and brestes rounde and hye.

Her nose is flat, like her father's. Her grandfather, the parson, plans to make her his heir and to marry her into some high blood of worthy ancestry.

The pride of this family is ridiculous enough, in view of its being based so largely upon the wife's illegitimacy, but it becomes infinitely more so when the two young scholars, John and Allen, come to the mill to have their corn ground and are forced to stay the night. It then appears that the daughter, for whom such high hopes are entertained, is no better than a wench, who, with easy virtue, is quite ready to do her part to sully still further a "lineage" already somewhat besmirched—"somdel smoterlich."

Allen and John are a pair of lusty youths who make holiday of their trip to the mill. As they dismount from their horse and set down their sack, they greet Symkyn gaily:

> "al hayl, Symond, y-fayth;
> How fares thy faire doghter and thy wyf?"

Their speech throughout has the vigor and tang of youth and the hearty cheer of country folk. It is well sprinkled with oaths and homely proverbs. Their tongues go with their nimble wits. And though their high spirits are considerably chastened when their horse, loosed secretly by the miller, runs off to the fen and the wild mares, and though they come back to the mill at nightfall

> Wery and weet, as beste is in the reyn,

it is only for a moment. The sight of the miller seated by the fire after the day's work, and the promise of meat and drink and a night's lodging, though at their expense, is enough to restore them and enable them again to chaff with him on equal terms.

The account of events from this time until all go to bed—at midnight and not, as we are prone to believe of the Middle Ages, shortly after dark—gives us an intimate picture of the manners and economy of a fourteenth-century household. The sending of the daughter into the town for bread and ale, the roasting of a goose, the securing of the horse for the night, the making of a bed for the young men in the room where the miller and his wife and daughter sleep (the only chamber in the house), their sitting down to meat, and after supper their talking and drinking strong ale until the crock is empty and the miller begins to grow pale and to hiccup and talk through his nose, and his wife, something less than drunk, becomes as light and jolly as a jay—all this is a bit of so-called seventeenth-century Dutch or Flemish realism done with a few swift strokes by a fourteenth-century English artist a hundred years or more before the so-called beginning of the English Renaissance.

* * *

The *Cook's Tale* is but a fragment, consisting of no more than the introduction or opening of a story, and perhaps not all of that. But in its fifty-seven lines we have a memorable character-sketch and a fascinating glimpse of the low life of London in Chaucer's day. Perkyn Reveller—so called because he dances so well and jollily—is a prentice, of the craft of victualers. He is a proper short fellow, as brown as a berry, with black hair neatly combed. As gay as a goldfinch and as full of love as a hive is of honey, he is a prime favorite with the girls—

> Wel was the wenche with him mighte mete.

He sings and dances at every bridal. He loves the tavern better than the shop, and when there is a parade or procession in Cheapside, out of the shop he leaps and with others of his sort dances and sings and makes merry and never returns until he has seen all there is to see and danced to his heart's content. He and his fellows set a time to meet in such and such a street to play at dice, and there is no prentice in the town who can cast a pair of dice better than he. He is an easy spender, too—in private places—and his master often finds the till empty and bare. Though chided early and late, he has lived with his master for years, until the long-suffering man can stand him no longer and bids him be off—"with sorwe and with meschance." Perkyn sends his bed and clothes to a crony of his—a married man whose wife, "for contenance," keeps a shop, and whose love of dice, revel, and "paramour" makes him a thoroughly congenial companion.

That Perkyn Reveller is a disreputable character is certain. His removal from his master's house has cut him off from his last connection with the forces of sobriety and respectability. He is now his own master and his choice is the downward path and the company of the sons and daughters of evil. If he is not already of "the criminal class," he soon will be, and it is a safe bet that he will come to no good. And yet there is something about him to admire after all. His wildness is so obviously that of a vigorous young animal, incapable of thought, given only to play! His pursuit of pleasure is so headlong and heedless! His energy is so intense, and his gayety so high-pitched! Life runs furiously in his veins. He is no product of modern slums, sodden and depressed, but a "jolly prentys" full of health and high spirits. If he is riotous, it is because he suffers from the pressure of youth and of the zest for life, not because he is really vicious. And as the tide of life is full and strong in Perkyn, so is it in the London revealed here. The tumbling of prentices out of the shops to see a procession go by, the dancing and singing in the streets, the gambling and thieving and whoring, the marching of riotous and disorderly persons "with revel to Newegate," are fourteenth-century parallels to many a low-life scene in Elizabethan comedy and in the novels of Dickens. If Chaucer had finished the *Cook's Tale,* it would almost certainly have been another masterful fabliau and one that would have given us, in all probability, an incomparably full and rich picture of London life in his day.

* * *

The *Summoner's Tale* is unmistakably one of the most brilliant of Chaucer's works. Its chief interest, as I have already said, is in the characters, not in the plot, nor in the trick played upon the friar by the bedrid Thomas. The chief character is the preaching, begging, overweening, hypocritical friar. But there are also Thomas and his wife; and in this tale, as in the *Miller's Tale,* the *Reeve's Tale,* and the *Merchant's Tale,* Chaucer has depicted a whole household and set before us a bit of domestic life in dramatic fashion.

The picture of the friar preaching and begging in the church and afterwards begging from house to house, writing down on his ivory tablets the names of those who give, promising to pray for their souls, and then erasing the names as soon as the door closes behind him, is vivid to a degree. But it pales beside the realism of the scene in the house of Thomas. Here the friar is very much at home. He enters with easy assurance and glib greeting. He is certain of a welcome, at least from the wife, and of a good dinner. And he is in great hopes of getting money from Thomas, as he has often done before. Wont to peer and pry in every house, he enters this one with a "Deus hic!" and an "O Thomas, freend, good day!"

> "Thomas," quod he, "god yelde yow! ful ofte
> Have I upon this bench faren ful weel.
> Here have I eten many a mery meel;"
> And fro the bench he droof awey the cat,
> And leyde adoun his potente and his hat,
> And eek his scrippe, and sette him softe adoun.

The fourth line here is one of the homeliest and most effective bits of realism in all Chaucer. As Lowell said of it, "We know without need of more words that he has chosen the snuggest corner."

Thomas greets the friar with feigned affection and respect. He calls him "dear master" and asks after his health. With an irony that is lost upon the friar, he remarks

> "I saugh yow noght this fourtenight or more."

When the wife comes in from the yard, the friar embraces her closely, kisses her, and vows that in all the church that morning he saw no wife so fair.

The greetings of friar, Thomas, and wife, the conversation of the friar, his pretended concern for Thomas's health and salvation, his immense superiority to all curates, the hearty, busy, housewifely, and gullible wife, the testy and long-suffering husband—these things make the scene one of unmistakable truth, the very life of the time.

The wife fairly drinks up the friar's words. She is a perennial type—the woman who dotes on the dominie. She is delighted to set before him his favorite dishes—a capon's liver, some soft white bread, and a roasted pig's head. Nothing is too good for him, or too much trouble for her. And I have no doubt that in winter she knitted him socks and mufflers. Half seriously, half humorously she bids him chide her husband well, for, as she says, "though he has all he can desire, he is always complaining and is as angry as a pismire. At night he groans like our boar in our sty, and nothing I do pleases him."

Thomas is a cantankerous sort, who, though he has spent many a pound on friars (probably through his wife's importunity), is a realist and a skeptic. He listens patiently while the friar preaches to him and at him on the evils of anger. The friar says,

> "I coude of Ire seye so muche sorwe,
> My tale sholde laste til to-morwe,"

and he piles up argument on argument and instance on instance. His long-winded discourse runs to three hundred lines, and he ends all with shameless begging for gold, Thomas meanwhile putting in only a word now and then. The oily tongue of the friar is feeding the flame of Thomas's wrath and all the while he is meditating a fitting revenge—with the result we know.

There is a minor character in this tale, tucked away in a corner near the end, who is worthy of note. He is a village Sir Thomas Browne. On a small scale he is possessed of the curiosity and tenacity of mind, the interest in the difficult and the occult, which characterized the great physician of Norwich. He is "the man of great honor" to whose house the friar in his rage hastens after suffering the insult at the hands of Thomas. He is at dinner, and there in the presence of his lady and his squire, the friar tells what has happened. The lady dismisses it with the sensible remark

> "I seye, a cherl hath doon a cherles dede."

But her lord is of a more speculative and imaginative turn. He sits like one in a trance while he rolls up and down in his mind the question, How did a churl have the imagination to pose such a problem to the friar? The devil must have put it in his head. In all arithmetic there was never such a problem before.

> "It is an inpossible, it may nat be!"

He philosophizes about it. The rumbling of a sound

> "Nis but of eir reverberacioun,
> And ever it wasteth lyte and lyte awey.
> Ther is no man can demen, by my fey,
> If that it were departed equally."

Finally he gives it up, but reluctantly, and with the pious wish that the churl may go hang himself. It is left to the squire, much to the astonishment and admiration of both the lord and the friar, to explain how the impossible may be accomplished. And one might smile to think that we may have here the germ of those humorous modern stories in which the omniscient butler or the very superior gentleman's gentleman answers all the questions.

* * *

In the *Merchant's Tale* Chaucer works on a more spacious canvas and spends his genius more lavishly than he does in any of his other fabliaux. In this we have no fewer than six characters. There is the Merchant himself, who tells the story and prefaces it with a bitterly ironical account of the advantages of marriage. There is the old roué, January, who wants to end his days in the holy state and security of wedlock. There are his two brothers, who offer him advice—Placebo, the yes-man and flatterer, who seconds all his thoughts and desires; and Justinus, the realist, who counsels caution. There is May, the young wife, who takes pity on Damian and wrongs her husband; and Damian, the fresh young squire and lover. There is, besides, a lively debate on marriage, an interesting picture of the household of an Italian nobleman, and a colorful description of a wedding with its old customs and ceremonies.

The portrait of January seems at first glance to be purely satirical. It is a perfect picture of a dotard, who, after a life of gallantry, decides at sixty, at the very brink of the pit, that he will marry and that his wife must be young and beautiful. His self-assurance is tremendous. He has no doubt that all will be well. He sends for his friends, but not to get their advice, only their help. He is in great haste and is convinced that he and they together will be able to find the suitable lady much sooner than he could alone. They give advice, it is true, but strong-headed and wilful, he accepts only what he likes and impatiently rejects the rest with a

> "Straw for thy Senek, and for thy proverbes."

His haste springs from a sudden doubt as to the safety of his immortal soul. All his life a man who "folwed ay his bodily delyt," he is still vigorous—

> "I fele me nowher hoor but on myn heed"—

and he wishes to marry in order that he may lead "in ese and hoolynesse his lyf," for, as he observes, "wedlock is so esy and so clene." He has but one fear, and that is that his bliss in marriage will be so great that he may miss the joys of paradise, for, as he has heard said, no man may have perfect bliss both on earth and in heaven. On this score Justinus reassures him, reminding him that his wife may prove to be his purgatory—a stroke of irony that seems to pass entirely over the old dotard's head.

The lady is found and the marriage celebrated, and as January sits in the midst of the festivities, doting on his wife's beauty, further ridicule is heaped upon him. He longs for the night, though he is distressed to think how he must offend this tender creature. He fears she may not be able to endure all the ardors of his love. He fortifies himself with wine and hot spices, and after the feasting, drinking, and dancing, he whispers to some of his close friends,

"For goddes love, as sone as it may be,
Lat voyden al this hous in curteys wyse."

Finally, when the bride is brought to bed and the bed is blessed by the priest and all have left the chamber, he takes to his arms

His fresshe May, his paradys, his make.
He lulleth hir, he kisseth hir ful ofte
With thikke bristles of his berd unsofte,
Lyk to the skin of houndfish, sharp as brere,
For he was shave al newe in his manere.
He rubbeth hir aboute hir tendre face.

When day comes, he takes a sop of bread in some fine old wine and sits up in bed.

And after that he sang ful loude and clere,
And kiste his wyf, and made wantoun chere.
He was al coltish, ful of ragerye,
And ful of iargon as a flekked pye.
The slakke skin aboute his nekke shaketh,

Whyl that he sang; so chaunteth he and craketh.
But god wot what that May thoughte in hir herte,
Whan she him saugh up sittinge in his sherte,
In his night-cappe, and with his nekke lene;
She preyseth nat his pleying worth a bene.

All this is humorous and satirical to a degree. The old man's delight in himself is as great as his delight in his young wife. He has no thought that he may be making a fool of himself, or that his bride on this first night of her wedded life has found anything but ecstasy. The picture of him here in the dawn, sitting up in bed in shirt and nightcap, full of chatter, singing a song in his cracked voice, the slack skin about his scrawny neck shaking as he sings, is downright cruel. Cruel too is his going blind later on, and his being wronged by the wife in whom all his happiness is centered and by the squire he values most—his "own squier," his "born man."

And yet, cruel as it is, the portrait of January is sympathetic, too. It is not true, as has been said, that January "has not a single redeeming feature." There is much that is admirable in him. I have already mentioned his magnificence, his almost royal way of living, his love of beauty, his generosity, the strain of poetry in him.[56] He is referred to as "a worthy knyght," "this goode man," "this noble Januarie free," "this olde, blynde, worthy knyght." He is fond of a song and has the excellent habit of singing himself, though it be with a cracked voice. On another occasion, in his garden with May, he

Singeth, ful merier than the papeiay.

There is, too, his patient acceptance of his blindness, after a little while; his generosity to May, to whom he gives all his heritage, "toun and tour"; and his genuine concern for Damian, who is sick. To this last matter Chaucer gives no less than thirty-five lines. Shortly after the wedding, as January and May are sitting in the hall, he suddenly bethinks himself

[56] See pp. 189–90.

that he has not seen Damian. "Saint Mary! how may this be?" he asks. "Is he sick, that he isn't here to attend me?" When other squires inform him that Damian is ill, he exclaims, "He is a gentle squire, by my troth. If he died, it would be great harm and pity. He is as wise, discreet, and trusty as any man I know of his degree; and manly and thrifty, too. After dinner, as soon as I can, I will go—and May too—to see him and give him what comfort I can." And he commands his wife to take her women and visit Damian to cheer and solace him. And the poet adds, everyone blessed him for his words, because in his bounty and courtesy he would comfort his squire in sickness—"for it was a gentil dede." The irony of it is that by this visit Damian is enabled to give May the letter that tells her of his love. January is undone by his own goodness and generosity. To the cynical this may seem but another instance of his folly. But it is rather a token of his "gentilesse" and of the trust he puts in both wife and squire. And clearly Chaucer is here bringing out one of the redeeming features of his character. In truth, the portrayal of January is an outstanding example of what may be called Chaucer's balanced realism. He refuses to allow his keen realization of a man's faults to blind him to the man's virtues. Ruthless though he is in revealing January's lechery, conceit, and folly, the poet is scrupulous enough as man and artist to record also his excellences.

In view of this sympathy with January—a sympathy that reveals the old man as a figure of pathos as well as folly—it is difficult to account for Chaucer's approval of the conduct of May. He praises her "gentil herte," which pities Damian and leads her to give him her love; and he condemns those tyrant women, with hearts of stone, who would have let him die rather than grant him their favor. The sentiment may be explained in part by one of the conventions of Courtly Love, but it is due also to that insight, that deep understanding of life, which enables Chaucer to see the two sides of January. He sympathizes with Damian, sick with love-longing, and with May, unhappy in her fate in being wedded to a man in his dotage. All goes by the law of life. It is in the course of nature that an old man who has married a young and beautiful wife should be made a cuckold, however fond and generous he may be. It is natural for May to desire a proper lover, and for Damian to fall in love with her. All is by the law of nature, "the law of kinde."

* * *

The *Nun's Priest's Tale* is not a fabliau, but certainly it belongs with the masterpieces of realism and humor. It is a fable in the mock-heroic style, and one that is done with the lightest and surest touch.

How Chaucer gives the story vividness is seen in his localizing the action in a definite setting—a poor widow's hen-house and yard. With highly specific details he describes her narrow cottage, her sooty bower and hall,

> In which she eet ful many a sclendre meel,

her three sows and three cows, her sheep named Moll, and her lordly cock with his seven hens.

But humble though it is, the scene is set against a background of the overruling heavens, of Fortune, Destiny, the Foreknowledge of God, and the powers of Venus, goddess of Love, whose servant Chanticleer is. And the story moves and has its being in an atmosphere of learning. It is shot through with references and allusions to medieval physiology and medicine, to the philosophy of dreams, to classical story and biblical lore, and in lighter vein, to popular song and romance, and even to recent uproars and riots when peasants swarmed in the streets of London during the Peasants' Revolt. All this adds to the mock-heroic quality of the poem. And most skilful is Chaucer's way of making it seem but a reflection of the well-stored and lively and humorous mind of this jolly priest,

This swete preest, this goodly man, sir Iohn

who "loketh as a sperhauk with his yën."

The great feature of the work is the characters of Chanticleer and Pertelote. They are cock and hen, no doubt, but cock and hen with very human attributes. Pertelote is described as a gracious lady. She is called "faire damoysele Pertelote," and from the first we are made aware that she is a lady in the high courtly tradition. But she is also the typical housewife who likes to manage her husband, lecture him, and keep watchful eye upon his diet. She passes easily from "Herte deere" to "Fy for shame!" and "fy on yow, hertelees!" She taunts him with his fear, swears he has lost her heart and all her love, for she cannot love a coward; and she asks him

"Have ye no mannes herte, and han a berd?"

As she warms to her work and her tongue gathers speed, she attacks his stupidity and folly in believing in dreams, and in a torrent of words launches forth on a learned discourse on the nature and causes of dreams. She has medieval physiology at her finger tips. She knows all about the humours and their effect. Her assurance is tremendous. There is nothing in heaven or earth that her philosophy has not dreamt of and comprehended. Nothing daunts her or gives her pause. She is a blue-stocking in her high pretensions to knowledge, and must certainly have been the president of the women's club in that barnyard. She ridicules Chanticleer's transcendental leanings and is pat with a full scientific explanation of dreams on a purely physical and materialistic basis. We are reminded of Pater's remark about the "female conscience," which "traverses so lightly, so amiably" the ground that the male conscience goes over so warily and "full of eyes." Her superiority is immense. There is much more she might say, she assures her husband, but she will pass over such matters as lightly as she can; that is, of course, in consideration of his masculine ignorance and stupidity. She belittles him, mothers him, treats him as a child. She prescribes a laxative and "digestives of worms," and undertakes to teach him what herbs he shall eat.

But Chanticleer is more than a match for her. He meets her on her own ground, answering her quotation from Cato by citing

> ". . . many a man, more of auctoritee
> Than ever Catoun was."

He overwhelms her with text and story, theory and instances —and all with the most finished and elaborate courtesy. He demonstrates that her reading and learning are in no way equal to his own. Four or five times he seems about to stop and allow her to reply. But his ready mind jumps to new illustrations of his point, and she cannot get in another word. She is completely silenced, and the last word is his. And what a word it is! one that flatters her and yet pricks the bubble of her pretended learning and her self-assurance:

> "Now let us speke of mirthe, and stinte al this;
> Madame Pertelote, so have I blis,
> Of o thing god hath sent me large grace;
> For whan I see the beautee of your face,
> Ye ben so scarlet-reed about your yën,
> It maketh al my drede for to dyen;
> For, also siker as *In principio,*
> *Mulier est hominis confusio;*
> Madame, the sentence of this Latin is—
> Womman is mannes ioye and al his blis."

With great emphasis he reaffirms his conviction that dreams are prophetic and that his is ominous, and he tells her he will have none of her laxatives,

> "For they ben venimous, I woot it wel;
> I hem defye, I love hem never a del."

Pertelote, it seems, has had before this no experience of her husband's stores of knowledge or power of argument. Otherwise she would have attacked him either not at all or with some caution and circumspection. She got more than she bargained for, more than she dreamt was there.

Her assurance and air of superiority bring out Chanticleer magnificently. He demonstrates not only his learning but his independence. He is cock of the roost and lord of his wife. And never is he more splendid than when, flushed with his victory and the success of the deadly stroke of wit with which he concludes his discourse, he flies down from the beam and with a cluck calls the attention of his wives to some corn he has found:

> Royal he was, he was namore aferd;
> He fethered Pertelote twenty tyme,
> And trad as ofte, er that it was pryme.
> He loketh as it were a grim leoun;
> And on his toos he rometh up and doun,
> Him deyned not to sette his foot to grounde.
> He chukketh, whan he hath a corn y-founde,
> And to him rennen thanne his wyves alle.
> Thus royal, as a prince is in his halle,
> Leve I this Chauntecleer in his pasture;
> And after wol I telle his aventure.

But in spite of his triumph in the argument and the firm stand he takes, Chanticleer's "aventure" at the hands of the fox is attributed to his having followed his wife's advice:

> My tale is of a cok, as ye may here,
> That took his counseil of his wyf, with sorwe,

These two lines, however, are the only evidence that supports this interpretation, and Chanticleer's downfall is rather to be ascribed to forgetfulness and to a false sense of security. He has not weakened, he has only become a little slack. He has not given in to his wife by subscribing to her view—not by one jot or tittle. It is simply that the effect of his dream has worn off. His fear is now a thing of the past. It is a fine May morning, and he is in an expansive and relaxed mood. The shining sun, the singing birds, the fresh flowers of spring, have filled his heart with "revel and solas." Pertelote and his other wives are bathing in the warm sand. On such a day, who would think of danger? Who would suspect that a beast "ful of sly iniquitee" is hiding in the bed of herbs? Certainly not Chanticleer. Free from care, he bursts into song and sings "murier than the mermayde in the see." When he is suddenly confronted by the fox, it is his vanity that arrests his flight and makes him listen to the words of the fox

> As man that coude his tresoun nat espye,
> So was he ravisshed with his flaterye.

Moreover, all happens by Destiny and the foreknowledge of God. It is

> By heigh imaginacioun forn-cast.

Chanticleer's magnificence on the physical side is obvious. His beauty is the beauty of the perfect cock, and is brought out by the things with which his parts are compared. His voice is merrier than the church organ; the timing of his crowing is more accurate than a clock; his comb is like fine coral and is battled like a castle wall; his bill shines like jet; his legs and toes are azure, his nails whiter than the lily, and his color that of burnished gold. And his manners and his mind are as magnificent and lordly as his appearance. He moves in a large intellectual freedom that quite transcends his narrow surroundings. He is learned in the classics, skilled in argument, a finished gentleman, and on a fine spring morning something of a poet. But he is also a coxcomb, a man of strutting vanity, easy prey to the flattery of the fox. And yet, by no means a fool, for he keeps his wits about him even in the jaws of the fox and saves himself by his wit. He is quick to profit by his experience, to learn his lesson. Once safe in the tree, he vows never again to be beguiled by flattery or tempted to sing and wink with his eyes when he should see—

> "For he that winketh, whan he sholde see,
> Al wilfully, god lat him never thee!"

And we are glad that such a princely person, such a precious specimen of the lordly species, is saved, though it be only after a bad fright and a disconcerting blow to his vanity.

II

TALES OF PATHOS

Though there are noteworthy instances of Chaucer's pathos in his earlier works, the outstanding examples are to be found in the *Canterbury Tales,* especially in the *Prioress's Tale,* the *Man of Law's Tale,* and the *Clerk's Tale.* Perhaps we should add also the *Franklin's Tale.*

Of these, the best known and most widely admired is the *Prioress's Tale.* Its appropriateness to the character of the Prioress has often been noted. And certainly it is distinguished by tenderness and delicacy of feeling. The prologue, or invocation to our Lord and His Virgin Mother, is of the essence of reverence and devotion. And the tale itself is distinguished by its utter simplicity of style and its deep sympathy with the innocence and beauty of childhood. The description of the school at the farther end of the Jewry where Christian children learn to sing and read

> As smale children doon in hir childhede,

the picture of the widow's little son, so young and tender of age, sitting at his primer, and as the other children begin to sing *Alma Redemptoris,* drawing nearer and nearer to them, as he dared, in order to hear the words and the notes; his learning the first verse in this way by his own effort, and afterwards getting the rest of the hymn from an older boy; and then, when he has it perfect, his singing it boldly and merrily each day as he goes to and from school—all this makes one of the most touching pictures of childhood to be found anywhere. Touching, too, is the figure of the widowed mother when, after a night of waiting in vain for her child to come home, she starts out at daybreak,

> With face pale of drede and bisy thoght,

to search for him. The child's habit of singing this hymn of praise to the Virgin twice each day as he passes through the Jewry seems suspiciously like a deliberate piece of Jew-baiting. But he is entirely innocent. He sings because he cannot help it, so deeply has the sweetness of Christ's mother entered into his little heart.

This tale of the martyred boy moved the company of pilgrims so much that every man

> As sobre was, that wonder was to se.

And it moves the modern reader too. But it is not alone a tale of innocent childhood and martyrdom, and of love for the Virgin. Nor is the Prioress by any means a woman who is all tenderness and compassion. The dainty and elegant lady pictured in the *Prologue,* who was so charitable and full of pity and so ready with her tears if she saw a mouse dead or bleeding, is here seen to be capable of bitter hatred and bigotry. Jews are to her the "cursed Iewes," the "cursed folk of Herodes." She describes Satan as having his wasp's nest in the hearts of Jews. And she seems to approve of the provost's action in punishing the guilty by having them put to torment and shameful death and afterwards drawn by wild horses and hanged. The *Prioress's Tale* is a story of martyrdom and of a miracle by the Virgin, beautiful in its feeling for childhood and innocence and in its rendering of the spirit of devotion. But it is also a story of religious bigotry, of the hatred of Jew and Christian, of vengeance, and cruel retribution. Neither the womanly compassion of the narrator, nor her truly religious temper, strong though they are, is sufficient to enable her to overcome the prejudices of her day and to accept the Christianity which stresses the brotherhood of man, the mercy of God, and the forgiveness of sin. Her choice of subject makes her tale less interesting to the modern reader than are the tales of many of the other pilgrims and she herself a less admirable character than the *Prologue* leads us to believe her to be. But even so, the sympathetic portrayal of the "litel clergeon" places the tale among the notable examples of Chaucer's pathos.

* * *

The *Man of Law's Tale* is another instance of a story which, unsatisfactory in some respects, owes its success to the way in which it presents the image of a single pathetic figure—the gentle and long-suffering Constance. In structure and design it is less closely knit than are the best examples of Chaucer's narrative art. It lacks the definiteness of setting of the *Miller's Tale,* the *Reeve's Tale,* the *Nun's Priest's Tale,* the *Summoner's Tale,* the *Merchant's Tale,* and the *Clerk's Tale.* The *Man of Law's Tale* sprawls over several widely separated lands and an indefinite number of years. The scene shifts from Rome to Syria, and by way of the "See of Grece," the Strait of Gibraltar, and "our occean . . . our wilde see," to Northumberland; and then by a course but vaguely indicated and with a pause at a "hethen castel" of unknown name, it returns to Rome. This fault is in the very nature of the tale, which deals with the wanderings and cruel sufferings of the persecuted Constance. It is in Chaucer's sources, and not even *his* powers of managing a story were equal, it seems, to the task of simplifying the action and giving to its various parts the desirable emphasis and appeal. In several scenes Chaucer is fairly successful—as in that in which Constance is leaving home to become the bride of the Sultan in far-off Syria; or in that of the wedding feast in Syria, at which all the Christians but Constance are slain; or in the scene of the reunion of Constance, King Aella, and the Emperor her father, in Rome. But these are widely separated in time and place, and have nothing in common save that they are episodes in the life of Constance. Moreover, the episodes are so numerous that the narrator is forced to slight some of them. The story is told largely in direct narrative, with much less dialogue than we find in Chaucer's greatest tales. And the characters are to some extent slurred in order that the ground of the mere plot may be covered. The characters involved in the Northumberland episode are more fully realized perhaps than are any of the others.

The story, too, draws heavily upon our credulity; it involves not only miracles but improbabilities. Would a sultan take such a romantic fancy to a Christian woman he has never seen and whose beauty and excellence he knows of only by the report of merchants? Would he renounce his religion and accept Christianity for himself and his people in order that he might marry her? Is it in the realm of probability that Constance should be spared when all the other Christians are slain? Is it possible for a woman alone and in an open boat to drift about the seas for "yeres and dayes," for "thre yeer and moore," and later for "fyve yeer and moore"? Would she have the strength to resist the renegade steward of the heathen castle and throw him into the sea? The answer of course is that these things happen by the power of God and are reported to the glory of God. But Chaucer, or the Man of Law, is thoroughly alive to the difficulties of the story; he anticipates the questions that spring to the mind of the realist and the skeptic, and in two passages devotes fifty lines to answering them. He is fully aware of the necessity of making the story credible. In short, the tale is a romantic Christian legend, and true to the spirit of romance it has improbable adventures, remoteness and vagueness of scene, and characters none too clearly defined.

But if the shortcomings of the *Man of Law's Tale* thrust themselves upon the reader's attention, it is only because one inevitably thinks of it in comparison with Chaucer's masterpieces. If we compare it with other tellings of the same story, with Gower's, for instance, in the *Confessio Amantis,* we gain a higher opinion of it, and we see how much Chaucer's greatness as a poet and as a master of narrative has done to make a difficult and untractable story such a success as his version of it is. In particular his superiority is seen in the first part of the story, which tells of Constance's proposed marriage, her leaving home, her arrival in Syria, her wedding, the feast given ostensibly in her honor by the Sultan's mother, and the slaughter of the Christians. Gower plods along with the mere facts, the plot and little more. Chaucer's narrative is full of feeling, of imaginative sympathy, and it betrays the true artist's patience and loving care for detail. Especially does he make vivid the pathos of Constance's position—about to leave home and native land, family and friends, for strange and distant parts and she knows not what fate:

> The day is comen of hir departinge,
> I sey, the woful day fatal is come,
> That ther may be no lenger taryinge,
> But forthward they hem dressen, alle and some;
> Custance, that was with sorwe al overcome,
> Ful pale arist, and dresseth hir to wende;
> For wel she seeth ther is non other ende.
>
> Allas! what wonder is it though she wepte,
> That shal be sent to strange nacioun
> Fro freendes, that so tendrely hir kepte,
> And to be bounden under subieccioun
> Of oon, she knoweth not his condicioun.
> Housbondes been alle gode, and han ben yore,
> That knowen wyves, I dar say yow no more.

"Fader," she sayde, "thy wrecched child Custance,
Thy yonge doghter, fostred up so softe,
And ye, my moder, my soverayn plesance
Over alle thing, out-taken Crist on-lofte,
Custance, your child, hir recomandeth ofte
Un-to your grace, for I shal to Surryë,
Ne shal I never seen yow more with yë.

"Allas! un-to the Barbre nacioun
I moste anon, sin that it is your wille;
But Crist, that starf for our redempcioun,
So yeve me grace, his hestes to fulfille;
I, wrecche womman, no fors though I spille.
Wommen are born to thraldom and penance,
And to ben under mannes governance."

In noble verse the poet apostrophizes the unpropitious stars and rebukes her father,

Imprudent emperour of Rome, allas!

for not consulting the heavens and seeing to it that his daughter was sent forth on her fateful journey at least in a more auspicious hour—

Allas! we ben to lewed or to slowe.

Finally, as the ship is about to sail and farewells are being said, we have the very human touch of Constance's pathetic little attempt to keep a brave face—

She peyneth hir to make good countenance.

The plot of the Sultan's mother is set forth; the array and pomp and ceremony of the wedding and the feast are described. And then, after four pages of this preliminary story, we come to the swift resolution:

For shortly for to tellen at o word,
The sowdan and the cristen everichone

Ben al to-hewe and stiked at the bord,
But it were only dame Custance allone—

a swift, dramatic resolution of a story, or of part of a story, which is worthy to be set beside that of the *Pardoner's Tale*.

Constance's subsequent hardships are told with the utmost sympathy. She is put into a ship and cast adrift, and Chaucer, thinking of her utter desolation, addresses her in terms of personal affection:

And forth she sayleth in the salte see.
O my Custance, ful of benignitee,
O emperoures yonge doghter dere,
He that is lord of fortune be thy stere!

We have a brief but fine picture of her ship cast upon the sand under a castle in far Northumberland, and we are told how the constable of the castle came down to view the wreck

And fond this wery womman ful of care.

Her helpless and lonely position when she is falsely accused of having slain Hermengyld is the occasion of another passage of noble pathos and sympathy, and in it occurs the striking comparison of her face, as she stands alone and friendless, with the face of a condemned man, showing pale and distinct among all the faces of the crowd about him:

Have ye nat seyn somtyme a pale face,
Among a prees, of hym that hath be lad
Toward his deeth, wher as hym gat no grace,
And swich a colour in his face hath had,
Men myghte knowe his face that was bistad,
Amonges alle the faces in that route?
So stant Custance, and looketh hire aboute.

But the finest example of pathos and tenderness in this tale of Constance is found in the scene in which she is about to be cast adrift again, this time with her infant son and by command, as she believes, of her lord and husband, King Aella, but really by the treachery of another mother-in-law.

> Hir litel child lay weping in hir arm,
> And kneling, pitously to him she seyde,
> "Pees, litel sone, I wol do thee non harm."
> With that hir kerchef of hir heed she breyde,
> And over his litel yën she it leyde;
> And in hir arm she lulleth it ful faste,
> And in-to heven hir yën up she caste.

She prays to the Mother of God and then turns again to her child:

> "O litel child, allas! what is thy gilt,
> That never wroughtest sinne as yet, pardee,
> Why wil thyn harde fader han thee spilt?
> O mercy, dere Constable!" quod she;
> "As lat my litel child dwelle heer with thee;
> And if thou darst not saven him, for blame,
> So kis him ones in his fadres name!"
>
> Therwith she loketh bakward to the londe,
> And seyde, "farwel, housbond routhelees!"
> And up she rist, and walketh doun the stronde
> Toward the ship; hir folweth al the prees,
> And ever she preyeth hir child to holde his pees;
> And taketh hir leve, and with an holy entente
> She blesseth hir; and into ship she wente.

In all Chaucer there is no more beautiful illustration of the sentiment of motherhood than this, not even in the *Clerk's Tale* of Griselda. Constance and Griselda are much alike, though one is an emperor's daughter and a queen, the other a peasant. Both are tried almost to the breaking-point—Griselda by her husband, Constance by an evil fate, or, more accurately, by a God bent on proving her excellence and His own power and glory to the furthering of the Christian cause. Both are women of infinite patience and resignation. And both are possessed of a gentleness and tenderness of heart that is revealed at its best in their feeling for their children.

Besides its pathos and tenderness the *Man of Law's Tale* is noteworthy for the number of instances it affords of Chaucer's indignation. In the prologue the Man of Law denounces stories of incest and other unnatural abominations and makes it one of Chaucer's merits that he never wrote of such cursed things. Later, in two stanzas of apostrophe and execration, he bursts out in righteous wrath against the Sultaness. In much the same way he damns Donegild, mother of King Aella; he has no English worthy to describe her malice and tyranny, and he resigns her to the Fiend as the only one with words to do her justice. And his account of the false steward who tries to make Constance his mistress is followed by an outburst against the "foule lust of luxurie." Chaucer is not often indignant. But in these instances his denunciation and hatred are unmistakable.

* * *

The *Clerk's Tale* of Griselda, like the story of Constance, is a tale made to the glory of woman. In particular it celebrates "this flour of wyfly pacience," Griselda, who is tested and assayed "as wel as evere womman was." But through her it praises her sex. Men speak of the humility and patience of Job, the poet says, but no man can acquit himself so well in humbleness as woman can, nor be half so true as women are. By her husband, the Marquis of Saluzzo, Griselda is subjected to four distinct tests, and always with the same result. Successively her young daughter and her young son are taken from her, to be murdered, as she supposes. Later she is informed she is to be discarded by her husband in favor of a younger and fairer wife of noble blood. And finally she is humiliated by being asked to prepare the chambers for the wedding guests and the tables for the feast, and to welcome and praise the bride who is to take her place. She suffers

these cruelties and insults with all meekness and patience. Her loyalty to her lord is steadfast throughout, and her love for him knows no change.

The characters of Walter the Marquis and of Griselda are difficult to believe in. With the infinite patience of Griselda the reader is likely to be out of all patience. He either considers her too good to be true or despises her for want of spirit. Her husband, he thinks, is impossible. Was ever man so persistent in cruelty, so relentless in persecuting, in cold blood and merely as a result of his having taken a notion into his head, a woman he really loves? These characters are not human. They are not credible. They are creatures of the moralizing tendency of those who tell stories. Such is very likely to be the reader's reaction.

We have already seen that Chaucer told the tale from Petrarch, that Petrarch got it from Boccaccio, and that Boccaccio seems to have made it from one or more popular stories or folk tales of his own day. Scholars have pointed to parallel stories in certain fairy tales, lays, and ballads, and, convinced that the Griselda story is of folk origin, have sought to discover folk elements even in the versions of Boccaccio, Petrarch, and Chaucer. In Walter the Marquis, in Childe Waters of the ballad of that name, and in Lord Thomas in the ballad of "Fair Annie"—all of them men who discard mistress or wife and put her to cruel tests and insufferable hardships and humiliations—students of folklore have seen a reminiscence or survival of some king of faëry, some creature of the other-world who is both more and less than human. And in the heroines of these stories—in Griselda, Ellen, and Fair Annie—some have found survivals of "an ancient type of supernatural woman."

The point is interesting and, as all students of folklore know, highly probable. But the fact remains that in the versions of the Griselda story by Boccaccio, Petrarch, and Chaucer, whatever supernatural elements may be present are present only in fossil form. In all three versions the story is put upon a purely naturalistic basis and deals with human beings, not supernatural beings. And in all three it stands or falls, and is meant to stand or fall, by the soundness or falseness of its psychology. Incidentally it may be observed that though in the original folk tale or fairy story one or both of the principal characters may have been of the other-world and therefore supernatural, their dominant traits of character—in the man, delight in inflicting torture; and in the woman, infinite patience and endurance—may themselves have been of natural origin and have become supernatural only through the exaggeration of traits that are entirely human and as a matter of fact not uncommon. If many modern stories are derived by a process of rationalization and humanization from old supernatural stories, we must remember that many of these must in turn have been derived, at least to a large extent, from a still older naturalism by a process just the reverse.

The *Clerk's Tale,* then, in spite of the studies of modern folklore specialists, should be to the present-day reader precisely what it was to Chaucer—a human tale of human beings. And it should be judged today as any other human tale is judged—by considerations of plot, character portrayal, motivation, and the like. Chaucer puts it squarely in the actual world of men and women, and the question the critic must decide is whether or not it is true to life, and whether Chaucer has succeeded in making his Walter and Griselda vital and convincing in spite of the fact that one or both may be of supernatural lineage, and in spite of the fact that the tale, as Chaucer or Petrarch or Boccaccio got it, may have been shaped in part by the influence of sermonizers bent on preaching of man's duty to be constant in adversity.

It is essential, first of all, to bear in mind that the action of the story takes place in the Middle Ages. Walter, though only a marquis, is really a king, an absolute ruler in his little domain, with power of life and death over his subjects. Constitutional and limited monarchy were as yet unborn. The rights of man, and of woman, had not been heard of, either in the council chambers of kings or in the halls of philosophy. An occasional woman here and there—like the Duenna in the *Roman de la Rose* or the Wife of Bath in the *Canterbury Tales*—uttered heresies on the subject of the rôle of woman in love and marriage, but there was no such thing as feminism. As Constance says in the *Man of Law's Tale,*

> "Wommen are born to thraldom and penance,
> And to ben under mannes governance."

And that was the normal, orthodox view. Both Constance and Griselda are medieval women, and of a time earlier than Chaucer's. The Clerk himself notes the change. In reference to Walter he remarks,

> "This world is nat so strong, it is no nay,
> As it hath been in olde tymes yore."

And of Griselda he says,

> "It were ful hard to finde now a dayes
> In al a toun Grisildes three or two."

Moreover, Griselda is of peasant stock, taken from a life of toil in cot and field to be the Marquis's bride, and she has to the full the peasant's humility and power of long-suffering patience and endurance. In one passage she herself explains her power to endure adversity in part by her being "a povre fostred creature." With these things in mind, a close study of the poem should convince even the present-day reader that the characters are drawn with entire plausibility and that their actions and reactions are given with perfect soundness and with the utmost care in motivation.

The Marquis is far from being a monster, even a human monster. He is young of age, fair and strong, a man full of honor and courtesy, discreet in governing. His people fear him, but they also love him. So well do they love him and all his works, that they would be perfectly happy, they declare, if only he would marry and beget an heir. His manner toward his proposed bride is stern, it is true, and before he marries her he exacts from her an oath of perfect obedience. But it is also considerate, and he calls her "Griselda mine." When her first child is born, he is glad, though it is not a son. Later, when he puts her to the successive tests, he is astonished at her patience and is moved to pity for her suffering. Despite his stern and cold bearing, his assumed "drery contenance," and his pretended cruelty, he is clearly in love with her; and his love is so great that only by strength of will does he succeed in going on with his diabolical plan to the end. Moreover, Griselda's love for him is of a kind that is a tribute to him as well as to her. Such is its strength that she would gladly die, she says, if she knew that her death would give him ease. And she adds,

> "Deth may noght make no comparisoun
> Unto your love."

Besides all this, Walter loves his children, and though he sends a villainous-looking "sergeant" to do his bidding and take her children from her, he sees to it that they are wrapped soft and warm and brought safely and tenderly to Bologna, there to be fostered in all "gentilesse" by his sister.

Thus Walter is at bottom an ideal husband and father. He is evil only in the evil purpose he conceives—of proving his wife though he has no doubt of her; to "essay in thee thy womanhood," as he tells her in the end when she is happily reunited to her children and reinstated as his wife. And even in this and in the persistence with which he holds to his purpose, he is acting within the bounds of the natural and the human. Chaucer, or the Clerk, comments upon this "marvellous desire" that has entered Walter's heart. He disapproves of it, but he is not surprised at it. In fact, he speaks of it as a not infrequent thing. Some men praise it for a subtle wit, he says, but as for me, I say it is an evil thing to assay a wife when there is no need, and to put her in anguish and dread. When Walter persists in his course, the poet observes that

> . . . wedded men ne knowe no mesure,
> Whan that they finde a pacient creature;

and again, that

> . . . ther ben folk of swich condicioun,
> That, whan they have a certein purpos take,
> They can nat stinte of hir entencioun,
> But, right as they were bounden to a stake,
> They wol nat of that firste purpos slake.

Chaucer thus finds nothing unnatural either in the purpose Walter conceived or in the determination with which he carried it through. And certainly many a man has tormented his wife or treated her brutally without even such an excuse as Walter had, without excuse at all save a vicious temper. Walter's purpose in doing what he did may have been an irrational one, but it was at least a purpose, and not the mere prompting of an evil and cruel character or of a sadistic delight in inflicting suffering and pain. To him it was even a rational purpose.

Griselda is described, before her marriage, as a girl of lowly and simple life. Her father was the poorest of the poor in their village, and her life was one of hard and constant labor;

> She wolde noght been ydel til she slepte.

She drank of the well oftener than of the tun. Her clothes were of the coarsest, her bed was hard, and her food consisted in worts and other herbs.

> But hye god som tyme senden can
> His grace into a litel oxes stalle;

and Griselda's virtue and womanhood stand out in her face and manner in spite of her mean surroundings—at least to the discerning eyes of the Marquis when he sees her as he rides a-hunting.

After her marriage she keeps her simplicity and goodness unspoiled. She wins the people's love by her goodness and wisdom. She aids her husband in governing his people and by her ripe and wise words is able to still all rancor, settle disputes, and right wrongs. In her great estate she is discreet and full of patient benignity and humility, without pride or pomp or semblance of royalty; and to her husband ever meek and constant.

Chaucer tells the tale of Griselda with perfect sympathy. He utters no syllable of criticism against her but is full of admiration of her goodness and love. He has only admiration and pity for her. And this is because he understands, as many a reader has failed to understand, that her actions spring not from weakness, supineness, or insensibility, but from a strength and sweetness that are heroic. She is the antithesis not only of the Wife of Bath but of all those bright, advanced women, whether medieval or modern, who love themselves more than their husbands and dwell much in their thoughts on women's rights, whether or not they are given to much talk on that subject. Her love for her husband is so intense, her loyalty to him so unswerving, that, like the king, he can do no wrong—or at least, no wrong that will change or diminish her love. She is not blind to his faults or his cruelty. She is keen and wise. And one suspects that her insight is such that she knows he really loves her, in spite of all appearances to the contrary. It is a mistake to suppose that because she so seldom cries out in her anguish she feels none. She is one of the most sensitive of women, as is seen in every word she utters. But such is her fortitude that she stifles her cries, except on one or two occasions when she can endure no more. And these outbursts, by their infrequency, reveal the depth and strength of her character and add to the poignancy of the reader's feeling for her. When her first child is to be taken from her, she makes no protest, but accepts meekly her lord's will. She lays the child in her bosom, kisses it and lulls it, and blessing it with the sign of the cross, hands it over to the sergeant, pathetically praying him to bury its little body in some place where neither beasts nor birds can disturb it. It is only when her second child is to be taken from her and, as she again thinks, to be slain, that a note of bitterness and complaint is heard in her speech; and then it is but for a moment. She cries,

> "I have noght had no part of children tweyne
> But first siknesse, and after wo and peyne."

Later, when she is to be displaced by a new wife, she reproaches her husband again, but in words so gentle that there is more love in them than reproach:

> "O gode god! how gentil and how kinde
> Ye semed by your speche and your visage
> The day that maked was our mariage!"

Both are cries from the heart, and both are eloquent of her womanly strength as well as her tenderness. She breaks down, swooning and weeping, only at the end of the story, when she at last learns the truth and finds her children before her and she herself is restored to her husband's arms.

The simplicity and nobility of Griselda's character and the depth of her humility are revealed at their greatest in the words she speaks to her husband when she renounces her marriage and is about to return to her father's house. And the pathos of the story reaches its climax when she tells him that she is leaving all her jewels, her wedding ring, and even her clothes, but begs that she may keep her smock, for, though she came naked out of her father's house and naked must return, surely her husband would not do so great a villainy as to expose to the gaze of the people the womb that bore his children.

> "Lat me nat lyk a worm go by the weye.
> Remembre yow, myn owene lord so dere,
> I was your wyf, thogh I unworthy were."

To dismiss Griselda as a woman too good to be true is to be hasty and unwise. Her like is by no means unknown. The annals of fiction and of real life record not a few instances of women who have stood by their men in spite of everything, in spite of hardness, neglect, persecution, cruelty, and brutality, and merely because they have loved them and borne their children. As to humility and power of endurance, Griselda's was hardly greater than that of certain women in modern fiction. One thinks of Olan in *The Good Earth* and of Hardy's Tess. Olan had been a slave, and Tess, like Griselda, was of the peasant class, in spite of her descent from the once noble D'Urbervilles. The modern reader accepts these as plausible characters, true to life. Why should he do less in the case of Griselda?

One of the highest tributes to the *Clerk's Tale* was penned by Leigh Hunt in an essay in *The Seer*. Its concluding words are these:

> And so, with feasting and joy, ends this divine, cruel story of Patient Griselda; the happiness of which is superior to the pain, not only because it ends so well, but because there is ever present in it, like that of a saint in a picture, the sweet sad face of the fortitude of woman.

* * *

The *Franklin's Tale* is not perhaps an outstanding example of pathos, but there is in it another true and gentle wife, to be placed beside Constance, Griselda, Blanche the Duchess, and the ladies in the *Legend of Good Women;* and the story of the married life of Dorigen and Arveragus is not without its touches of the pathetic. Moreover, it is the tale in which Chaucer gives his solution of the marriage problem.

In contrast to all the words Chaucer puts into the mouths of the Host, the Merchant, and the Wife of Bath concerning the unhappiness and even the hell that may exist in marriage, we must remember the words he puts into the mouth of the Franklin:

> "Who coude telle, but he had wedded be,
> The ioye, the ese, and the prosperitee
> That is bitwixe an housbonde and his wyf?"

Dorigen and Arveragus are deeply in love with each other; so much so, indeed, that Dorigen, in her husband's long absence in England, is grief-stricken and disconsolate. She mourns and watches and complains, and nothing that her friends can do will assuage her grief. She walks on the high rocky cliffs by the sea, and seeing many ships and barges sailing their courses, exclaims, "Alas, is there no ship will bring home my lord?" The grisly black rocks scattered along the treacherous coast unnerve her, and she asks why a wise and reasonable God ever made them to destroy so many of God's creatures. She wishes they were all sunk in hell.

> "Thise rokkes sleen myn herte for the fere."

A fine scene is that in which Dorigen is found weeping by her husband upon his return from a second absence and confesses to him the cause of her woe. In a rash moment she had promised the young and importunate squire Aurelius to grant him her love provided he removed all the rocks from the coast of Brittany, and now he has done this impossible thing and demands that she keep her word. Her husband is so true a knight that he insists that she fulfill her promise. "Truth," he says, "is the highest thing man may keep," and he bursts out weeping and exclaims, "As I may best, I will my woe endure."

In one sense it may be said that the tale is told for the purpose of posing the question, which of the three men was the most noble and generous—Arveragus in insisting that his wife keep her vow, Aurelius in releasing her from it, or the clerk, by whose magic the rocks were removed, in excusing Aurelius from the payment of the thousand pounds. But the story's real interest is in the three leading characters and in the picture of the wedded bliss of Dorigen and Arveragus as an example of the ideal of matrimony.

The solution of the marriage problem is given at the beginning of the tale. After telling of the vows exchanged by Dorigen and Arveragus at the time of their wedding—to the effect that they will ever live in mutual forbearance, without jealousy and strife, and without sovereignty the one over the other—the Franklin pauses in his narrative to comment upon the wisdom of this arrangement:

"For o thing, sires, saufly dar I seye,
That frendes everich other moot obeye,
If they wol longe holden companye.
Love wol nat ben constreyned by maistrye;
Whan maistrie comth, the god of love anon
Beteth hise winges, and farewel! he is gon!
Love is a thing as any spirit free;
Wommen of kinde desiren libertee,
And nat to ben constreyned as a thral;
And so don men, if I soth seyen shal.
Loke who that is most pacient in love,
He is at his avantage al above.
Pacience is an heigh vertu certeyn;
For it venquisseth, as thise clerkes seyn,
Thinges that rigour sholde never atteyne.
For every word men may nat chyde or pleyne.
Lerneth to suffre, or elles, so moot I goon,
Ye shul it lerne, wherso ye wole or noon.
For in this world, certein, ther no wight is,
That he ne dooth or seith somtyme amis.

Ire, siknesse, or constellacioun,
Wyn, wo, or chaunginge of complexioun
Causeth ful ofte to doon amis or speken.
On every wrong a man may nat be wreken;
After the tyme, moste be temperaunce
To every wight that can on governaunce.
And therfore hath this wyse worthy knight,
To live in ese, suffrance hir bihight,
And she to him ful wisly gan to swere
That never sholde ther be defaute in here."

This is the heart of the matter, and it will be noted that Chaucer, or the Franklin, goes beyond the mere question of married life and is giving his views on the subject of human relationships in general, stressing the necessity of patience and tolerance and of our recognizing that at one time or another we are all guilty of offense. He is particularly wise on the subject of love. "Love will not be constrained by mastery." It is "a thing as any spirit free." And in insisting that women, by nature, desire liberty fully as much as do men and are not to be held as thralls, the poet is well in advance of his age.

CHAPTER X

"Well of English Undefiled"

THE phrase is old and threadbare. But of the thousands who have used it, few probably have known that the words were Spenser's and that they were uttered in praise of Chaucer, and more particularly, of Chaucer's style. They serve to remind us of a fact too often forgotten, even by readers of Chaucer, that Chaucer is one of the greatest of all masters of style and the fountainhead or well of that tradition of purity and simplicity in style which characterizes the greatest English poetry and is often the feature which distinguishes it from the lesser.

Spenser did not particularize. He made no mention of the characteristics of Chaucer's style which, in his opinion, warranted such praise. But what he meant is fairly clear. And today the special student, with the history of the English language, of English prosody, and of English literary criticism before him, can look back over the centuries and affirm the absolute rightness of Spenser's judgment, and affirm, furthermore, that in some respects Chaucer is as much and as truly a well of English undefiled to us as he was to Spenser, though Shakespeare, Milton, Dryden, and Wordsworth have intervened.

A well is both a source and a reservoir. And Spenser was thinking of Chaucer at once as the founder of a great tradition in the matter of style and as a model to whom other writers had turned and might still turn, even as Spenser himself was turning, in order to steep themselves in that tradition and thus keep alive and perpetuate a high and noble artistic ideal. To him the great feature of Chaucer's style was that it is undefiled. But undefiled by what? We cannot know with certainty, but by comparing Chaucer's work with that of his contemporaries, and of his successors down to Spenser's day, we can see that Spenser may have had in mind a number of things. Chaucer's style is a style undefiled by the provincialisms and archaisms, or what were rapidly becoming provincialisms and archaisms, of some of the other writers of Chaucer's time; undefiled by the "colors of rhetoric" and the "high style" of rhetoricians in his day and before; undefiled by the excessive alliteration of the alliterative poets of the West Midlands; undefiled by the Renaissance importations of heavy Latin and Greek words, which so often weight and muddy the style of Shakespeare; undefiled by the euphuisms and conceits of many of the Elizabethans; [57] and undefiled by the grandiloquence, rhetoric, and bombast found in many an Elizabethan tragedy. Spenser may have been thinking too of the ease and grace of Chaucer's verse. But fundamentally his tribute is a tribute to Chaucer's purity of diction and to that purity and simplicity of taste which led him to seek, and enabled him to achieve, effects of the greatest beauty by use of the simplest means. No doubt Dryden had in mind much the same things when he said, "from Chaucer the purity of the English tongue began."

Let us look at some of these points more closely.

Turn at random to any passage in *Sir Gawain and the Green Knight,* which is generally considered to be one of the most truly poetical things done in the age of Chaucer outside of the works of Chaucer himself. The poem is written in the alliterative long line, with its four heavy beats, made heavier by alliteration—a measure that points backward to Old English times rather than forward to Spenser, Shakespeare, and Milton, and one that was already moribund if not dead in spite of the efforts of the Gawain poet and others to revive it. One finds a goodly number of words that not only

[57] As Landor said, "Chaucer was born before that epidemic broke out which soon spread over Europe, and infected the English poetry as badly as any."

have not come down to modern standard English but are not to be found in Chaucer—words that belonged to an old and outworn tradition, the poetic tradition of Old English, rather than to the living poetic style and the living speech of the author's day. Frequently this use of old words has been dictated by the exigencies of the alliteration and is the result of the poet's having adopted a measure better suited, one feels, to Old English than to Middle English, and of his lacking the necessary mastery of language and of versification to harmonize the old poetic form with the living speech of his day—if indeed that were possible. The language of *Sir Gawain* seems greatly older than Chaucer's and more like Old English, or even a foreign tongue. And the modern reader can read it only in translation or glossed, though he may read Chaucer in the original.

Chaucer escaped both these pitfalls. He avoided the old outworn words and meanings, and he avoided the outmoded alliterative verse scheme. The *Gawain* poet, though in writing of Arthur's court and of the Christmas festivities at the castle of the Green Knight he shows that he was familiar with courtly ways, was not "at the center." Chaucer, on the other hand, was in London and at the court. He was not only born and bred in London, but bred in the court circle. And he seems to have followed the traditionally best English of the city and the court as he followed the verse schemes and patterns and poetic subjects that were the vogue at court.

Chaucer's avoidance of words that were archaic or provincial, or that were rapidly being made archaic or provincial by Chaucer's works themselves and by the works of other poets writing in London English, may have been a lucky accident—the accident of his having been born and bred in the birthplace of the modern standard speech. But there can be no manner of doubt, I think, that his preference for the simple word over the ornate or rhetorical or learned word was a matter of his personal taste. Chaucer can be as learned and scientific and technical as you please—as when he describes the Doctor of Physic in the *Prologue* of the *Canterbury Tales,* or has occasion to use the jargon of astrology or magic or alchemy, as in the *Treatise on the Astrolabe* or the *Canon's Yeoman's Tale*. But these are special occasions and special subjects, which demand a scientific or technical vocabulary. In general, Chaucer chooses the simple style and avoids whatever smacks of the high-flown, the grandiloquent, or the pompous.

In several passages Chaucer definitely protests that he is no "rethor excellent" and knows nothing of the colors of rhetoric. It is true he puts these protests, these indirect criticisms of the rhetorical, into the mouths of his characters—of the Eagle, of the Host, the Squire, and the Franklin—but they seem none the less to be Chaucer's own views and to have a definite bearing upon the question of his taste and of his idea of an excellent style.

In the *House of Fame* the Eagle plumes himself on the simplicity with which he has explained to Chaucer the way in which all speech, carried upward from the world, reaches the House of Fame. He has put it

"... simply,
Withouten any subtiltee
Of speche, or gret prolixitee
Of termes of philosophye,
Of figures of poetrye,
Or colours of rethoryke.
Pardee, hit oghte thee to lyke;
For hard langage and hard matere
Is encombrous for to here ..."

This preference for simplicity, this objection to subtlety, prolixity, terms of philosophy, figures of poetry, colors of rhetoric, and to hard language because it is "encombrous for to here," is avowed here in the relatively early *House of Fame* and again in several places in Chaucer's last work, the *Canterbury Tales.*

When the Host calls upon the Clerk to tell a tale, he asks for "some merry thing" and requests him to tell it in plain terms so that "we may understand what ye say" and to keep his rhetorical devices in store until he indites in high style, as when men write to kings:

> "Telle us som mery thing of aventures;—
> Your termes, your colours, and your figures,
> Kepe hem in stoor til so be ye endyte
> Heigh style, as whan that men to kinges wryte.
> Speketh so pleyn at this tyme, I yow preye,
> That we may understonde what ye seye."

Again, at the beginning of the *Squire's Tale,* the Squire says he cannot describe the beauty of Canacee, because he lacks the necessary command of style and is no rhetorician:

> "But for to telle yow al hir beautee,
> It lyth nat in my tonge, nin my conning;
> I dar nat undertake so heigh a thing.
> Myn English eek is insufficient;
> It moste been a rethor excellent,
> That coude his colours longing for that art,
> If he sholde hir discryven every part.
> I am non swich, I moot speke as I can."

Later, the Squire protests that he cannot do justice to the way in which the strange knight in the story delivered his message to King Cambyuskan. He cannot "sound" the messenger's style, "cannot climb over so high a stile." And yet he proceeds to give the long message of the stranger knight, explaining the magical horse, mirror, ring, and sword, in the simplest possible words. The passage is too long to quote, but it is in the best of all styles—simple, clear, swift, and flexible—and achieves its purpose of giving a full and forthright explanation of the magical properties of these objects better than could all the devices of rhetoric and fine writing. Moreover, it is astonishingly modern. With only a few changes it would be perfectly good English of today.

Another criticism of rhetoric is found in the words of the Franklin:

"But, sires, by-cause I am a burel man,
At my biginning first I yow biseche
Have me excused of my rude speche;
I lerned never rethoryk certeyn;
Thing that I speke, it moot be bare and pleyn.
I sleep never on the mount of Pernaso,
Ne lerned Marcus Tullius Cithero.
Colours ne knowe I none, with-outen drede,
But swiche colours as growen in the mede,
Or elles swiche as men dye or peynte.
Colours of rethoryk ben me to queynte;
My spirit feleth noght of swich matere.
But if yow list, my tale shul ye here."

The Franklin, as a plain man, can and will speak only as a plain man. He has never learned rhetoric, never slept on Mt. Parnassus or studied Cicero. And perhaps we should not be wrong in applying those last words of his to Chaucer himself:

"Colours of rethoryk ben me to queynte;
My spirit feleth noght of swich matere."

Chaucer will not write as men do when they write to kings.

"Thing that I speke, it moot be bare and pleyn,"

and at times he is as plain and homely and Saxon as can be. I am thinking not only of such things as the Manciple's words to the drunken Cook:

"Hold cloos thy mouth, man, by thy fader kin!
The devel of helle sette his foot ther-in!
Thy cursed breeth infecte wol us alle;
Fy, stinking swyn, fy! foule moot thee falle!"

but of the homely figures of speech scattered through Chaucer, as that in which Troilus is compared with "proude Bayard"; [58] and of the hundreds of instances of vivid colloquial speech in the conversation of Pandarus and in the Wife of Bath's monologue; and of such masterful examples of the pure style as the Clerk's statement about Petrarch:

> "He is now deed and nayled in his cheste."

These criticisms of the high style of rhetoric are directed, it seems, against the high-flown, inflated, and pompous style rather than against what Matthew Arnold was later to call the grand style. And yet, the grand style itself is not infrequently allied to rhetoric. Arnold, it will be remembered, distinguished between the "grand style simple," the best example of which is Homer's, and the "grand style severe," of which perhaps the best model is Milton's. That is an important distinction and, to my mind, one between something admirable and something less admirable. When the grand style gets on stilts, becomes stiff or wooden, wordy or grandiloquent, or uses the diapason too much, it becomes something less than the grand style; it becomes rhetoric, and it passes out of the realm of poetry into the realm of prose, or even of oratory.

The "grand style severe" is in greater danger of doing this than the "grand style simple." And not even Milton succeeds always in keeping on the right side of the line that divides poetry from rhetoric. Arnold refuses to admit this. He says, "From style really high and pure Milton never departs," and again, "Milton, from one end of *Paradise Lost* to the other, is in his diction and rhythm constantly a great artist in the great style." [59] But there is not a little bombast and rhetoric in the grand style of Milton, and not a little prose that goes

[58] *Troilus and Criseyde,* I. 211–24.

[59] Matthew Arnold, *Essays in Criticism, Second Series,* London, 1905, pp. 61–62.

masking under the name and reputation of poetry. Clothes are

These troublesome disguises which we wear.

Adam is "our general ancestor," "our general sire," "our great Progenitor," "the Patriarch of mankind." There is nothing so wooden and lifeless as this in Chaucer. Chaucer calls him simply "Adam oure fader." In Milton, Eve is "our general mother," and God "the universal Maker," "the sovran Planter." These things come pretty close to being "tall talking" and in their stilted wordiness are not far removed from journalese.

One weakness of the grand style is its lack of flexibility. It may easily become monotonous and inappropriate, as it does in parts of *Paradise Lost.* There is no change with the change of subject. Adam and Eve in the garden of Eden talk very much like the fallen angels in hell—in set formal speeches. There is no real dialogue between them, no intimacy and familiarity. The dignity and elevation of the grand style does not permit it. Nor does the supposed epic tradition. Adam addresses his wife as "Sole Eve, associate sole," "Daughter of God and Man, accomplished Eve," "Fair Consort." And Eve addresses Adam as "My author and disposer." Lamb, it will be remembered, complained of Milton's Adam and Eve that they talk and act too much like married people. That is not it. They talk and act too *little* like married people, too little like lovers, or anything else human. Milton in heaven or Milton in hell or Milton almost anywhere between heaven and hell—in the realms of Chaos and Old Night—is superb, and especially in hell. But Milton in Paradise, with "troublesome disguises which we wear" and "rites mysterious of connubial love" is wordy, pompous, and not a little wooden. The grand style has lost its grandeur and become rhetoric.

Chaucer never made the mistake of committing himself to

any one style—least of all the grand style. He had too strong a sense of life, and too strong a sense of humor. Furthermore, it was not in his nature to take himself too seriously. In two or three places he ridicules his own too figurative language, as he does in *Troilus and Criseyde* when, after referring to the sun by such conventional figures as "honor of day," "heaven's eye," and "foe of night," he explains, "Al this clepe I the sonne"; [60] and again in the *Franklin's Tale,*

> But sodeinly bigonne revel newe
> Til that the brighte sonne loste his hewe;
> For thorisonte hath reft the sonne his light;
> This is as muche to seye as it was night.

One of the chief merits of Chaucer's style is its flexibility, adaptability, and variety. It is adequate to all uses—to reporting the words of the Host or the Pardoner or the Wife of Bath or the Prioress or the Clerk of Oxford or the Man of Law. It is always appropriate, whether his matter is the ribaldry of the *Reeve's Tale* or Troilus's lofty meditations on Predestination and Free-Will. And it is always musical and poetical, even in his lightest and most humorous moments.

Still another excellence of Chaucer's style is its freedom from the heavy Latinity that mars so much Elizabethan verse, especially in the drama. Chaucer came too early to be influenced by the changes wrought in the English vocabulary by the Renaissance; but even if he had come later, even if he had been an Elizabethan, it is most unlikely that he would have succumbed to the temptation to write in the heavy style or to load his lines with big words. His taste was too pure for that.

Renaissance borrowings profoundly changed the English vocabulary. They were mostly Latin and Greek words, abstract and philosophical, often heavy and polysyllabic; and they began to come in on an extensive scale at about 1550. The Age of Elizabeth, in its exuberance, delighted in these

[60] *Troilus and Criseyde,* II. 904–6.

brave new words, as it delighted in conceits, in word-juggling and wit-snappery. It welcomed them with open arms and proceeded to scatter them lavishly and recklessly over comedy, tragedy, and narrative poem, in spite of the protests of a few critics. The lyric to a great extent escaped the contamination; in it, the tradition of simplicity in style for the most part prevailed. But in comedy and tragedy, and especially in tragedy, the big words made holiday, with the result that even in the works of the greatest dramatist of his time, and of all time, passages of sheer rhetoric, turgid and pretentious in style, stand shoulder to shoulder with noble and poetic passages of perfect purity, simplicity, and restraint.

It was Arnold who said that there is "not a tragedy of Shakespeare but combines passages in the worst of all styles, the affected style," and who noted the fact that Shakespeare's gift of expression at times degenerates "into a fondness for curiosity of expression . . . an irritability of fancy, which seems to make it impossible for him to say a thing plainly." One need not go far to find examples; they occur on nearly every page:

Nor windy suspiration of forced breath,
No, nor the fruitful river in the eye—HAMLET, I. 2. 79–80

In filial obligation for some term
To do obsequious sorrow: but to persever
In obstinate condolement is a course
Of impious stubbornness.—IBID., 91–94

Come, let's do so;
For every minute is expectancy
Of more arrivance.—OTHELLO, II. 1. 40–42

It was a violent commencement, and thou shalt see
An answerable sequestration—IBID., I. 3

And heaven defend your good souls, that you think
I will your serious and great business scant
For she is with me: no, when light-wing'd boys
Of feather'd Cupid seel with wanton dullness

My speculative and officed instruments,
That my disports corrupt and taint my business,
Let housewives make a skillet of my helm,
And all indign and base adversities
Make head against my estimation!

—IBID., I. 3. 266–74.

To make a recordation to my soul
Of every syllable that here was spoke.
But if I tell how these two did co-act,
Shall I not lie in publishing a truth?
Sith yet there is a credence in my heart,
An esperance so obstinately strong,
That doth invert the attest of eyes and ears,
As if those organs had deceptious functions,
Created only to calumniate.

—TROILUS AND CRESSIDA, V. 2. 116–24

Why did Shakespeare write in this fashion so often? Partly because it was characteristic of the tradition in which he was working—the tradition of tragedy in his age. Sometimes, as in this quotation from *Troilus and Cressida,* it seems to be due to the dramatist's feeling that he must convince the groundlings that this is veritably a hero speaking, a son of Priam, a great warrior, and a lofty and noble character. But above all, it was because of a deficiency of taste in Shakespeare and in the whole Elizabethan Age, a want of classical feeling and restraint, an insufficient or undeveloped sense of form.

To say this is to say nothing new. I have already quoted Arnold. And Bagehot voices much the same idea. He says of Shakespeare, "His works are full of undergrowth, are full of complexity, are not models of style; except by a miracle, nothing in the Elizabethan Age could be a model of style; the restraining taste of that age was feebler and more mistaken than that of any other equally great age." He justly adds, however, that "there is an infinity of pure art in Shakespeare, although there is a great deal else also."

Bagehot explains the fact by the difficulty that confronted Shakespeare and other dramatists in attempting to delineate in five acts and under stage restrictions and by mere dialogue a whole set of characters, of characters enough for a modern novel and with the distinctness of a modern novel. Shakespeare would "hold the mirror up to nature." And he succeeded. But it is no wonder that in letting "the fullness of his nature overflow, he sometimes let it overflow too much, and covered his pages with erroneous conceits and superfluous images."

There is some plausibility in this, but it is not a complete explanation, for the same faults appear in other works of Shakespeare than his plays—in the *Rape of Lucrece,* for instance, where he is dealing with only three or four characters. No, the fault was in the age and was due to the enormous inrush of new knowledge and ideas, to the complexity and ardor of Elizabethan life, to the heterogeneous mixture of new forces and new elements—from the Renaissance, the Reformation, the new world, the new science. It was an age too new, too youthful, too ardent and impatient, to have much concern for restraint and form, or to have learned the value of simplicity and congruity. Shakespeare is at times guilty of juggling words and dallying with ideas even in the most tragic situation. When Lucrece finally blurts out the name of her ravisher before her husband and his attendant lords, and stabs herself with a knife, the poet says:

> Even here she sheathed in her harmless breast
> A harmful knife, that thence her soul unsheathed.

And no doubt both he and his readers were delighted with the contrast and play between "harmless" and "harmful" and "sheathed" and "unsheathed." This is a pretty rhetorical trick, but it is not poetry. In bad taste anywhere, it is especially bad at a moment of such tragedy. The poet then proceeds to dally with the picture of her blood gushing from the wound.

But here he is playing with ideas rather than words, and we have a succession of conceits, and of conceits that are not pretty. The blood is a purple fountain, which chases the knife as the knife is withdrawn; her body is an island surrounded by this fearful blood; some of the blood is red and that is what still remains pure; but the rest, which looks black, is that which Tarquin has stained; the black blood has a mourning face and seems to weep; and ever since, corrupted blood some watery token shows, and untainted blood is ever red, blushing at blood that is putrified.

Elizabethan wit, one feels, was often too nimble, and at times unseasonable. There is something childish in this dallying with words and ideas, as well as a defective taste. With all their sophistication, the Elizabethans never quite outgrew the child's love of play nor the youth's passion for mere cleverness.

The objection is not to long words as such, for Shakespeare and Milton, like many another poet from Chaucer down, get most happy effects at times by means of polysyllabic words. Such lines as these from Milton—

> In Vallombrosa, where the Etrurian shades
>
> Aloft, incumbent on the dusky air
>
> With blackest insurrection to confound

are magnificent, and their effect is in part due to the combination of the long and sonorous word with the simple, short word. But in Milton's

> Tasting concoct, digest, assimilate
>
> Ominous, conjecture on the whole success
>
> In whose conspicuous countenance, without cloud

and in Shakespeare's

> My speculative and officed instruments

In obstinate condolement is a course
Of impious stubbornness

the poet's familiarity with big words has got the better of his judgment and even of his ear.

Mrs. Meynell, in her essay "Composure," speaks of the way in which, in a master's phrase, words of different origin and race encounter as gay strangers and add to the beauty of the style. "The most beautiful and the most sudden of such meetings," she observes, are in Shakespeare, and she cites "superfluous Kings," "a lass unparalleled," and "multitudinous seas." She speaks of the "splendour of such encounters, of such differences, of such nuptial unlikeness and union."

There is much truth in this, and undoubtedly in all the great English poets there are these happy effects brought about by the union or alternation or harmonizing of the short word with the sonorous long word, which is generally a Latin word. Chaucer is full of them, and he is perhaps the first English poet to realize their full possibilities:

Almighty and al merciable quene

Hast thou to misericorde receyved me

Uncircumscript and al maist circumscrive

The issue is not between short words and long words, nor between Saxon words and Latin words, but between words needed to express the thought and words that are surplusage; between a straightforward style and a verbose or inflated style; and between combinations that are musical and those that are awkward and cacophonous. As soon as long words predominate or come in too quick succession, the style becomes heavy, awkward, or pompous. When Shakespeare writes, "If children predecease progenitors," which is "If children die before their fathers" writ large, he is indulging a taste which we of today associate with the half-educated.

It must not be inferred that Chaucer was ignorant of the "colors of rhetoric" or that he always eschewed rhetorical devices; or that his style is without polysyllabic words. There were many such words of Latin origin in the language of his day. They had come in mostly through the French, and Chaucer himself seems to have been responsible for the introduction of some of them. But he uses polysyllabic words with discretion and restraint. His preference is overwhelmingly for the simple word, and he seems to have had a horror of prolixity, of the least suspicion of pomposity, and of language that is involved, indirect, or highly figurative.

The greatest poetry is always in the simple style. The glory of English poetry is the English lyric, for it is there that English poetic genius has kept most strictly and consistently to the ideal of pure poetry—that is, of poetry that has no axe to grind and therefore belongs to the category of the fine arts. And if one takes an anthology of English lyrics—such as the *Golden Treasury* or the *Oxford Book of English Verse*—and goes through it, one sees that the great poems of the race, the poems we cherish most, are miracles of simplicity and purity of style. To study them closely is to marvel at the simple means by which the great poets have achieved the greatest beauty. Take single lines at random—

> My true love hath my heart, and I have his
>
> Fair and fair and twice so fair
>
> Calm was the day and trembling through the air
>
> Full many a glorious morning have I seen
>
> That time of year thou may'st in me behold
>
> How should I your true love know
>
> Take, O take those lips away
>
> Go and catch a falling star

Shall I, wasting in despair,
Die because a woman's fair?

Gather ye rosebuds while ye may

When I consider how my light is spent

Go, lovely rose,
Tell her that wastes her time and me

Tell me not, sweet, I am unkind

Oh braid no more that shining hair

It is a beauteous evening, calm and free

Earth has not anything to show more fair

Milton, thou should'st be living at this hour

Away, the moor is dark beneath the moon

Oh wild West Wind, thou breath of Autumn's being

Silent, upon a peak in Darien

Or, passing to recent times and taking any anthology of poems by the great British and American poets of the present day, one finds the same thing—in Hardy, Bridges, Housman, Yeats, A.E., Davies, Ralph Hodgson, Masefield, Stephens, E. A. Robinson, Amy Lowell, Robert Frost, Sara Teasdale, Edna Millay, and others. The poems chosen as representing the best of each poet's work are, in the vast majority of cases, poems in which the highest beauty is accompanied by the utmost simplicity—by the use of simple, familiar words and a minimum of ornament. The highest beauty in poetry lies neither in the heavy combinations of Shakespeare and Milton, nor in the excessive alliteration and verbiage of Swinburne, nor in the chiming and jingling of words which is so characteristic of Tennyson's earlier poems, of Poe's *Raven* and *The Bells,* and of Mr. Noyes's *The Highwayman* or the *Forty Singing Seamen*. It is, in fact, incompatible with these things.

But what its elements are it is perhaps impossible to say. We cannot define it or anatomize it. We can only quote lines that have it, and speak, with the critic, of "the unmistakable accent of genuine poetry." We can say with certainty, however, that it is a beauty simple rather than ornate; chaste, restrained, and almost bare of ornament; and that what ornament it wears is of the less obvious, more subtle kind.

Now Chaucer, it seems to me, was the founder of this great tradition of simplicity in English poetry; or perhaps we should say, of the tradition of beauty with simplicity. I do not imply that no examples of the combination are to be found before Chaucer, for they occur here and there in various early lyrics and occasionally in early narrative work. But with Chaucer, this lyrical style, as it may be called—this style of perfect ease and grace, of perfect blending of the simple, the melodious, and the beautiful—which in subsequent times became the characteristic of lyric poetry more than of any other kind, and especially of the greatest lyrics, was habitual. He used it in poems of many kinds, in descriptive and narrative verse as well as lyric, in long poems as well as short. It was as if he said, for the guidance of his successors, "This is the style to aim at, the style that is chary of big words and still more so of combinations of big words; the style that is free from pretense and affectation and goes unadorned save by its simple ease and grace and melody. Poetry is in the right way when it keeps to this ideal, and this is true for epic and drama as well as lyric." The splendor of Chaucer's verse is its music. His verse is always musical and always simple. His is a sustained simplicity, not an occasional one. And in this combination of melody and sustained simplicity his verse has never been equaled in narrative poetry since; not by Shakespeare in drama, or Milton in epic, for these poets at times fall into the pompous and affected style. On coming to Shakespeare or Milton from a reading of Chaucer, one is frequently forced to smile at the awkwardness and cumbersomeness of either. It is in such striking contrast with Chaucer's simple ease. Chaucer's style is without effort. It is untortured. It is eloquent of a mind at ease, and this ease of mind seems to be the result of the poet's complete mastery of his subject, whatever it is. Possibly Chaucer's verse is equaled by Spenser's in melody and simplicity, but Chaucer's has the advantage in flexibility and adaptability, for the demands upon it were so much greater by reason of the greater variety of his matter.

Likewise, one is struck by the contrast between Chaucer and Dryden. Long ago Leigh Hunt put side by side a passage from the *Knight's Tale* and Dryden's modernization of it, and remarked upon "the saliency and freshness and natural language" of the original, and the artificial character of Dryden's version.[61] Recently A. E. Housman did much the same thing, contrasting Chaucer's direct and admirable lines with Dryden's rendering of them in a style often grossly padded or "fortified," the "false style" that prevailed for more than a century.[62] To Wordsworth's reaction against the artificialities of the pseudo-classical style, revealed in *Lyrical Ballads* and explained in the famous Preface to the second edition of that work, Chaucer was a contributing influence. Wordsworth was a great admirer of Chaucer. He calls him "the ever-to-be-honoured Chaucer," and in the Preface he remarks, "It is worth while here to observe that the affecting parts of Chaucer are almost always expressed in language pure and universally intelligible even to this day."

Like Wordsworth and the other great lyric poets of later times, Chaucer gets the finest effects by the simplest means:

> The lyf so short, the craft so long to lerne
>
> Love is thing ay ful of busy drede [63]

[61] "Specimens of Chaucer," no. II, in *The Seer*.
[62] *The Name and Nature of Poetry*, Macmillan, 1933, p. 20–23.
[63] A translation of Ovid: *Res est solliciti plena timoris amor*.

Biseching him to doon hir that honour

Have ye nat seyn som tyme a pale face

Of olde stories, longe tyme agoon

Lat me nat lyk a worm go by the weye

I have, quod he, herd seyd, ful yore ago

I may yow nat devyse al hir beautee

But it is not a matter of a single line here and there, but of unfailing melody and simplicity through all his works, or at least in all that came after the *House of Fame*. It is a sustained and flowing melody, varied in accent and movement, and of such virtue that it can clothe with beauty prosaic matters of fact and if necessary make use of words usually thought to be harsh and unpoetic, without any loss of its characteristic excellence.

It is often said that Chaucer is not a lyric poet, that his genius was descriptive and narrative rather than lyrical. This is in one sense true, but, like so many of the commonplaces of Chaucerian criticism, it is hasty and much too sweeping. It fails to take into account a number of important considerations.

Chaucer wrote many more lyrics than have been preserved. This is clear from his words in the Prologue of the *Legend of Good Women*. There the good Alceste, in defending the poet against the God of Love's accusations, calls attention to the works he has composed in honor of Love and of Love's servants. Among them she mentions

"... many an ympne for your halydayes,
That highten Balades, Roundels, Virelayes."

This evidence is confirmed by Lydgate, by Gower, and by the fact that in the famous *Retraction* at the end of the *Canterbury Tales* Chaucer mentions among his "enditings of worldly vanities" many a song and many a lay.[64] The "balades, roundels, virelayes" noted in the *Legend of Good Women*—songs or lyrics in honor of Love's holy days, such as St. Valentine's Day—have not come down to us, unless one or two of them may be included among the Minor Poems of the canon, which is unlikely.

From another passage in the *Legend of Good Women* we learn of the existence at the English court of two rival parties, or orders, of lovers—those of the Flower and those of the Leaf; and we are told that both were given to the making of "fresshe songes." Indeed, Chaucer protests, these courtly makers of songs have written so much that they have reaped the harvest of "making" and left nothing for him to glean but a single ear here and there. The remark is not to be taken too seriously; it is evidence of Chaucer's modesty rather than proof that he wrote but few such poems. It is evidence that the practice of making love songs was widespread in the court circle, and that there was rivalry in the art between the two factions of the Flower and the Leaf. Under such circumstances it would be strange if the greatest poet of his age, who was himself a court poet and an avowed poet of love, were not one of the most prolific and successful of the writers of such songs.

The lyrics of Chaucer that we do possess are found in the Minor Poems and here and there in the narrative poems which constitute his major works. Among the Minor Poems there are light, humorous lyrics such as the *Complaint to His Empty Purse* and the *Words Unto Adam,* and poetical epistles in humorous and lyric vein, such as *Lenvoy to Scogan* and *Lenvoy to Bukton*. The *Balade Against Women Unconstant* and *Merciless Beauty,* though usually classed among the poems of doubtful authenticity, in spirited and humorous way strike the note of the Defiant Lover and may well be by Chaucer. The *Balade to Rosemund,* though it may not be

[64] See Robinson, *Works,* pp. 612 and 959.

his, is noteworthy for its perfect blending of the serious and the humorous. It is as light and courtly, and as perfect in its grace, as a Cavalier lyric. In loftier vein there are moral and philosophical lyrics, or lyrics of exhortation. In *Fortune* we hear the voice of defiance and of stoic courage in such lines as

> Yet is me left the light of my resoun.

Truth, or A Balade of Good Counsel is an eloquent plea to man to abandon the world and seek after truth, to

> Flee fro the press, and dwelle with soothfastnesse.

The Former Age, with its complaint of the corruptions of the day in contrast with the virtues of the golden age of the past, has something in it of the spirit of Wordsworth's "The world is too much with us," or, better still, of "Milton! thou should'st be living at this hour." And the same is true of *Lack of Steadfastness.*

But the most lyrical of Chaucer's lyrics are to be found not in the Minor Poems but embedded in the major works as lyrical interludes or adornments in poems that are narrative. The best-known examples are "Now welcome, somer, with thy sonne softe," which the birds sing in the *Parliament of Fowls* before the parliament breaks up and they fly away, and "Hyd, Absolon, thy gilte tresses clere," which is sung by the company of fair ladies in the *Legend of Good Women* in praise of "Alceste the debonaire." But there are others. In the *Medea* there is the complaint of Medea against the false Jason. This is but six lines long and is a translation from Ovid, but it has the genuine lyric accent—

> "Why lyked me thy yelow here to see
> More then the boundes of myn honestee?"

In *Anelida and Arcite* Anelida's Complaint runs to the length of 140 lines and, besides being an elaborate and successful metrical experiment with complex and balanced structure and varied metre and melody, is of sustained lyrical excellence.

A poem, to be a lyric, need not be the expression of the poet's personal emotion, though one may easily fall into the habit of thinking so, because so many modern lyrics have been subjective in this sense. It may be the expression of an emotion felt by one of the poet's characters. Thus we have lyric lines and lyric passages in the drama, in the ballad, and, as in the last-mentioned lyrics by Chaucer, in the narrative poem. Chaucer was not a lyric poet in the sense that he wrote of himself and made his own joys and sorrows the subjects of his lyrics. He never carried his heart on his sleeve, nor bared his bosom to the world. His muse commanded him not to look in his heart and write, but to look in the hearts of others—a more difficult and perhaps a nobler thing to do. Chaucer wrote of the sufferings of the Knight in Black, of Troilus, of Constance and Griselda, of Anelida and Canacee and the ladies of the *Legend of Good Women,* and not of the sufferings of Chaucer. And in so doing he frequently wrote great lyrics.

Troilus and Criseyde contains a number of songs and complaints. In Book I we have Troilus's song on the torments of love; at the end of Book III, his song in praise of love; and in Book V, a third, on the loss of love. In Book IV there is Criseyde's formal complaint against the fate that is to separate her from her lover,[65] and in Book V there is Troilus's passionate complaint at the absence of his lady, beginning

> "Wher is myn owene lady, lief and deere?"

Besides these things, there are passionate outbursts in great number in which we hear the genuine lyric cry, as in Troilus's long lament in Book IV (260–336), with such memorable lines as that in which he addresses his own spirit—

> "O wery goost, that errest to and fro"

[65] IV. 743–98.

or the line addressed to Calkas, the evil and absent father of Criseyde—

"O oold, unholsom and myslyved man."

In Book V there are Troilus's apostrophes to Criseyde's empty palace, to the moon, and to the wind blowing from the Greek camp where Criseyde is (650–58; 669–79). There is, too, Criseyde's lament as she looks toward Troy and thinks of the city and the lover she has left (731–65).

In the *Clerk's Tale* there is an excellent one-stanza lyric in protest against the thoughtless and fickle mob:

"O stormy peple! unsad and ever untrewe!
Ay undiscreet and chaunging as a vane,
Delyting ever in rumbel that is newe,
For lyk the mone ay wexe ye and wane;
Ay ful of clapping, dere y-nogh a Iane;
Your doom is fals, your constance yvel preveth,
A ful greet fool is he that on yow leveth!"

This might just as well be Chaucer's own comment or outcry, but he puts it in the mouths of the more stable and serious-minded citizens—

Thus seyden sadde folk in that citee.

In addition, Chaucer's works contain numerous examples of single lines, uttered by this or that character, in which we hear the unmistakable lyric cry. In these instances, as in the more extended lyrical passages mentioned above, the lyric cry is dramatic, but that does not alter the fact that they are highly lyrical and are noble examples of lyric verse. The Wife of Bath's

"Allas! allas! that ever love was sinne!"

is as much a triumph of lyric genius as it is of dramatic. The same is true of Pandarus's great line, addressed to Criseyde,

"Allas, that God yow swich a beaute sente!"

and of the Host's comment upon the *Physician's Tale* of Virginia,

"Allas! to dere boghte she beautee!"

It is true also of the glad cry of Griselda in the *Clerk's Tale,*

"O tendre, o dere, o yonge children myne."

These embedded lyrics, as they may be called, whether single lyrical lines or longer units in the form of song or complaint, must be put down to Chaucer's credit as a lyric poet as well as the separate or independent lyrics among the Minor Poems. Considered rightly, they belong with the great body of great English lyrics, hidden or obscured by their position though they are, and they prove conclusively that Chaucer possessed the lyric gift in high degree.

Chaucer, then, is a lyric poet in the sense that he was one who wrote courtly love songs in the conventional modes (and their number, we believe, was great) and whose narrative works afford numerous examples of lyric lines, lyric passages, and set lyrics in the form of songs, apostrophes, and complaints, that testify to his lyrical genius. Chaucer's age, though not a subjective age, was an age in which many lyrics were written, but it was above all, and overwhelmingly, the age of the narrative poem. It was to the narrative poem that his powers were chiefly devoted. And it was on his narrative poems that he spent much of his lyrical genius. The lyrical element is strong even in the *Canterbury Tales,* and *Troilus and Criseyde* is so rich in lyrical passages that it may be classified as lyric narrative, in much the same way as certain dramas may be termed lyric drama. Witness especially Books III, IV, and V. Likewise, Chaucer was possessed of great dramatic powers, and these too he lavished upon his narrative poems. Into the narrative poem he introduced as many lyrical and dramatic elements as he could, and as many as that literary mode could well accommodate.

Moreover, if what has been said above is true concerning the lyrical grace and simplicity of Chaucer's style, then, in one sense at least, Chaucer is a lyric poet throughout, because he writes in what I have called the "lyric style." Fragment H of the *Canterbury Tales* begins with the lines,

> Wite ye nat wher ther stant a litel toun
> Which that y-cleped is Bob-up-and-doun,
> Under the Blee, in Caunterbury weye?

These are merely an indication of place in a narrative which goes on to tell how at Bob-up-and-down the Host rallied the pilgrims, jested at the Cook's expense, and finally got the story-telling going again. But they might as well be the opening lines of a lyric, of a lyric by Wordsworth, let us say, commemorating in immortal verse some personal experience that had stirred his heart and flashed upon the inward eye. They have the lightness and grace and sweet simplicity of lyric verse at its best. For another instance take these lines from the *Knight's Tale:*

> The bisy larke, messager of day,
> Saluëth in hir song the morwe gray;
> And fyry Phebus ryseth up so brighte,
> That al the orient laugheth of the lighte,
> And with his stremes dryeth in the greves
> The silver dropes, hanging on the leves.

They give the setting and the time of Arcite's going into the fields and groves to do observance to May. They are descriptive, but they could do service in a lyric, for many a lyric is in part descriptive, and these lines are full of light and song and lyric joy. Chaucer wrote no lyric to the skylark, as did Wordsworth and Shelley, but he wrote lyrically of the bird, and of her song at dawn, of the gray morning, and of the sun's flooding the east with light.

CHAPTER XI

"This Green Earth"

I am in love with this green earth. . . .
I would set up my tabernacle here.
Charles Lamb, NEW YEAR'S EVE.

OF all that Chaucer wrote, the best-known lines are the opening lines of the *Prologue* of the *Canterbury Tales.* And this is as it should be, for though they may seem trite from much repetition, they illustrate some of the characteristics of Chaucer's poetry which we cherish most. They are lines that tell of April and her sweet showers, of the young sun, of the sweet breath of the west wind, of tender shoots springing in wood and heath, and of small birds stirred to song as their great mother, Nature, warms and gladdens their hearts. They breathe of spring and the youth of the year, of the renewal of life in field and bird and man. They speak of Chaucer's love of nature, of flowers, sun, and rain; of his love of England, of England when April is there. His tenderness is in them, and his sweetness. The word "sweet" occurs twice in the first five lines, and "tender," "young," and "small" in the next four. The passage is full of Chaucer's delicate feeling and of his fresh, unspoiled joy in a world that still seems young, a world that is sunny and new-washed by the rain. Above all, it is steeped in that open-air quality which is characteristic of so much of Chaucer's poetry and which he possesses to a greater extent than any other English poet.

Chaucer is not a poet of the out-of-doors. He is not a nature poet. Though his love of nature was great, he did not make poems on the seasons, on clouds and winds, or cuckoos and nightingales. His details of nature, which so delightfully reveal his delicate observation and tender feeling, are incidental and introduced by the way. He is a poet of men and women. Except in the *Parliament of Fowls* his subjects are men and women and their stories. But his poetry none the less lives in the out-of-doors, in something of the same way as do the poems and novels of Hardy, and the action in most of his stories takes place in the open. Chaucer's world is an out-of-doors world. The drama of the Canterbury pilgrimage takes place on the road. In the *Book of the Duchess* the dream introduces us to a hunt, and the Knight in Black tells his story sitting under an oak in a forest. In the *House of Fame* the whole of Book II is of the out-of-doors, describing the poet's flight through the heavens in the talons of the Eagle. The *Parliament of Fowls* and the Prologue of the *Legend of Good Women* are obviously of this category. And if in *Troilus and Criseyde* many of the scenes are laid in Troilus's or Criseyde's palace or in the house of Pandarus, much of the action takes place in the streets of the town, in the Greek camp, or on the walls; and we are never allowed to forget that the plains of Ilium are not far away.

To some extent the interest in nature revealed in Chaucer's poetry is a conventional one. The May morning, the lovely garden, the singing birds were features of the dream poetry and poetry of Courtly Love which influenced him so profoundly and which he wrote so successfully. But with all due allowance for this traditional element, there is also in Chaucer's poetry a large love of nature that is entirely genuine and personal. Even when he introduces details that may have been suggested by this or that poem in French or Italian, he makes them his own.[66] The widely admired passage on the daisy in the Prologue of the *Legend of Good Women* is in part inspired by marguerite poems by Deschamps and other French poets. But no one can doubt Chaucer's love of

[66] See above, p. 54.

> . . . these floures whyte and rede,
> Swiche as men callen daysies in our toun,

flowers which are

> . . . ever ylyke fair and fresh of hewe,
> As wel in winter as in somer newe.

Nor can one doubt his love of "the smale softe swote gras," embroidered with sweet flowers, as he kneels on it to watch the daisy unclose. He notes its delicacy, its softness and fragrance, and as his senses delight in the beauty around him, he thinks how the earth has forgotten its poor estate of winter and now is clad all new again by influence of the temperate sun. And in this whole passage, all the objects of nature that are mentioned—flowers, grass, the earth, winter, the sun—are spoken of in terms of affection, of an affection personal and intimate, and almost, as it were, the affection of one of God's creatures for another. They are thought of as living, sentient beings, with a spirit within. There is more in this than the usual commonplace personification of poetic imagery. It is a survival, in a weakened, refined, and almost unrecognizable form, of the old animistic belief in the existence of spirit, and even of personality, in all living things. Animism, the old spiritual theory, is of course at the bottom of all poetic personifications, whether in ancient poetry or modern. But in Chaucer the sense of the spirit within is real and strong, with the result that these personifications are something more than fossilized figures of speech. They are evidence of a living belief, of a belief which, though not so strong as the similar beliefs of the Greeks and Romans or of primitive peoples today, was still widespread in the folklore of Chaucer's time and must have permeated to a greater or lesser extent the thoughts of practically all men in his day and is by no means unknown in England, America, and other civilized lands today.

It is this belief—held more or less unconsciously perhaps by Chaucer and mixed with the merely conventional literary acceptance of the classical personifications, but nevertheless, as I have said, a living thing—that explains, I believe, the exceptional tenderness, sympathy, and love which we note in his attitude toward natural objects. Chaucer's delight in nature is partly an aesthetic delight; his aesthetic sense was a highly developed one. But while his aesthetic sense will explain his response to beauty, it will not explain the peculiar tenderness, love, and what amounts to a feeling of kinship, revealed in his descriptions of nature. That can be due only to his belief in the spiritual nature of life. It is a belief that was held also by W. H. Hudson, and Hudson, it seems, recognized it in Chaucer when he surmised that Chaucer was "nearer to primitive man physically than we are" and when he asked, "Does he, Chaucer, speak only for himself when he writes thus of the daisies and of the smale fowles . . . or is he expressing feelings which were more common in his day than in ours?" [67] It explains much of Hudson's writing on nature—much of *his* tenderness and loving sympathy, of his vital feeling for nature—as it does of Chaucer's.

Chaucer took especial delight in birds. He wrote an entire poem on birds, the *Parliament of Fowls,* and in it one sees his knowledge of many kinds of birds—from the royal eagle

> That with his sharpe look perceth the sonne,

to the dove "with hir eyen meke," and to

> The cok, that orloge is of thorpes lyte.

In many of his works he makes incidental mention of birds—in bits of description and in figures of speech, some of them homely and proverbial figures of speech. When Troilus at last has Criseyde fast in his arms, the poet asks,

[67] *Hind in Richmond Park,* N.Y., 1923, pp. 64–66.

What myghte or may the sely larke seye,
Whan that the sperhauk hath it in his foot?

Later, when Criseyde's fears are stilled and she pours out her heart to her lover, she is like

. . . the newe abaysed nyghtyngale,
That stynteth first whan she begynneth to singe,
Whan that she hereth any herde tale,
Or in the hegges any wight stirynge,
And after, siker, doth hire vois out rynge.

In the *Knight's Tale,* after Arcite receives the promise of victory in the temple of Mars, he fares to his inn

As fayn as fowel is of the brighte sonne.

In the *Squire's Tale* we have a picture of the gladness of the birds in the spring sun:

Ful lusty was the weder and benigne,
For which the foules, agayn the sonne shene,
What for the seson and the yonge grene,
Ful loude songen hir affecciouns;
Hem semed han geten hem protecciouns
Agayn the swerd of winter kene and cold.

And in the *Legend of Good Women* the birds sing their songs of love loud and clear

. . . for the newe blisful somers sake,
Upon the braunches ful of blosmes softe,

Chaucer's out-of-doors is full of sunshine, and it is the sunshine of spring and summer, and often of the early morning. The air is clear and fresh.

Bright was the sonne, and cleer that morweninge

when Emily walked in the garden and the two young knights saw her for the first time.

The morwening atempre was and fair

when Jason and Hercules after their long voyage came to land at Lemnos. And Canacee, in the *Squire's Tale,* rises in the morning

As rody and bright as dooth the yonge sonne.

In *Troilus and Criseyde* there is a fine description of a sunset, in which the poet notes the way white things grow dim as the light fails. The sun

Gan westren faste, and downward for to wrye,
As he that hadde his dayes cours yronne;
And white thynges wexen dymme and donne
For lak of lyght, and sterres for t'apere.

But Chaucer also notes sights and sounds of nature in her less benign seasons and aspects: the whistling wind that makes the Monk's bridle jingle; the way the stars twinkle on a frosty night. When Troilus learns that Criseyde must go to the Greeks in exchange for Antenor, he is as desolate and forlorn as the bare trees in winter:

And as in wynter leves ben biraft,
Ech after other, til the tree be bare,
So that ther nys but bark and braunche ilaft,
Lith Troilus, byraft of ech welfare,
Ibounden in the blake bark of care.

In the *Franklin's Tale* there is a scene in

The colde frosty seson of Decembre,

which, in its use of specific details characteristic of winter, reminds us of Shakespeare's "When icicles hang by the wall."

Phebus wex old, and hewed lyk latoun,
That in his hote declinacioun
Shoon as the burned gold with stremes brighte;
But now in Capricorn adoun he lighte,

Wheras he shoon ful pale, I dar wel seyn.
The bittre frostes, with the sleet and reyn,
Destroyed hath the grene in every yerd.
Ianus sit by the fyr, with double berd,
And drinketh of his bugle-horn the wyn.
Biforn him stant braun of the tusked swyn,
And "Nowell" cryeth every lusty man.

Chaucer's life was one which must have kept him much in the open. Though he was a man of the court, we must not think of him as spending his days at court. Nor, though he was Controller of the Customs for twelve years, who kept his accounts himself and not by deputy for most of that period, must we picture him as a clerk confined to his desk. As a member of Prince Lionel's household he did considerable traveling and went to the wars in France. As esquire in the King's household he executed numerous missions at home and abroad, traveling by horseback when he was not at sea. As Controller he spent much time by the river. And as sometime Clerk of the Works, commissioner to survey the walls, ditches, bridges, etc., along the Thames, and Sub-forester of the King's forest in Somerset, he was responsible for the upkeep, repair, or preservation of various royal properties, which must have necessitated much journeying to and fro.

Perhaps it is in such a life that we are to find the explanation of the open-air quality of Chaucer's poetry, of his love of birds, flowers, and sunshine, and of his frequent references to beasts and animals, usually the homely domestic animals of farmyard and field. Perhaps too we are to see in it the secret of his heartiness. Heartiness is born of the open air. It is found oftenest in country folk or those who are separated from the land by not more than a generation or two, or those who live much in the open. Chaucer was born in the city and was of the middle class, but his life, as I have said, must have kept him much out-of-doors. In any case, he is the heartiest of English poets, and he loves all that is "fresh," "lusty," "green," "merry." I have already commented upon the fresh beauty of Blanche the Duchess, and upon the "lusty," "fresh" folk—knights and ladies—in the Legends of the *Legend of Good Women*.[68] Likewise, Emily and Canacee and Alisoun and May are all memorable for the freshness of their beauty. When, at the end of the *Clerk's Tale,* the Clerk sings a song—the grave clerk who "loked holwe, and therto soberly"—he does so

> . . . with lusty herte fresshe and grene.

Within less than twenty lines in the Prologue of the *Canon's Yeoman's Tale* there are a half-dozen instances of words like "jolly" and "merry." The Canon's Yeoman has ridden furiously to join the company of pilgrims, and both he and his horse are in a great sweat. And here occurs the famous line which is one of the best of all examples of Chaucer's gusto and zest. The poet exclaims,

> But it was ioye for to seen him swete! [69]

Chaucer takes joy even in seeing a man sweat, if he sweats well and heartily.

Likewise full of gusto are the greetings in Chaucer. They speak of joy and high animal spirits. The Canon's Yeoman hails the company with a greeting that is heartiness itself—

> "God save," quod he, "this ioly companye!"

And this should be compared with the greetings of Allen and John and Symkyn the Miller in the *Reeve's Tale*.[70] Another example is the "Hail, and wel atake!" with which the summoner in the *Friar's Tale* salutes the "gay yeoman" he meets by the way. The yeoman's reply is:

[68] See above, p. 52 and p. 163.

[69] Commented upon also by Professor Lowes, *Geoffrey Chaucer,* p. 238, and previously by Aldous Huxley, *On the Margin,* p. 202.

[70] See above, p. 249.

"Welcome," quod he, "and every good felawe!
Wher rydestow under this grene shawe?"

Each is glad to meet a fellow traveler. The yeoman's welcome is so broad as to include "every good felawe," and his added words, "under this grene shawe,' which are strictly unnecessary, suggest his joy in the woodland paths and the open air. Later, in the same tale, they meet a carter, stalled in the mire with a load of hay. Because of the mud and the stones his horses cannot, or will not, pull the cart out. He lashes them and curses them, and with the greatest relish in the world wishes the whole concern to the devil—horses, cart, and hay:

The carter smoot, and cryde, as he were wood,
"Hayt, Brok! hayt, Scot! what spare ye for the stones?
The feend," quod he, "yow fecche body and bones,
As ferforthly as ever were ye foled!
So muche wo as I have with yow tholed!
The devel have al, bothe hors and cart and hey!"

But when the horses pull with a will and the cart moves, he turns completely about and with equal heartiness calls down upon their heads the blessings of Jesus Christ, God, and Saint Loy:

This carter thakketh his hors upon the croupe,
And they bigonne drawen and to-stoupe;
"Heyt, now!" quod he, "ther Iesu Crist yow blesse,
And al his handwerk, bothe more and lesse!
That was wel twight, myn owene lyard boy!
I pray god save thee and sëynt Loy!
Now is my cart out of the slow, pardee!"

The carter is a thorough man. For him, "Devil take you!" is not enough. He must add, "body and bones" and "as ferforthly as ever were ye foled." And as if this were not enough, he concludes with great force and passion, "The devel have al, bothe hors and cart and hey!" This triple-bound curse is then followed by a triple-bound blessing. He calls down upon his horses not only the blessing of Jesus Christ, but of "al his handwerk" and "bothe more and lesse"; and, for good measure and running over he prays God and Saint Loy to save them. The carter's blessing is as thorough and hearty as his cursing. It was a thorough and hearty age, when men cursed and blessed with equal gusto.

Tradition has it that Swift once compiled a list of the curses in Chaucer. One can well believe it. It is a thing worth doing, and the list would be a pretty one. But it would be eloquent of the vigor and robust spirits of the age much more than of its profanity.

Nothing in Chaucer better illustrates his incomparable vividness than this little episode of the carter stalled in the mud with his two horses and his load of hay. The man is alive there on the page, a veritable peasant from that old England, saved from oblivion by Chaucer's dramatic art—vigorous, passionate, earthy, salty, religious, profane, full of temper, but full also of love. How close is the bond between him and his beasts! We even know their names. How full of affection are his words of praise, "That was wel twight, myn owene lyard boy!" How full of satisfaction and relief is his naïve exclamation, "Now is my cart out of the slow, pardee!"

Similarly in the *Pardoner's Tale* Chaucer lavishes his power of vivid portrayal upon a mere episode and in the full gusto of his art gives us details in measure heaped up and overflowing that we may see the thing in three dimensions. The scene is the one in which the youngest of the three revelers goes into an apothecary's shop to buy poison to kill his two fellows he has left behind under a tree to guard the gold they have found. There is no real need for this little scene. It adds nothing to the plot of the story, nor to the revelation of character. The poet might have told us simply that the man bought poison of an apothecary. Instead, he takes us into the shop and we witness the whole transaction. The man asks for some poison with which to kill his rats; also, he says, there is a polecat in his hedge that has slain his capons; and further, he would avenge himself on vermin that destroy him by night. Any one of these reasons would have sufficed, one would think. But this is a thoroughgoing liar and villain, and none too shrewd; so, to make his story plausible, he gives three. The apothecary answers,

> ". . . and thou shalt have
> A thing that, also god my soule save,
> In al this world ther nis no creature,
> That ete or dronke hath of this confiture
> Noght but the mountance of a corn of whete,
> That he ne shal his lyf anon forlete;
> Ye, sterve he shal, and that in lasse whyle
> Than thou wolt goon a paas nat but a myle;
> This poyson is so strong and violent."

Apparently it is the best poison in the world, and the apothecary will stake his soul on it. He is as explicit and as emphatic in recommending his poison as the villain is in giving reasons for wanting it.

Here, as in the episode of the carter, the use of homely details counts heavily in producing the effect. The rats, the polecat, the capons, and the fleas serve to remind us that life does not change through the ages. The same is true of the description of the poor widow's cottage and mode of life in the *Nun's Priest's Tale*. She lives in a narrow cottage, with hall and bower that are sooty. She has two daughters, three large sows, three cows, a single sheep named Moll, and a cock and hens. Her simple diet is of milk and bread and broiled bacon, with sometimes an egg or two. And in a later episode in the same story we have a third illustration. When the fox runs off to the woods with Chanticleer in his mouth, the widow and her daughters run after him, raising the hue and cry, and the whole farm and countryside are in an uproar. Men with staves, Colle our dog, Talbot and Gerland, and "Malkin, with a distaf in hir hand"—all join the chase.

> Ran cow and calf, and eek the verray hogges.

The ducks cry as if they are about to be killed; the geese fly over the trees, and the bees swarm out of the hives. And to the yelling, barking, and shouting is added the noise of horns and trumpets—of horns and trumpets made of brass, box, horn, and bone. How very homely all this is! And how human! It is the perfection of mock-epic, and also the soundest of classical art. "Malkin with a distaf in hir hand!" Chaucer was there. He saw it happen. And he puts *us* there.

These are illustrations of the homely, human quality of Chaucer's poetry, as well as of his heartiness and out-of-doors freshness. Chaucer loves all these animals and these country folk living close to the soil. The matter of his poetry is the common stuff of everyday life. Like Homer in describing Odysseus's swineherd, or Ovid in painting the humble cottage of Baucis and Philemon, he understands that vividness is best achieved by the use of specific details and that the homelier and more familiar they are the better. He knows, too, that the eternally interesting subjects of art are the simple everyday things. As Max Beerbohm reminds us, it is the "primitive and essential things" that have "power to touch the heart of the beholder . . . a man plowing in a field, or sowing or reaping; a girl filling a pitcher from a spring, a young mother with her child, a fisherman mending his nets, a light from a lonely hut on a dark night." These are "the best themes for poets and painters." [71] And, we may add, the list of primitive, homely, essential, and eternal things which the great poet can make effective use of includes such lowly creatures as Chaucer's vermin that destroy one by night and as Mase-

[71] Max Beerbohm, "The Golden Drugget" in *And Even Now,* N.Y., 1920, p. 117.

field's cockroach which "scuttled where the moonbeam crossed." [72]

These passages, with many others that might be cited, are examples of the gusto of Chaucer's art, of the intensity of his vision and of his power to convey that vision to others by means of words. And this intensity and vividness in his art is the result fundamentally of the intensity of his feeling for life, of his zest for life. In all gusto, whether in art or in life, there is a strong element of joy as well as of power. The one springs from the other. The heartiness of Chaucer's poetry, its homeliness, its tenderness and sweetness, its gladness and humor, its vividness, are really one. At bottom they are but different manifestations of his love, of his almost all-inclusive love. He wrote as he did because he loved as he did. His poetry moves and has its being in the principle of love rather than hatred, of attraction not aversion, of joy not disgust. The things that Chaucer hates can be counted on one hand. He is often called a satirist, but he is not a satirist, because he is not a reformer. The satirist is inspired by hate, or at least by aversion or distaste. Chaucer sometimes resorts to satire or to the satirical method but only the better to reveal the humors of life and to add to his own and his reader's enjoyment. His satire itself is a phase of his love. It springs from his delight in the quirks and foibles, the vanities and rascalities, of human nature. Not by one jot or tittle would he have the Monk or the Pardoner or the Host other than they are. No more than he would change Constance or Griselda. His joy in them as he finds them is too great. This is not to say that Chaucer was a man of no judgment or discrimination, nor that he lacked a proper sense of values. On the contrary, he was one of the most discerning of men, and of poets. It means that he was one who made it his business to enjoy and portray, not to judge. It means that along with his tremendous capacity for noting the characteristics of things, he possessed an un-

[72] *The Dauber,* N.Y., 1916.

failing power of taking joy in them. There is no poet more catholic than he, and none more human. He could tolerate, and perhaps find pleasure in, the Parson's endless sermon and the long-winded moral discourse of the tale of Melibeus and Prudence, which he himself tells. To him it was "a heaven" to hear the birds sing, and a joy to see a man sweat. He could listen to and report the Wife of Bath's outrageous account of her married life or the Pardoner's confession of his rank hypocrisies and villainies with the greatest profit and delight. He watched the squirrels sitting and eating high up in the trees. He loved the freshness of a May morning or of Blanche's and Emily's beauty. He knew the fragrance of Alisoun's breath—as sweet as hoard of apples laid in hay or heather. And though it would be too much to say that he had joy in the cursed, stinking breath of the Cook, he used the one as he used the other, with the zest of the perfect artist. All these things he loved, or at least welcomed and rejoiced in as an artist. He is at home with all this warm humanity, even though at times it is coarse, ribald, or obscene. And he writes about it with such a personal touch, with so much of his own tenderness, sympathy, humor, or joy, that we find him in every line. There is no poet who is to such an extent at once both objective and subjective, who while writing so constantly of the world about him, contrives so constantly to make that world his own and to bring into his work so much of himself. The Chaucerian note that we hear is unmistakable. It convinces us that here is one who wrote not in the spirit of artistic virtuosity nor in the spirit of showmanship, so frequent among dramatists, but in the fullness of his joy in so much life. It is the note of one who, as he stood upon earth, found the scene before him so warm and rich and varied as to have felt no desire to be rapt above the pole. Swinburne held that the sublimity of Wordsworth is worth all the excellences of Chaucer put together. That is one point of view. From another, and to another temperament, it would be as true to say that Troilus, Criseyde, Pandarus, the Wife of Bath, the Host, Constance, Griselda, and the others, are of greater price than all the sublimity of Wordsworth. He writeth best

> . . . who loveth best
> All things, both great and small.

Index